FOUNDATIONS OF ENVIRONMENTAL ETHICS

Eugene C. Hargrove
University of Georgia at Athens

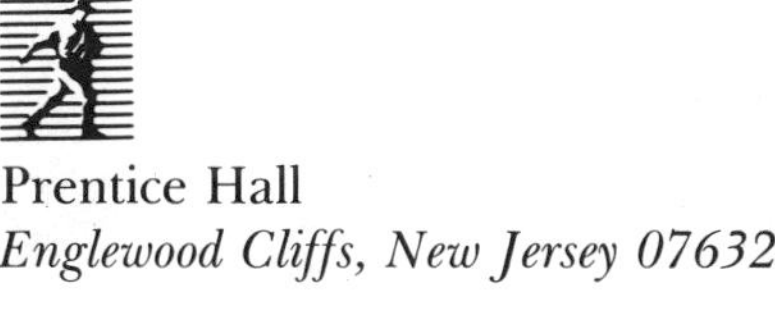

Prentice Hall
Englewood Cliffs, New Jersey 07632

Library of Congress Cataloging-in-Publication Data

HARGROVE, EUGENE C., (date).
Foundations of environmental ethics.

Bibliography: p.
Includes index.
1. Human ecology—Moral and ethical aspects.
I. Title.
GF80.H37 1988 179'.1 88-25484
ISBN 0-13-329574-5

Editorial/production supervision and
interior design: Mary A. Araneo
Cover design: Ben Santora
Cover photo: E.J. Muybridge: Falls of the Yosemite, from Glacier Rock, No. 36, 1872. Department of Special Collections, University Research Library, UCLA.
Manufacturing buyer: Peter Havens

Chapter Two originally published in *Environmental Ethics* 2 (1980): 121-48, under the title "Anglo-American Land Use Attitudes"; Chapter Three originally published in *Environmental Ethics* 1 (1979): 209-40, under the title "The Historical Foundations of American Environmental Attitudes"; Chapter Four originally published in *Inquiry* 30, nos. 1-2 (March 1987): 3-31, under the title "Foundations of Wildlife Protection Attitudes," with permission of the publisher Universitetsforlaget As.

Printed in the United States of America

10 9 8 7 6 5 4 3 2 1

ISBN 0-13-329574-5

Prentice-Hall International (UK) Limited, *London*
Prentice-Hall of Australia Pty. Limited, *Sydney*
Prentice-Hall Canada Inc., *Toronto*
Prentice-Hall Hispanoamericana, S.A., *Mexico*
Prentice-Hall of India Private Limited, *New Delhi*
Prentice-Hall of Japan, Inc., *Tokyo*
Simon & Schuster Asia Pte. Ltd., *Singapore*
Editora Prentice-Hall do Brasil, Ltda., *Rio de Janeiro*

To Richard A. Watson

CONTENTS

Chapter Six
AN ONTOLOGICAL ARGUMENT FOR ENVIRONMENTAL ETHICS 165

Afterword
BEYOND ECONOMICS: TOWARD A BALANCED VALUE SYSTEM 206

INDEX 217

PREFACE

Although environmental concern is a major characteristic of Western society in the twentieth century, the philosophical and ethical foundations of modern environmental thought are poorly understood both by environmentalists and by their opponents. Indeed, the environmental perspective is frequently characterized as being contrary to Western traditions—in particular, Western philosophy, science, and political theory—and as such a threat to the continuation of Western civilization. In this book, I examine the history of ideas that has produced this conflict. In Part I, I look at the philosophical, scientific, and land use attitudes that have inhibited environmental thought. In Part II, I show that important Western aesthetic and scientific attitudes support an environmental perspective and that they are as well grounded historically in Western traditions as the attitudes discussed in Part I. In Part III, I develop a traditionally oriented foundation for environmental ethics that reconciles the conflicting elements of Western thought as described in Parts I and II. In this context, I reject Barry Commoner's third law of ecology, "Nature knows best," in favor of an ontological philosophical position that takes account of the basic environmental intuitions implicit in the frequently heard, but philosophically unsupportable, claim by environmentalists that living and nonliving nature has a "right to exist." In the afterword, I discuss various contemporary social, political, educational, and economic perspectives that still inhibit the development of a balanced value system and prevent Western civilization from becoming fully reconciled with its own environmental roots.

Research for Chapters 2, 3, and 4 was undertaken as a Rockefeller Foundation Fellow in Environmental Affairs. I wish to thank the Rockefeller Foundation for its support during the fellowship period. In addition, I am grateful for the help and cooperation of the following research institutions: the Missouri Historical Society, the National Archives, the Smithsonian Institution, the Library of Congress, the Yale Historical Manuscript Collection, the Yale Western Americana Collection, the Huntington Library, the Rush Rhees Library of the University of Rochester, the American Philosophical Society, the Marietta College Archive, the University of Wisconsin Division of Archives, the New York Public Library, the Jefferson Expansion Memorial, the Cooper-Hewitt Museum, and the Yosemite National Park Library. Finally, I wish to thank the following people for their support, criticism, and encouragement: Judy Blankenship, Susan Power Bratton, J. Baird Callicott, Frederick Ferré, Gerald G. Forney, Frank B. Golley, John Granrose, Hans Huth, Gertrude Ilming, Roderick Nash, R. J. Nelson, Lawrence R. Pomeroy, H. Ronald Pulliam, Holmes Rolston, III, and Dennis Trombatore—and most of all, Richard A. Watson, to whom this book is dedicated.

INTRODUCTION
APPLIED ETHICS AND ENVIRONMENTAL CONCERN

This book is a contribution not only to the field of environmental ethics but also more generally to what is called applied ethics. We have lived for some time in an applied period in the humanities. Many disciplines currently have applied areas. Although the applied movement is controversial, especially in philosophy, philosophy is, nevertheless, the most applied discipline of all at the moment, and historically a period beginning in the early 1970's and continuing into the future to a time as yet undetermined will probably be characterized as the applied philosophy period.

It is customary in philosophy for all new ideas to be greeted with scorn and denounced on the grounds that they will destroy philosophy, and applied ethics is no exception. Nevertheless, applied ethics is a direct outgrowth of the philosophical periods that have preceded it. At the beginning of this century, a scientific philosophy, called logical positivism—for the most part a philosophy of science, but with bigger ambitions—devastated ethical theory. According to the positivists, ethical statements, like religious statements, are scientifically unverifiable and therefore have no meaning. Thus, they concluded, ethical statements and ethics in general are just expressions of emotion.[1]

After World War II, the logical positivists came under attack. In philosophy of science, critics started looking into what scientists really do and compared what they found with what the postitivists said about them. This examination of what came to be called the "logic of discovery" disclosed that it was possible to distinguish between the activities that scientists engaged in when making discoveries and those that they engaged in when justifying those discoveries. It turned out that the activities were quite different and accounts of one could not be substituted for the other. Parallel to these discussions in the philosophy of science, similar research was undertaken in ethics. Philosophers began looking into the logic of ethical inference, and it turned out, to the surprise of many philosophers, that people were not simply expressing their emotions when they made ethical decisions and that making decisions was different from justifying them. Work in this area was initially called practical ethics. As philosophers became more and more interested in examining specific ethical issues, practical ethics gradually transformed itself into applied ethics.

Applied ethics emeged at a time when doctors were increasingly concerned about ethical issues related to their medical practices. Medical ethics was therefore the first applied ethics to be developed, and it continues today to be the most successful and influential. Doctors and medical ethicists have worked very closely over the years, and in many cases their results have found their way into law and public policy.

In addition to medical ethics, there are several other prominent subdisciplines in applied ethics. Business ethics, engineering ethics, and other professional ethics are all very important. In many respects, feminist philosophy can be regarded as part of applied ethics. The area closest to environmental ethics is animal rights or animal liberation, which shares much common ground, but is nevertheless based on different principles.

In comparison with these other areas in applied ethics, environmental ethics is somewhat unusual, for unlike the others, it is not focused primarily on ethics. Rather it encompasses pieces of most of the more traditional fields within philosophy: in particular, aesthetics, metaphysics, epistemology, philosophy of science, and social and political philosophy. Whereas the other parts of applied ethics will likely remain distinct subject areas, as subdisciplines in philosophy, I expect that eventually environmental ethics will disappear as the various mainstream subject areas adjust and take account of the problems environmental ethics deals with. In other words, when the environment is properly taken into account in the basic fields within philosophy, there will be little need for environmental ethics as a distinct subject.

Although one might conclude from my projections about the pending demise of environmental ethics that it is not a very important subject within philosophy, such a conclusion would be an error. No area in applied ethics deals more fundamentally with philosophical issues than environmental ethics. It is a very serious challenge to philosophy as a whole because many of the basic elements of any environmental ethic adopted by Western civilization will almost certainly be incompatible with fundamental positions in the history of philosophy. It is because the basic assumptions in environmental ethics conflict with the basic assumptions of traditional Western philosophy that many philosophers argue that environmental ethics is not philosophical. If environmental ethics succeeds in overturning and replacing the flawed assumptions sprinkled throughout classical and early modern philosophy, the result will be a transformation of philosophy as we have known it, or, depending on how you look at it, philosophy and environmental ethics will become one.

This point would probably be easier to grasp if environmental ethics as a subject was not misnamed. A more appropriate name would have been environmental philosophy. Unfortunately, however, the field has taken the name of my journal, which was named *Environmental Ethics*, rather than *envirnomental philosophy*, to emphasize the value dimension and to discourage the submission of philosophy of science papers on evolution and the like without specific environmental and ethical implications. For various reasons, discussed in Chapter 1, philosophy has traditionally refused to acknowledge or directly face up to the physical existence of the Earth. Greek philosophers decided that the world as we experience it was not real. Modern philosophers devoted several centuries to doubting its existence. As a result, in both periods of the history of philosophy, the environment was left out. Once environmental ethics or environmental philosophy finishes putting the environment back into philosophy, it will be significantly different from what it is now.

In 1974, shortly after philosophers began working on environmental ethics, a book challenging the propriety of such research was published in England. The book was *Man's Responsibility for Nature: Ecological Problems and Western Traditions* by John Passmore, a noted social and political philosopher in Australia.[2] The basic argument of the book was that environmental ethics, not yet formally named, was inconsistent not only with Western philosophy but with Western traditions as a whole. It remained for many years the only book-length discussion of environmental ethics and was not formally answered on a comparable scale until 1983, when *The Ethics of Environmental Concern* by Robin Attfield, a British philosopher, was published.[3] Attfield's book goes over much the same material, drawing more favorable conclusions from it as far as environmental ethics is concerned. For example, Attfield argues that the stewardship tradition is more significant, or dominant, than the dominion tradition in Western thought and is therefore a better foundation for environmental ethics than Passmore allows in his treatment of these issues.

This book, like Attfield's, is intended as an answer to Passmore's position, but, unlike Attfield's, it covers new material that is not dealt with in Passmore's book. This material was overlooked by Passmore and others critical of environmental ethics because it is not part of the official history of Western philosophy, even though it touches on that history now and then. The material is primarily aesthetic and scientific and is thoroughly

Western. Although it is not part of traditional philosophy, it should have been, and would have been, if philosophers had not been too busy doubting the existence of the external world. This material shows conclusively, I argue, that environmental ethics is compatible, after all, with Western traditions.

I have called this book *Foundations of Environmental Ethics* for a very specific reason. The word *foundations* in the title is important. This book is not intended as an introduction to environmental ethics; nor is it intended as a definitive position on the subject. Rather it is an exploration of the roots of environmental ethics in Western thought together with the various ideas and philosophical positions that appear to make it non-Western. In *Man's Responsibility for Nature,* Passmore argues that for an environmental ethic to be successfully developed and adopted, it must be fully grounded in Western traditions. As he puts it:

> an ethic . . . is not the sort of thing one can simply decide to have; 'needing an ethic' is not in the least like 'needing a new coat.' A 'new ethic' will arise out of existing attitudes, or not at all.[4]

In this book, I demonstrate that there are existing Western attitudes and that they are the appropriate foundations for an environmental ethic. We do not need a new coat; the coat we have just needs a significant amount of tailoring.

This book is not concerned with the exact formulation of the ethical principles that will ultimately make up our environmental ethic. I expect that these principles will be a subject of debate for decades to come. Moreover, their final form will not be settled by philosophers but by ordinary people when they start using these principles to make decisions and to justify their actions.

Developing new ethical principles is not a matter that ethicists have had much experience with. Although there have been changes in our ethical principles and our moral values, these changes have, for the most part, simply happened in the real world and later been reflected in the writings of philosophers. This is the case with environmental ethics and animal liberation. The moral viewpoint of most North Americans and Europeans changed in the middle of the nineteenth century in a such a way that their treatment of animals and nature began to be noticeably different. These changes, however, were changes in moral intuition that could be expressed only fuzzily in language. As a result, both in animal liberation and in environmental ethics, we are still trying to find appropriate principles for behavior that is now more than a hundred years old.

The selection of principles is complicated by the fact that conflicting principles can often equally well account for the main features of our new ethical behavior. With regard to animal liberation, for example, the decision of most Westerners to conclude that it is morally wrong to inflict unnecessary suffering on animals can be accounted for either as a dim recognition that animals have rights—specifically, a right to life without unnecessary suffering—or as a restriction of human rights to inflict suffering on animals without any attribution of rights to the animals themselves. Though contradictory positions, they produce the same behavior in most cases. Only in tough or special cases in which our intuitions are not yet clear do the two positions on rights point us in different directions. Deciding how to select the right principle from two contradictory versions will be one of the difficult problems that will have to be faced as we gradually develop the principles of environmental ethics.

Elsewhere I have developed a model for ethical decision making through an examination of the way in which humans play chess.[5] Chess is an appropriate model because since 1850, when a large number of strategic and tactical rules were discovered in the play of a chess player from New Orleans named Paul Morphy, a great deal of theoretical activity has aimed at working out the rules for playing chess well. The history of rule development in chess provides some insight into the turns that rule development in environmental ethics is likely to take.

The first set of rules, gleaned from Morphy's play, were rules for the open game, in which pieces are exchanged to keep the board clear and the remaining pieces very mobile. These rules were followed by rules for the closed game, in which pieces are locked into stationary positions and very little movement is possible. It was believed for a time that all the rules were settled with the development of the rules for the half-open game and that the three sets of rules, taken together, constituted the scientific solution to the game of chess. As it turned out, however, this belief was shattered by the hypermodern reaction in which chess players emerged at the beginning of the century who could play by rules that were the contrary of the established rules and still win. For example, instead of moving their pieces to the center of the board, where they would, according to conventional wisdom, be more powerful by having more move opportunities, they conceded the center, allowing their opponents to become so powerful that they became weak. The hypermodern rules thus produced theoretical conflict in chess theory comparable to the conflict between animal rights accounts and restricted human rights accounts in animal liberation.

In practice, some of the hypermodern theory was assimilated into the general pool of strategic and tactical rules. However, not all of it could be, for most of the rules were too difficult to understand and apply. I, for one, after any extensive exposure to hypermodern theory, usually temporarily lose the ability to win a game. Such difficulties with hypermodern rules show that there are clear differences between various formulations of rules—some are easier to understand and use than others. What this means is that the determination of basic strategic and tactical rules depends more on their intelligibility than their theoretical precision. Rule development in environmental ethics will almost certainly be affected in the same way.

When contradictory rules accounting for the same behavior arise in theoretical discussions, the ultimate winner will most likely be the one that is most easily understood, and this may mean either easy to use or most in conformity with the individual's basic intuitions and moral world view.

Although usefulness and conformity to one's world view may at first seem like very different grounds, in actuality they are not. It is generallly supposed that rules are useful because they produce good results when we follow them. The teaching of chess rules, for example, is based on this belief. Chess books provide rules and examples. The reader tries to learn how to apply the rules to the sample situations in the hope of being able to do so in future situations that are similar. Curiously, however, close attention to what goes on in the mind of a person playing chess reveals that a chess player rarely follows a rule in any straightforward sense.[6] The player simply examines situations, mumbling something like, "If I do this, he'll do that." The player resorts to following a rule only when it becomes impossible to find any move that provides a definite advantage. Then the player thinks, "Since I can't think of anything else to do, and since doubling rooks on an open file is supposed to be a good idea, though I don't see any advantage in this case, I guess I'll do that for want of something better."

The absence of the rules in the decision process, however, does not mean that the teaching of the rules is an error, for when someone asks why a player made a particular move, the answer, when it is not simply "Because I could win a piece," is almost invariably in terms of rules and their application. The player will say that the situation is one in which this or that rule applies. What this means is that rules function most explicitly as aids in learning and as principles of justification. This does not mean that the rules are not involved in the making of decisions, but it does mean that they are usually not involved consciously.

In a study of the way that chess players make moves, Adriaan de Groote had players of varying skill examine a board situation in which exchanging a knight for a bishop produced an even result while exchanging a bishop for a knight won a piece.[7] The winning exchange was against the common textbook rule that it is better to trade a knight for a bishop than a bishop for a knight, since the value of a bishop increases during the game as its mobility increases and the value of a knight decreases as it becomes more vulnerable to attack. Although they did not consciously think about this rule, players of average and below-average ability did not consider the winning exchange at all. Players of above-average ability saw the winning move possibility almost immediately. What this kind of example shows is that even though the rules are not usually applied consciously, they unconsciously affect perception during the decision-making process. In light of this phenomenon, it is clear that the purpose of studying rules when one is a beginner is not to learn how to apply those rules but rather to improve perception.

The making of a decision in chess, and I believe equally so in life, is a very perceptual or intuitive process. The first step that de Groote identifies is *favorite formation,* in which a small group of possible solutions appears, basically out of nowhere. The second step is an *empirical investigation* in which possible results of each solution are examined. These results are evaluated in terms of what de Groote calls *maximum and minimum feelings of expectation,* feelings concerning the best and the worst that might be achieved. The empirical investigation proceeds in accordance with what de Groote calls *progressive deepening,* in which the favorite solutions are reexamined repeatedly in terms of the feelings of expectation. Although this continual reexamination of the same possibilities on the surface seems pointless, and de Goote thought at first that it was an indication of poor memory, it is the key element in the decision-making process of humans. The problem being solved is actually only very dimly perceived when the investigation begins, but it becomes clearer as the investigation proceeds. Each attempt to solve the problem also contributes to a better understanding of the problem, which, as a result, goes through a series of changes as it approaches its final form. The reinvestigation of previously rejected solutions is periodically necessary to determine whether one of them is now the solution to the problem in its newest form. Because the problem is in flux until it is solved, the decision maker cannot simply apply the appropriate rule by rote.

This kind of thought process, though rule-governed, is not rule-following. Although the justification of a decision can and should be a presentation of rules as they relate to a specific situation in a rule-following format, the decision process itself does not conform to this pattern. The inappropriateness of a rule-following characterization of decision making is especially clear when one considers the phenomenon of favorite formation. First, the group of favorite solutions that emerges at the beginning of the decision process is almost never enlarged. The decision maker reexamines the group of favorites with the intention of including new ones only as a last resort, when extensive investigation of the favorites has produced results that are below the minimum level of expectation. Second, the favorites in the group usually also appear in ranked form, and the highest-ranked favorite is usually the solution ultimately selected. It is for this reason that good chess players are still able to play quite well when they play quickly, as in lightning chess. Finally, the accuracy of the ranking increases dramatically with experience and skill level. An international grandmaster sees more on the chessboard in a few seconds than an average player sees in thirty minutes. This aspect of the decision process makes it absolutely clear that decision making is primarily a kind of seeing, not a kind of rule-following activity.

Although rules are, of course, valuable, they cannot fully account for the subtleties expressed unconsciously in the perceptual dimensions of the decision process. The lists of rules in beginning chess books do not form a rational system of interlocking rules of action. For the most part, each rule is independent. There is no definite hierarchy. There is no order of precedence between rules like "Don't move your queen out too early in the game," "Double your rooks on an open file," or "Exchange bishops for knights but not knights for bishops." The rules themselves are so general that numerous examples can easily be brought forward in which following them would miss a win or even lose the game. There is also nothing in the rules that provides assistance in choosing between them when more than one applies and there is no way to take them all into account. The exceptions to these rules, moreover, are generally far too numerous to list exhaustively and as a result are only implicitly (unconsciously) connected up with them. They rise to the surface only when they are consciously needed. What holds the rules together like a kind of glue, provides the necessary order, and makes them appear to be a system for learning and justification is not something in the system of rules itself; rather it is the experience of the individual, which is best expressed as perception or interpretation, as a kind of world view, so to speak.

Although it is commonly believed that environmental ethics will ultimately produce a tight, rationally ordered set of rules that can automatically be applied with great precision, I think that the likelihood that such an environmental ethic will ever be produced is zero, or very close to it. If such systems of rules were possible, chess theoreticians in the past 120 years would certainly have produced such a system for chess players. Instead they have produced a hodgepodge of rules that are useful in learning and justification but play no direct role in decision making. This situation, I argue, is not the result of some sort of failure on the part of those working on chess theory; rather it is a reflection of the fact that such a system is not needed and, given the manner in which the human mind actually decides, would not be useful even if it did exist.

In making these points, I am not suggesting that the quest for an environmental ethic is hopeless, for it is not. I am only stressing that our environmental ethic, when we really have one, will be a collection of independent ethical generalizations, only loosely related, not a rationally ordered system of ethical prescriptions. People who want to understand and follow this environmental ethic will have to study the application of these generalizations to specific situations, as if they are learning to apply rules, but in fact they wil be internalizing these rules or generalizations and in this way learning to see the world aright from the standpoint of environmental ethics. In a manner exactly analogous to the way that chess players become good chess players, they will be developing an environmental world view.

The creation of such a collection of independent ethical generalizations will take a long time, probably longer than it took to create the body of chess rules that beginners use today. These rules will have to be argued about at length, and real people in the real world will have to try them out to see if they work.

In bits and pieces, this book makes some contribution to this rule development process, but that is not its primary purpose. In my own experiments with chess learning, I have found that the direct study of rule application is not the only way in which one's chess perception can be improved. A beginner who is given a book of rules will undoubtedly make substantial improvement. However, greater improvement can be expected if the beginner is also given a book of the theoretical history of the rules. The book of beginning rules and the book of theoretical history complement each other, the first providing the details to be sweated out and transformed into perception, the second the overview that explains in part at least the how and sometimes even the why of the rules.[8]

It is in this context that this book has been written, as a historically-oriented theoretical overview. As such, it is in part a response to Passmore's claim that environmental thought has no history in Western traditions. In this regard it may also be helpful to readers who would like to know why they and other people, both in favor of enviromental protection and against it, say the kinds of things they do. Primarily, however, it is intended as a foundation for efforts to formulate principles or rules for environmental ethics that will clarify our basic environmental intuitions and provide guidance for ethical education, decision making, and justification. In this regard, its object is not the selection and perfection of those rules out of conflicting alternatives, as they now exist intuitively in the minds of environmentalists, but rather the establishment of a theoretical framework in which the selection and perfection of the rules can take place and be facilitated.

In looking over the subjects covered in this book, some people may conclude that it fails to provide background for some of the most important arguments in environmental ethics—for example, that nature ought to be protected because it is instrumentally valuable to human life, health, and welfare. To be sure, arguments of this sort are fundamentally important to environmental ethics. They are probably even the best and most convincing ones. I have not dealt with these arguments, however, except indirectly and, from time to time, critically, because from the standpoint of environmental ethics they offer no theoretical problems except when they are presented as the *only* arguments needed.[9] These arguments are really the foundations of what might be called, in opposition to environmental ethics, traditional ethics. To say that they are in opposition, nevertheless, is not quite right, for it is better to think of environmental ethics as an extension of traditional ethics, covering matters to which Westerners have traditionally been blind. Since the instrumental arguments for the protection of nature are so well grounded that they need little or no defense, I have not treated them at any length. Thus, narrowly speaking, this book really constitutes the foundations of nature preservation, taken as a group of arguments calling for the protection of nature on noninstrumental grounds, independent of considerations about the life, health, and welfare of humans. It provides the foundations of environmental ethics more generally only when it is viewed in the context of traditional ethics, as modified to accept appropriate noninstrumental environmental arguments.

This focus on noninstrumental or intrinsic value arguments may be confusing to those readers who, following the lead of the deep ecologists, exclusively identify instrumental values with anthropocentrism and intrinsic values with nonanthropocentrism. As I argue in Chapters 5 and 6, both instrumental and intrinsic values can be either anthropocentric or nonanthropocentric. Traditional ethics is usually considered to be anthropocentric in the sense that nature is valued only to the degree that it is instrumentally valuable to human beings. This is, however, an oversimplification. Although it is true that nature is so valued by most human beings, it does not follow that all instrumental values in nature are anthropocentric or that all intrinsic values are nonanthropocentric. There are, first of all, innumerable instrumental relationships in natural systems that are completely independent of any possible instrumental value to human beings, and these (or similar) nonanthropocentric instrumental values would exist whether humans had ever evolved and will continue to exist even after humans become extinct, so long as life itself persists. With regard to intrinsic value, humans have for nearly three centuries valued natural beauty for its own sake and without regard to its human uses, and this human or anthropocentric valuing has never depended on any nonanthropocentric factors or arguments.

In environmental ethics it is frequently contended that instrumental value arguments are an inadequate foundation and must be supplemented or replaced by nonanthropocentric intrinsic value arguments. I am sympathetic to this position but do not attempt to deal with it in any significant way in this book, since I find no support for the view in the history of ideas out of which contemporary environmental thought has evolved. Instead, I focus on anthropocentric intrinsic value arguments, which no one in the anthropocentric/nonanthropocentric debate seems interested in but which, nevertheless, are strongly supported by the history of ideas that actually shaped our basic environmental attitudes.

I harbor no illusion that the foundations explicated in this book will be fully satisfying to anyone. Although they are only "weakly anthropocentric," since they allow for anthropocentric intrinsic value arguments, they are anthropocentric nonetheless and therefore not likely to be well received by readers who hold that nothing short of a nonanthropocentric foundation will do. I ask of such readers the willing suspension of their disbelief, for it is not my intention in this book to do anything to discourage research into the development of nonanthropocentric foundations. I wish here merely to put our environmental house in order historically, constructing or reconstructing arguments based on the actual evolution of our environmental attitudes, so that further research can proceed without unnecessary confusion or delay. The clarification of these matters is, I believe, of importance whether nonanthropocentric arguments ultimately triumph or not. If they do, these weak anthropocentric foundations will serve only as a temporary defense against anthropocentric positions that are exclusively instrumental and will eventually become nothing more than historical curiosities. Should the quest for foundations based primarily on nonanthropocentric intrinsic value fail, however, and we be forced to align our preservationist arguments with the actual history of ideas that created our basic intuitions and attitudes, the foundations described in this book may achieve a more lasting importance in the long-term debate over the nature and character of environmental ethics.

The main body of this book is divided into three parts. In the first, I examine the positions that inhibit the development of an environmental ethic; in the second, I provide accounts of the history of ideas that has produced environmental thought; and in the third, I develop a general argument, in the context of Parts I and II, in favor of the preservation of nature. In Chapter 1, I discuss the role of philosophy in debates about environmental ethics and show why most philosophers usually claim that environmental ethics is in conflict with Western philosophy and the traditions of Western civilization. In Chapter 2, I examine land use attitudes that are closely connected with Western conceptions of private property and that have historically inhibited the development of concern about the environment. It is these attitudes, rather than the philosophical ones discussed in Chapter 1, that, in practice, exert the greater influence, although they, through the social and political writings of Locke, in particular, may be said to be philosophical attitudes as well. In Chapter 3, I present an account of the aesthetic and scientific attitudes that provide the fundamental intuitions upon which environmental thought and environmentalism in general are based. In Chapter 4, I examine wildlife protection attitudes as a special case of the general position developed in Chapter 3. In Chapter 5, I consider and reject an instrumental argument for protecting nature based on the belief that we humans will never develop the technical ability to manipulate nature without unforeseen side effects. I argue that the environmental defense of nature should not, for prudential reasons, be based on speculations about the limitations of ecological science but rather should be based more positively on our environmental values. In Chapter 6, I present an argument, in terms of our traditional environmental values and based on the history of ideas discussed in Chapters 3 and 4, that we humans have a duty to preserve nature in general because the existence of natural beauty, defined very broadly, represents a positive good in the world. I conclude the book with an afterword in which I discuss the relationship of environmental ethical and political action in democratic societies, provide a context in which public education in environmental ethics may be possible, and suggest a way in which the conflicts between environmental and economic values can be reconciled so that we may eventually be able to act and live in accordance with an environmental ethic.

Though it may not be obvious at first glance, much of the book comes very directly out of my experiences trying to protect a cave in Missouri, called Devil's Icebox, from water pollution in the early 1970s. Chapters 3 and 4 present my research on the history of ideas behind the kinds of arguments that I used in trying to protect the cave. Chapter 2 deals with the history of ideas behind the arguments that local landowners presented in reply. Chapter 1 recounts many of the aspects of the history of Western philosophy that made it difficult for me as a philosopher, when I first started thinking about environmental ethics, to recognize that there is a philosophical and ethical dimension to environmental problems.

The last two chapters and the afterword, in contrast, do not reflect my personal experiences to any significant degree. Chapter 5 is, in important respects, an evaluation of Barry Commoner's third law of ecology, "Nature knows best." Chapter 6 is a new position of my own creation intended as a substitute for the environmentalist's frequently heard argument that nature has a right to exist. Although I do not present a rights argument, I do try to take into account the special significance of natural existence in the environmentalist's world view. The afterword is primarily my response to Passmore's claims in *Man's Responsibility for Nature* that environmentalism is undemocratic and that economic arguments in theory will always override environmental arguments in management situations.

The foundations of environmental ethics that I identify in this book are in the broadest sense Western, meaning European, but more specifically they are American, that is, Western environmental attitudes as they have ultimately developed in the United States. This emphasis deserves some explanation. One of the reasons for this focus is that my interest in environmental ethics is tied directly to the American environmental world view. The primary reason, however, is that the book is intended as an answer to John Passmore's critique of environmentalism and environmental ethics as presented in his book *Man's Responsibility for Nature*, in which Passmore frequently depicts the positions he is attacking as American.

While this focus on American attitudes is historically correct, it can nevertheless lead to some misunderstandings and confusions about what environmental ethics is and should be. Despite the American contribution to environmental ethics and environmental thought internationally, it should not be suppposed that there will be, or ought to be, at some definite time in the future, an American-based environmental ethic for the whole Earth. The establishment of such an ethic would not, I believe, serve any useful purpose, for it could not possibly capture the basic environmental intuitions of all the peoples on this planet. In my view, what is needed is not a single universalizable environmental ethic but rather a family of them, customized to take into account the national and cultural differences in Western society and between East and West. It is in this global context that this book should be read: as a contribution to the development of an environmental ethic in the United States and as a model for similar efforts in other countries and cultures around the world.

NOTES

1. See A.J. Ayer's "Critique of Ethics and Theology" in A.J. Ayer, *Language, Truth and Logic* (New York: Dover Publications, 1950), pp. 102–120.
2. John Passmore, *Man's Responsiblity for Nature: Ecological Problems and Western Traditions*, 2nd ed. (London: Duckworth, 1980).
3. Robin Attfield, *The Ethics of Concern for Nature* (New York: Columbia University Press, 1983).
4. Passmore, *Man's Responsibility*, p. 56.
5. Eugene C. Hargrove, "The Role of Rules in Ethical Decision Making," *Inquiry* 28 (1985): 3–42.
6. For a more comprehensive account than I give here, see Hargrove, "Role of Rules," pp. 12–19.
7. Ibid., p. 14; Adriaan de Groote, *Thought and Choice in Chess,* ed. George W. Baylor (The Hague: Mouton, 1965), p. 90.
8. The best set of rules, in my opinion, is Reuben Fine, *Chess, the Easy Way* (New York: Cornerstone Library, 1942); the best theoretical history is Richard Reti, *Modern Ideas in Chess* (New York: Dover Publications, 1969).
9. See, for example, Passmore, *Man's Responsibility*, pp. 54–57.

Part I
Traditional Positions

CHAPTER ONE
PHILOSOPHICAL ATTITUDES

In his famous essay "The Land Ethic," Aldo Leopold states his conviction that environmental problems are ultimately philosophical in nature and require a philosophical solution before there can be much hope of environmental reform. Although he is aware that philosophers have taken little or no interest in the environment, Leopold does not blame them for their inactivity but rather faults contemporary environmentalists, who, he says, have failed to make conservation something worthy of philosophical attention. He writes:

> No important change in ethics was ever accomplished without an internal change in our intellectual emphasis, loyalties, affections, and convictions. The proof that conservation has not yet touched these foundations of conduct lies in the fact that philosophy and religion have not yet heard of it. In our attempt to make conservation easy, we have made it trivial.[1]

While this general criticism of twentieth-century environmentalists and their methods may be deserved, it is an exaggeration to claim that they had anything to do with Western philosophy's insensitivity and lack of interest in environmental issues. Actually, the ideas and attitudes that have kept philosophy and religion from paying attention to the environmental movement have been part of Western civilization and thought for thousands of years and transcend all recent environmentalist activity. The simple truth is that philosophy in particular has always been either irrelevant or incompatible with environmental thinking since Western man first began philosophizing almost three thousand years ago.

It is, however, perhaps a little harsh to *blame* philosophy and philosophers for the modern environmental crisis, since we normally assess blame for doing something wrong when it is possible to determine that it could and should have been done in another way. Philosophers living hundreds and even thousands of years ago can hardly have been expected to have foreseen our present troubles, which in large measure stem from the presence on the Earth of enormous numbers of people—numbers inconceivable in earlier times. Yet philosophy, which is the primary source of most Western ideas, is in some less passionate and morally reprehensible sense *responsible* for the ideas and attitudes that inhibit environmental protection today, and a close look at the origins and history of Western philosophy can help clarify these matters even though it may not resolve them.

Religion, in contrast, though often criticized by environmentalists as the chief culprit, has played a much less fundamental role. Most of the environmentally offensive ideas in Western religion originated not in religion but in Western philosophy. It could easily be argued that religion, by continually borrowing from philosophy, was itself victimized by it. Charges that religion is responsible for our environmental problems usually depend on special interpretations of early passages of Genesis involving the claim that God intended man to have dominion over the Earth.[2] It can be argued that Genesis caused human beings to begin the transformation of nature that has continued to the present day with disastrous consequences. The weakness of this accusation is, as John Passmore has noted, that Genesis was written long after this transformation began and thus could hardly be the initial cause.[3] At most Genesis merely states a view of man's relationship to nature that was commonly accepted at the time the book was written and probably predated the Old Testament by many thousands of years.

It can still be argued, however, as Passmore suggests, that Genesis was intended as a justification for the human modification of the Earth and as such was an attempt by man to "salve his conscience."[4] While this interpretation may place religion at the center of an almost prehistoric guilt-ridden debate over human impact on the environment, it too is difficult to defend. It is hard to imagine that human beings at the dawn of civilization could have perceived the damaging influence of their actions so clearly when their descendants have only begun to achieve a dim understanding of the relationships involved in the past hundred years. It is probably more reasonable to speculate that early humans were more concerned with salving their fear of nature than their guilt and that Genesis served less as a justification of environmentally offensive actions than as a comfort and hope for people unsure of their place in the natural world and therefore preoccupied with survival.

Most likely Genesis did not become environmentally troublesome until the late Middle Ages, when church philosophers interpreted it in accordance with the writings of Aristotle, a newly rediscovered Greek philosopher who thought that the purpose of the world was the service of man.[5] Later it also became entangled in political philosophy, for example, when it was used by John Locke, an English philosopher of the seventeenth century, to help justify his theory of property—a theory that was to have important influence on environmental debates in nineteenth-century America.[6] The association of these philosophical ideas with the passages in Genesis transformed them into primarily philosophical rather than religious doctrines.

Two periods in the history of philosophy have been most instrumental in shaping philosophical attitudes toward the environment: classical Greek philosophy and early modern European philosophy. Although they are closely related, they need to be dealt with separately.

GREEK PHILOSOPHY

Greek philosophy is normally divided into two parts: the two hundred–year period before Socrates and all subsequent philosophy after Socrates until the Roman conquest. Its high point came at the beginning of the second period with the work of Plato and Aristotle. Although these two men have probably had a greater impact on Western thought than all other philosophers combined, they were working within an established philosophical tradition that had in large measure already determined the general direction of Western philosophy. Thus the pre-Socratic period needs to be examined first before turning to them.

Basic Presuppositions

Pre-Socratic philosophy was almost exclusively concerned with speculation about the natural world. Some attention was focused on biological matters, rather amazingly with results that anticipated the theory of evolution. Anaximader, one of the earliest known philosophers, for example, claimed that man came from a fish.[7] About a century later, Empedocles proposed an evolutionary theory anticipating the "survival of the fittest" doctrine.[8] These ideas, however, though interesting, did not find a permanent place in Western thought and apparently had no influence on nineteenth-century evolutionary biologists. Much more important historically were early Greek speculations about the nature of matter and its interactions with mind. The latter remains one of the major unresolved problems still confronting philosophers today. The former was an essential ingredient in the development of natural science. However silly and simplistic the actual ideas offered by these early philosophers may seem by modern scientific standards, they served admirably as preliminary studies that helped make possible physics as we know it today.

The first philosopher of whom we have any record was Thales, born in Miletus in 640 B.C. His most spectacular accomplishment was the predication of a solar eclipse in 585 B.C. Unfortunately, none of his writings have survived, and his views are known only from criticism of his ideas found in the writings of later philosophers. Only three statements have been directly attributed to him: (1) The first principle of all things is water, (2) the lodestone has a soul because it draws iron, and (3) all things are full of gods.[9] Admittedly, these remarks do not provide us with enough information to determine what Thales' philosophical views were as a whole, but they do shed some light on the kinds of problems and questions that Thales was concerned with and the assumptions he made about the natural world.

Judging by these fragments, Thales was primarily interested in the nature of the physical world and its interrelationships with mind. He conceived of the world in material or physical terms and was fundamentally committed to the idea that objects encountered in the world were made out of some kind of material substance or matter. One of the problems that he set for himself was the identification of this underlying substance. When Thales said that the first principle was water, he was hypothesizing that water was the substance out of which all physical objects were formed. In addition, he was curious about how the soul or mind influenced physical objects. According to Aristotle, Thales believed that mind was the source of motion and could move objects. In this sense, the ability of the lodestone or magnet to move iron was supposed to be an indication that it might have a soul. Thales' statement that all things were full of gods, Aristotle adds, might mean that mind or soul is distributed throughout the world and intermingled with it.[10]

The concept of matter in Thales' philosophy, whether it originated with him or not, has been one of the most influential contributions of Greek thought to Western philosophy. Although no one accepted Thales' conclusion that water was the ultimate substance, everyone agreed that there was an underlying substance of some kind, and each major philosopher after Thales offered his own speculations about what it might be. Anaximander, a contemporary of Thales' in Miletus, called it the "infinite." Anaximenes said it was air. Pythagoras, enraptured with mathematics, said that it was "number." Heraclitus suggested fire, and Xenophanes, earth. Empedocles proposed four elements: earth, air, fire, and water. According to Anaxagorus, it was an infinity of infinitely divisible "seeds". Democritus, going one step further, claimed that it was an infinity of atoms, which were not themselves further divisible. Despite occasional lapses of interest, the physical composition of the world has continued to fascinate and puzzle Western philosophers and scientists ever since. Atoms, electrons, protons, neutrons, and now quarks are only the most recent answers to the problem Thales raised nearly 2500 years ago.

Equally important to the future of Western philosophy and science, however, were three other assumptions implicit in Thales' philosophy: (1) that the world has a rational structure, (2) that this structure is knowable, and (3) that it is relatively simple and easy to understand. Thales believed that the world was organized in an orderly manner and that the principles describing or governing this order were true in all parts of the universe. Furthermore, he was convinced that these principles could be discovered and comprehended through the use of reason. In other words, man, by engaging in *rational* activity, could uncover the secrets of a *rational* world. Finally, Thales undertook his investigations with an almost arrogant optimism. He did not humbly set out to learn something about the workings of nature but rather immediately sought the *first* principle upon which all the rest of the structure or order depended, confident that everything else would fall into place once it was found.

Although pre-Socratic philosophers after Thales did not challenge any of his basic assumptions, they did consider his characterization of matter naive. Subsequent work in philosophy during this period thus focused on efforts to develop a fuller account of the nature of matter. According to Anaximander, it was foolish to suppose that the ultimate substance was one of the more obvious elements—earth, air, fire, or water—for none of these was very fundamental since one could be observed turning into another.[11] The true underlying substance, he argued, had to be something that was not itself encountered in ordinary experience. While all this may seem little more than common sense to people in the twentieth century who are used to the idea that physical objects, such as tables and chairs, are made out of atoms, it was this aspect of Anaximander's philosophy that provided the foundation for the type of scientific inquiry that would centuries later produce modern physics and chemistry. Anaximander's position, moreover, although critical of Thales' theory of matter, was nevertheless supportive of his basic assumptions about the nature of scientific inquiry. The idea that the underlying substance was not identifiable in the world as we perceive it through the senses further encouraged the pre-Socratics to seek knowledge through reason alone and disregard sensation. This assumption was challenged only once many years later, when Anaxagorus proposed that matter was composed of "seeds", tiny replicas of observable objects, which would therefore have sensible properties, though too small to be seen. Ultimately it proved very useful, with the emergence of modern physics at the end of the Middle Ages, specifically, in the context originally intended by Anaximander, the investigation of physical matter.

The Problem of Change

Most of the pre-Socratic period was devoted to a debate about the nature of motion and change, and it is in terms of this controversy that the Western conception of matter achieved its final form. Although one pre-Socratic, Heraclitus, tried to base his philosophy on change, stating at the outset that the world was in flux, most philosophers of the time were profoundly troubled by change, for it seemed to them to be logically impossible for change to take place at all. They reasoned that for something to change, it was necessary at some moment in time for the object that was changing to stop being what it was and start being something else. Since time was held to be infinitely divisible, this meant that at some tiny moment of time the object would no longer be what it had been and still not yet be what it would soon be, and at that moment it would be nothing at all. This argument reinforced the Greek suspicion that material objects as encountered in experience through the senses were illusory and nonexistent, and it led them to a conception of matter that was permanent and unchanging.

The arguments against change culminated in the philosophy of Parmenides, who believed that something could not come from nothing and that what existed could not cease to exist. What is, is, he declared; what is not, is not; what is, cannot not be; and what is not, cannot be. Since the world of change violated these principles, he concluded that it could not exist and must therefore be an illusion. What really existed, Parmenides claimed, must be "without beginning, indestructable, entire, single, unshakable, endless." He called this the "One," arguing that the idea of a world of *many* objects was just one more illusion. This position not only denied the existence of the world but also set strict limits on language and thought. The object of thought and language must physically exist, Parmenides argued, and since the One was the only existent object, only one sentence was possible: "Being is." All other thoughts and statements were nonsense because they referred to things that did not exist. To say, for instance, that an object was red was ridiculous, since the statement "This object is red" for Parmenides also asserted that it was *not* blue, *not* brown, and so on, all assertions of nonbeing or nonexistence.[12]

Strange though these arguments may sound to modern ears, they were taken very seriously by Greek philosophers and were strongly defended by Parmenides' supporters, particularly Zeno and Melissus of Samos. Zeno is well known for his many interesting paradoxes about arrows that cannot move in flight and slow-moving tortoises that cannot be overtaken by the fastest runner, all designed to illustrate the logical absurdity of more conventional views of the world and the consequent necessity of accepting Parmenides' philosophy of the One. Although Greek philosophers eventually rejected Parmenides' philosophy, they adopted his general conception of matter as eternal, unchanging, permanent, indivisible, indestructable, and immovable. By way of the Greek and Roman atomists, Parmenides' monism was converted into a pluralism of atoms, in which change was explained in terms of the rearrangement of atoms, and was in this form adopted by modern physics. Not only did the original atom of physics conform to Parmenidian specifications as an indivisible, unchanging, and indestructable entity, but so has every new subatomic entity that has ever been proclaimed the ultimate building block of the universe.

The most immediate effect of Parmenides' philosophy, however, had nothing to do with the atomic theory. In denying the possibility of language and thought. Parmenides was also denying the very possibility of epistemology, metaphysics, and science. Had his conclusions been allowed to stand in full, it would have meant the end of philosophical and scientific speculation, with devastating impact on the course of Western civilization.

Plato and Aristotle

Although the philosophies of Plato and Aristotle are much richer and more diverse than any of the pre-Socratics, they may for our purposes here be treated primarily as answers to Parmenides. Plato accepted Parmenides' claims that real entities must be eternal, permanent, immovable, indestructable, and so on, but he argued that epistemology and metaphysics were not impossible. According to Plato, the universality of concepts suggested that there were "forms" or "ideas" that governed our perception of the world and our thought. These forms did not exist in the world of experience but were outside of it and could be reached or perceived only through the use of reason. The world of the senses was in turn what shadows were to the world of the forms. The relationship of the conceptual and physical worlds was one of "participation." We know and understand a concept like equality, Plato claimed, by seeing the participation of objects in the natural world in this concept. Of course, no two objects are exactly equal, but they suggest the idea of equality to us. Geometric objects are suggested to us in the same way, as, for instance, when triangular objects participate in triangularity. Similarly, physical objects, such as trees, participate in the form of tree, and human beings participate in the form of man.

Metaphysically, this theory was rather disappointing. Although the mental realm of the forms, since it was unchanging and indestructable, was fully real or existent, Plato, like Parmenides, conceded that the world of experience did not really exist, since change and becoming necessitated moments of nonexistence; nevertheless, he did make some improvement even here by allowing limited reality to physical objects to the extent that they participated in the forms. In epistemology, however, Plato managed a major breakthrough by providing an adequate basis for knowledge and rational thought while still working within the framework of Parmenides' fundamental assumptions. By claiming that all the forms were logically connected to all the others—and as a group subsumed under the ultimate form, the Beautiful and the Good—Plato was able to meet the Parmenidian requirement for unity, which, taken together with the permanence and indestructability of the forms, saved knowledge, thought, and language from Parmenides' arguments. As such, it represented an epistemological solution to the problem of change.

The metaphysical solution, in turn, was achieved by Aristotle. Rejecting Plato's two-world concept of reality, Aristotle brought the forms down into the natural world, where he joined them with matter forming natural objects, which were combinations of matter and form. Form existed in these objects in a double sense—potentially and actually. The actual form was the set of properties exhibited by an object at a given moment. Potential forms latent in the matter of the object were forms that could be actualized in the future. On one level, change was characterized as the actualization of these potential properties. On another level, it was also characterized as a superficial movement and rearrangement of matter in space. By arguing that matter and form did not themselves change at either level, Aristotle succeeded in producing a credible explanation of change that did not violate Parmenides' arguments that absolute change was impossible.

Aristotle's solution to the problem of change brought to a close a very fruitful period on epistemological and metaphysical speculation. As should be obvious, this period prepared the way for the emergence of modern science in the seventeenth century. What may be less obvious, however, is that it also prepared the way for attitudes toward nature that are very much incompatible with modern environmental thinking. It is to these matters that we now turn.

GREEK INFLUENCE ON ENVIRONMENTAL THINKING

Using the preceding sketch as a guide, I shall now argue that Greek philosophers approached natural phenomena in a way that (1) prevented the development of an ecological perspective, (2) discouraged the aesthetic appreciation of the natural world, and (3) promoted a conception of reality that made the idea of nature preservation conceptually difficult, if not impossible.

The Ecological Perspective

Because of the general direction that Greek philosophy took from its very beginnings, in Asia Minor, it was virtually impossible for Greek philosophers to think ecologically in any systematic way. To begin with, the Greeks would not have considered an understanding of ecological relationships in nature to be knowledge. Objects of knowledge, like the ultimate objects of reality, were believed to be permanent, eternal, and unchanging. Ecological relationships, in contrast, are concerned with objects that are impermanent, perishable, and in a constant state of change. By Greek standards, therefore, an understanding of such objects could at best be good opinion, not knowledge, and could have no place of importance in the quest for the ultimate principles governing the nature of existence.

Similarly, the belief that the world has a rational structure also pointed the Greeks away from an ecological awareness of the world by discouraging firsthand observation. Wary of information gathered by the senses, the Greeks sought first principles from which they could deduce all other knowledge by reason. Because sensory data was considered a hindrance to the exercise of reason, it was seldom the starting point for metaphysical speculation and almost never used as a check on the validity of conclusions drawn by logical inference. In the *Phaedo*, for example, Socrates is portrayed as eagerly awaiting his own death so that he may at last employ his powers of reason free from the annoyances and distortions of the world of the senses.[13] This preference and reliance on reason and disdain and disregard for the senses made it unlikely that the results of philosophical reasoning would bear much similarity to actual ecological relationships and processes in the natural world.

A good example of the inhibiting effects of this rational approach to nature is found in the Greek conceptions of earth, air, fire, and water—all of great importance in modern ecological science. Since the Greeks frequently spoke of these phenomena and made some attempt to investigate their interrelationships, one might expect that they would have discovered a few ecological principles and relationships and developed a rudimentary ecological perspective. Greek philosophers, however, were not really interested in these phenomena as phenomena but only as stand-ins for ultimate substances or elements, and since matter was supposed to be something outside of immediate experience, its study was always suspect. In other words, study of the physical elements merely as encountered in nature and perceived through the senses was considered superficial, peripheral, and inconsequential, of no philosophical significance.

Equally damaging was the belief that change was impossible and therefore illusory. Because earth, air, fire, and water, the elements that were supposed to make up the world as we encountered it, were the phenomena most often observed in association with change, the logical implication was that they, like the rest of the world, were not real either. Interest in these elements persisted, but they were commonly viewed as superfluous sensory phenomena that veiled reality and did not partake of it in any significant degree. Aristotle's separation of metaphysics and physics permitted their reintroduction as subjects worthy of investigation, but even then they remained makeshift elements to be discarded when more suitable elements could be found. With the rise of modern science at the end of the Middle Ages, they dropped out of physics altogether to become part of astrology and alchemy. When scientific method was at last applied to these elements, the result was chemistry, not ecology.

Compare, for example, the Greek philosophical conception of fire with its counterpart in ecology in the twentieth century. Ecologists today find the study of fire in nature to be a complex and fascinating subject. They sometimes see it as part of an ecological cycle in which forest periodically becomes open grassland, allowing the reintroduction for a time of various animals that need specific habitats represented by distinct stages in the conversion of the grassland back into forest. Other times they see it as an instrument of the status quo, keeping adjacent forested areas from overrunning steppes and prairie. On still other occasions they even see it as a necessary step in the reproduction of plants, for example, sequoia saplings in the western United States that only grow on ground that has first been cleared by fire. Although in principle the Greeks could have drawn similar conclusions, their general philosophical orientation made such discoveries virtually impossible. When a Greek philosopher looked at fire in nature, it raised questions in his mind about the physical and chemical principles governing combustion, not about the effect of the fire on the natural history of the area.

Still another obstacle to the growth of an ecological point of view was the assumption that the rational structure of the world is simple. The complexity of the world did not fascinate the Greeks as it does us today; rather it bewildered and frustrated them, seemingly denying them the access to the first principles of nature that they so fervently desired to possess. The simplicity assumption encouraged the Greeks to ignore complex relationships in favor of simpler ones and contributed to the development of a method of investigation, the reductionist method, that concentrated on parts in isolation from the complex whole. This method was based on the idea that complex interactions and relationships could be broken down into a series of simple ones. Although this approach was undoubtedly essential to the development of the scientific method and the discoveries of physics and chemistry, it was not true of the world as a whole and unsuitable for ecological investigation, since, as we know today, most ecological interactions and relationships are too complex to be studied in isolation as simple and independent parts.

To a very large degree, even the kinds of relationships that the Greeks were looking for in their search for rational structure were inappropriate for the development of an ecological perspective. Because the Greek method of inquiry involved a step-by-step deductive procedure, philosophers tended to seek out and focus on relationships that were necessary and universal—that is, relationships that cannot be otherwise than they are and that are true in all times and places.[14] These can be dealt with very easily in deductive arguments because they are always true regardless of the circumstances. Most ecological relationships, however, are not of this kind. They are the product of a specific evolutionary history that could have happened in many other ways and are thus contingent or accidental, dependent on the circumstances in particular states of affairs. Such relationships cannot be discovered by the use of reason alone; extensive and painstaking observation and experimentation are required, approaches that the Greeks viewed with suspicion. Moreover, the large number of possibilities involved in such relationships limits their usefulness in deductive arguments. Knowledge of the existence of the panda, for example, cannot be deduced from knowledge of bamboo, or vice versa. Nor does knowledge of the dietary dependency of the panda on bamboo provide us with enough information to deduce the specific properties or characteristics of either organism. All kinds of animals could have developed a dependency on bamboo, and if bamboo had never existed, the ancestor of the panda could have turned to some other plant. If the Greeks had stumbled across ecological relationships of this kind, they probably would have discarded them as marginally interesting but useless bits of opinion and returned to their search for necessary and universal relationships more in tune with their deductive approach.

Of all the major Greek philosophers, Aristotle was the only one who came close to approaching nature from an ecological perspective. Although he never abandoned his metaphysical interests, he argued forcefully in *De Partibus Animalium* that the study of ultimate substances in the pre-Socratic manner had to be supplemented by the investigation of natural objects, plants, and animals as they are encountered in nature:

> But if men and their several parts are natural phenomena, then the natural philosopher must take into consideration not merely the ultimate substances of which they are made, but also flesh, bone, blood, and all other homogeneous parts; not only these, but also the heterogeneous parts, such as face, hand, foot; and must examine how each of these come to be what it is, and in virtue of what force.[15]

This shift of focus permitted Aristotle to make the transition from pure metaphysical speculation to pioneer work in biology and botany.

In addition, Aristotle developed an interest in geology and in this connection made observations that indicated that he was very much aware of environmental change. In the *Meteorology*, for example, he notes that the plain of Egypt was formed by deposits of silt left by the Nile, and generalizing on such observations, he concludes that from time to time major changes have taken place both locally and over vast regions of the Earth's surface. Many of these changes have gone unnoticed, he writes, because they have occurred over immense periods of time, sometimes longer than the histories of particular peoples or civilizations.[16]

Despite his recognition that environmental changes occurred frequently, however, Aristotle does not seem to have developed any interest in nature protection. On one occasion, for instance, Aristotle mentions that the Egyptians abandoned work on a canal linking the Nile and Red Sea when engineers determined that the Red Sea was higher than the Nile valley and might therefore flood the valley with salt water, spoiling the river and the land.[17] This example could have given Aristotle an excellent opportunity to say something about environmental protection, but instead he presents it merely as evidence in favor of his general views on changes in coastlines.

Although Aristotle's attitudes toward the environment, like those of other Greek philosophers, were undoubtedly shaped most fundamentally by his general metaphysical perspective, his belief in purposes or final causes in nature probably also played an important role. Noting that change in nature, particularly biological and botanical nature, usually occurred in specific ways involving specific stages, Aristotle concluded that certain kinds of objects, especially living organisms, existed for particular purposes as part of a design built into nature. The purpose or final cause of the existence of an acorn, for example, is an oak tree. Generalizing still further, he concluded that lower organisms existed for the benefit of higher organisms, and they all could be ranked into an order of being, with humans at the top. As he puts it in his *Politics*, in a section on property:

> Property, in the sense of bare livelihood, seems to be given by nature herself to all, both when they are first born, and when they are grown up. For some animals bring forth, together with their offspring, so much food as will last until they are able to supply themselves; of this the vermiparous or oviparous animals are an instance; and the viviparous animals have up to a certain supply of food for their young in themselves, which is called milk. In like manner we may infer that, after the birth of animals, plants exist for their sake, and that other animals exist for the sake of man, the tame for use and food, the wild, if not all, at least the greater part of them, for food, and for the provision of clothing and various instruments. Now if nature makes nothing incomplete, and nothing in vain, the inference must be that she has made all animals for the sake of man.[18]

Since the entire hierarchy exists, in this view, for the benefit of humans and this order is itself supposed to be permanent and unchanging, there is little need for environmental concern. Although, as Aristotle was quite aware, individual organisms frequently fall victim to mishaps that prevent them from fulfilling their purposes, enough could be expected to survive that humans at the top of the pyramid would not be unduly inconvenienced.

To have achieved an ecological perspective that could generate environmental concern, Aristotle probably needed, as a minimum, to abandon this belief in set purposes in nature. As J. Donald Hughes has pointed out, Theophrastus, a student of Aristotle's, did in fact develop a significant understanding of many ecological relationships in connection with his studies of plants and in doing so rejected the Aristotelian doctrine that animals, plants, and the earth existed solely for the sake of man. He claimed that they had their own purposes independent of the needs and interests of human beings. In connection with his specific botanical discoveries, for example, that many plants are dependent on specific habitats, this observation could have spurred the development of a Western ecological perspective.[19] Theophrastus' work, however, went unnoticed and had no influence on the course of Western philosophy and thought. As a result, the environmentally sound aspects of his philosophy are of historical interest only and irrelevant to the history of ideas that produced modern attitudes toward nature.

The Aesthetic Perspective

Although Greek philosophers did have feelings of appreciation and admiration for the world, those feelings were not primarily aesthetic. The characteristic of the world they most strongly reacted to was its order, not its beauty. Their emotional response was much like that of an automobile mechanic looking over a well-engineered motor or a mathematician going over a complex proof. Evidence of the lack of any genuine aesthetic feeling can still be found in the modern word *cosmetic*, which is derived from the Greek word *cosmos*, the technical philosophical term for the world or universe. *Cosmetic* does stand for a kind of beauty, but it is a superficial beauty that hides or veils the actual appearance of a thing or person. This sense of beauty originated in the Greek idea that ultimate reality is concealed and distorted by sensation and as such has nothing to do with beauty in its primary Greek sense in connection with the fundamental nature of reality, the human soul, and moral goodness.

There is ample evidence in the surviving poetry, drama, and art of ancient Greece to conclude that periodically throughout Greek cultural history, a deep appreciation and love of nature was fashionable.[20] Judging by the existent philosophical writings, however, Greek philosophers never shared these feelings with their artistic and literary counterparts. This difference in attitude seems to have resulted from the fact that writers and artists concentrated on the world of the senses, drawing inspiration from it in a way that philosophers could not, obsessed as they were with their efforts to uncover the ultimate reality that they believed was hidden by sensation. Put another way, philosophers developed no aesthetic appreciation for nature because they were too busy speculating about matter, atoms, and other hypothetical entities that could not be experienced directly by the senses and therefore possessed no visual or aesthetic aspects. Since Greek philosophy was reintroduced into Western thought much earlier than Greek art and literature, this indifference to the beauty of nature was passed on to medieval and early modern philosophers and theologians, who mistook it for a characteristic of Greek culture as a whole and at first tried to emulate it.

Plato came closest to bridging the gap between the aesthetic interests of the literary and artistic community and the metaphysical concerns of the philosophical community. His dialogues reveal not only his philosophical abilities but his literary skills as well. In his theory of forms, moreover, he succeeded in fusing the metaphysical, aesthetic, and ethical together in his ultimate form, the Beautiful and the Good. Yet he too was so enmeshed in the quarrels, controversies, and presuppositions of pre-Socratic philosophy that he could not carry his aesthetic insights very far, and no true appreciation or love of nature emerged in his philosophy.

Plato's dialogues occasionally show that he greatly appreciated nature, but his general philosophical viewpoint forced him into a position that largely ignored the world of nature or treated it contemptuously. In the *Phaedrus*, for example, Socrates and Phaedrus decide to leave the city and hold a philosophical discussion under one of Phaedrus' favorite plane trees in the country. On the way, favorable comments are made about the beauty of the countryside and, reaching the tree, Socrates exclaims:

> Upon my word, a delightful resting place, with this tall, spreading plane, and a lovely shade from the high branches of the *agnos*. Now that it's in full flower, it will make the place ever so fragrant. And what a lovely stream under the plane tree, and how cool to the feet!

Although these statements seem to suggest genuine delight in nature, their superficiality is revealed a few lines later when Phaedrus, attempting to continue the conversation in the same vein, is abruptly cut off by Socrates, who says, "You must forgive me, dear friend; I'm a lover of learning, and trees and open country won't teach me anything." This remark is quite serious and follows directly from Plato's epistemological belief that knowledge is gained by dialectical reasoning and contemplation of the forms, not by study of the world of nature.[21]

Metaphysically and aesthetically, Plato's commitment to the theory of forms led him straightforwardly to an antipathy to natural objects. In the *Parmenides*, we find Socrates admitting to Parmenides that he feels that some natural objects are too trivial and undignified to participate in the world of the forms.[22] Since natural objects in Plato's philosophy exist only to the degree that they participate in a form, those without forms have no metaphysical status—they do not exist. Aesthetically, the situation is much the same. Beauty is grounded in the form of the Beautiful and the Good, and natural objects are beautiful only insofar as they participate in it.

According to Plato's *Phaedo*, the beauty of the world of the forms is so magnificent that anyone who truly comprehends it must conclude that there is nothing of beauty in the natural world:

> If someone could reach to the summit, or put on wings and fly aloft, when he put up his head he would see the world above, just as fishes see our world when they put their heads out of the sea. And if his nature were able to bear the sight, he would recognize that that is the true heaven and the true light and the true earth. For this earth and its stones and all regions in which we live are marred and corroded, just as in the sea everything is corroded by the brine, and there is no vegetation worth mentioning, and scarcely a degree of perfect formation, but only caverns and sand and measureless mud, and tracts of slime wherever there is earth as well, and nothing is in the least worthy to be judged beautiful by our standards.[23]

In the world of the forms, in contrast, the colors are brighter, the trees perfectly proportioned, and the surfaces of rocks and other natural objects smooth, shiny, and unbroken.

As mentioned earlier, one of the most positive aspects of Plato's philosophy is the Beautiful and the Good, which as the ultimate form serves as the source of both fact and value or, put another way, as the source of science and ethics. This position, which gives ethical and aesthetic value a fully objective status, would be very useful to environmental philosophy except for the fact that Plato insists on locating the Beautiful and the Good outside and beyond the physical world. The beauty of the world of the forms needs no protection since it is already permanent, indestructable, and unchanging. The beauty of the natural world, however, cannot be preserved or protected in part because it is not truly beautiful but primarily because it does not really exist.

The same kinds of problems arise in terms of the theory of participation with regard to degrees of beauty. In this context, nature is less beautiful and less valuable because it lacks the perfection of the forms. Aesthetically, Plato's notion of perfection translates into a preference for mathematical proportions and ideal geometric shapes. This kind of perfection is responsible for much of the sixteenth- and seventeenth-century distaste for mountainous scenery, which for a time inhibited the development of modern nature appreciation. Thomas Burnet, for example, infected by such a Platonic aesthetic perspective, came close to losing his faith in God when, arriving in the vicinity of the Alps in 1671, he found that he was unable to discern any regularity, proportion, or symmetry in the slopes and shapes of the mountains before him. His conclusion that God could not have made such irregular and disorderly piles of rocks eventually cost him his career as a theologian and clergyman, which might otherwise have included appointment as the Archbishop of Canterbury.[24]

Platonic philosophy seems less incompatible with an environmental point of view today because we are usually first exposed to it in the romantic nature poetry of the late eighteenth and early nineteenth centuries. In this poetry, however, emphasis is placed directly on the beauty of the natural objects that are supposedly trying to conform to the even higher aesthetic and spiritual standards of the Beautiful and the Good. In a sense, the forms are still there, but the objects participating in them have preempted the spotlight. In addition, the metaphysical position attributing reality to the forms and little or no reality to natural objects is gone for the most part, and there is no longer any question that the world we live in exists.

Plato himself would undoubtedly have objected strongly to this misuse of his philosophy, since these metaphysical degrees of reality and perfection were of major importance to him and were the basis of his own rejection of all nature poetry and art in his own time. In the *Republic* he argues that nature as depicted in literature and art is two levels away from the truth, beauty, goodness, and reality of the forms. It is imitation of natural objects that are themselves but pale and imperfect reflections or shadows of the forms. Nature poets and artists, he adds, are unworthy of being part of the ideal society sketched in the *Republic* because their work turns men's minds away from the forms and feeds the irrational elements of the soul at the expense of the rational.[25] This position is essentially a forerunner of the medieval view that the aesthetic appreciation of nature should be discouraged because love of nature will detract from love of God and is probably at least in part its source. In this context, concern for the environment certainly cannot flourish and probably cannot develop.

The Metaphysical Perspective

Although Plato's philosophy generally suggests that he neither knew nor cared about environmental problems, one passage in the *Critias* shows that he was very much aware of at least one problem: the effect of deforestation on soil quality in Greece during his own lifetime. Speaking of the erosion that followed the cutting of the trees on the mountainsides, Plato writes that "what is left now is, so to say, the skeleton of a body wasted by disease; the rich, soft soil has been carried off and only the bare framework of the district left." In addition, he notes, in a moment of ecological insight, that before the trees were cut down,

> the soil got the benefit of the yearly "water from Zeus," which was not lost, as it is today, by running off a barren ground to the sea; a plentiful supply of it was received into the soil and stored up in the layers of nonporous potter's clay. Thus the moisture absorbed in the higher regions percolated to the hollows and so all quarters were lavishly provided with springs and rivers.[26]

These observations are especially interesting not so much because they show that Plato had some ecological understanding of the relation of trees, soil, and water but because Plato has Critias discuss the sudden transformation of the Greek landscape into its modern form *matter-of-factly*, simply as a curious historical event. Although Plato makes it quite clear that he understands not only what happened but also the environmental consequences, there is absolutely no suggestion of the modern concern and alarm that would arise if such an event occurred today.

This indifference cannot in this case be attributed to lack of ecological knowledge, for Plato's understanding of this particular situation is probably as good as that of most natural history scientists in the nineteenth century. Nor can it simply be a matter of aesthetic distaste for nature, since Plato specifically speaks of the problem in terms of the instrumental agricultural value of the land. It is of course possible that Plato was unconcerned because he thought that enough remnants of the original land remained that the destruction of much of Greece's soil did not matter. Even if that is so, however, it seems likely that his attitude was also shaped very significantly by the metaphysical perspective that he inherited from the pre-Socratics: the view that the natural world was an illusion and did not exist as experienced in any fundamental sense.

Given the emphasis that Greek philosophers from Thales on placed on the physical existence of the world and their obsessive attention to the problem of change, it is safe to say that the Greeks were very much concerned about the continuing existence of the world. I want to suggest, however, that it was probably much more than just that: that the Greeks were probably chronically suffering from a case of what might be called existential angst, that they were deeply bothered by the possibility that matter might pop into and out of existence. Feeling terribly insecure, they wanted proof that the world could not stop existing, that it was permanent, indestructible, eternal, and unchanging. In other words, some sort of existential distress may well have been what the problem of change was really all about.

This interpretation is supported, in particular, by Aristotle's reference to "men of narrow outlook" who thought that changes in the environment, for example, the drying up of the seas, represented a change in the amount of physical matter existing in the world.[27] While it might be objected that Plato's indifference about environmental change is evidence that no such angst existed, I would reply that more likely his indifference is simply proof that he, unlike the pre-Socratics, already had a philosophical theory—according to which the world is only an illusion—that permitted him calmly to accept and ignore environmental change as inconsequential.

If this hypothesis is correct, then the problem of change in early Greek philosophy was in reality a curious version of the problem of nature preservation that is solved by defining the problem out of existence. On the one hand, the world as experienced cannot be destroyed because it does not really exist. On the other hand, the world as it really exists cannot be destroyed, or even damaged, because it is already indestructible and unchanging. For most of the Greeks, including Aristotle, this second, unseen world is composed of some kind of physical matter. Plato differs with them in that he hypothesizes a mental world, the world of the forms, rather than a physical one. In either case, however, the environmental implications, or lack of them, are the same.

Actually, the proper division is not between Plato and the pre-Socratic materialists, who all agreed that the world as experienced is an illusion, but rather between Aristotle and his predecessors, including Plato, since, to the contrary, Aristotle believed that the world as experienced is real. In terms of pre-Aristotelian positions, whatever is taken to exist, to paraphrase Parmenides, as well as the first law of thermodynamics, simply is and cannot not be; whatever is considered not to exist simply is not and cannot be. Since, in this view, the world of sensation or experience fundamentally involves nonbeing, as things in it pop into and out of existence from moment to moment as part of the process of change, nothing in that world has enough permanence for nature preservation to make any sense. In the world of ultimate reality, material or formal, on the other hand, given its indestructible and unchanging nature, there is too much permanence for nature preservation to make any sense.

When we turn to the metaphysics of Aristotle, in which the world of experience really does exist, the situation becomes more complicated but still does not produce conditions that are conducive to nature preservation attitudes. According to Aristotle's metaphysics, the world is a gigantic conglomeration of matter undergoing perpetual change through an infinite period of time as a result of movement generated and guaranteed by an eternal source of movement, the Unmoved Mover. In the *Meteorology*, Aristotle concedes that many parts of the Earth are deteriorating, but he emphasizes that all deterioration is balanced by improvements in environmental conditions elsewhere. As land in one place dries up and becomes uninhabitable desert, other land becomes inhabitable, because the water has to go somewhere.[28] Given that time is infinite and the universe eternal, no part of the Earth can be expected to remain in any particular state. This situation, however, does not produce the need for efforts to preserve nature; it simply requires that humans relocate very slowly over time as the habitability of various parts of the Earth changes.

Although these cyclic environmental changes on the Earth's surface are massive and probably beyond human control, they are not a matter of chance and are not entirely unpredictable. All of these changes are either simple movement of matter through space or the actualization of potential form in particular substances. For the most part, the changes are even reversible. Presumably, given the size of the universe, and assuming, as Aristotle believed, that the universe exists for the sake of man, there will always be a suitable amount of appropriately actualized matter to fulfill human needs. As a result, there is no cause for environmental alarm.

In Aristotle's system, there is really only one way in which preservationist concern could reasonably have developed—with regard to the preservation of species. Although in rejecting the theory of evolution Aristotle concluded that the forms for each species of animal and plant were eternal and unchanging, he did recognize that most plants and animals needed actual parents to come into existence. Thus if all individuals capable of having offspring in a particular species were lost, presumably their form would never be actualized again. Although Aristotle considers this possibility in his *Metaphysics*,[29] such an occurrence did not seem very likely to him and did not suggest any need for concern. For all practical purposes, in Aristotle's time, the extinction of a species was and could only be a theoretical possibility. Since the classification of plants and animals had not been carried very far and since most of the world remained unknown and unexplored, the ranges of animals and plants already classified could not have been determined with any accuracy, and without that information, it would have been impossible to tell if a local decline in a species was having an effect on the survival of the species as a whole.

Moreover, even though the recognition that species extinctions could occur seems to suggest that human beings could also become extinct, opening up the possibility of some concern for future generations, humans are a special case in Aristotle's philosophy. In his ethics Aristotle rules out any moral concern for future generations on the grounds that including posterity into ethical deliberation would make the decision process too complicated.[30] In addition, there are metaphysical and religious reasons for not being concerned. The general Greek position, held by Plato and most, if not all, of the pre-Socratics, was that the human soul was immortal and indestructible. As mentioned earlier, Plato depicts Socrates in the *Phaedo* as looking forward to his physical death as a release from the world of sensation that would allow him to be able to reason more clearly. In Aristotle's philosophy, a human being is an unmoved mover, something that can move other things without itself being moved, which in environmental terms translates into an entity that can affect its environment without itself being affected. In this way, Aristotle, like all the other Greek philosophers, attributes absolute permanence and indestructibility to humans and removes them from the kind of dependency on the natural world needed to support any concern for the preservation of nature on instrumental grounds.

Although I have treated the incompatibility of Greek philosophy and modern nature preservation attitudes in terms of three perspectives, the fundamental source of all the difficulties discussed is the metaphysical perspective, for the problems that prevented the development of the ecological and aesthetic perspectives are really metaphysical. Ecological knowledge did not develop in any significant way in Greece because ecological nature was not fundamentally real from the standpoint of Greek metaphysics and therefore could not be the object of knowledge. Likewise, following Plato, who draws the conclusion most clearly, nothing in the nature world is beautiful because metaphysically, once again, nature is imperfect and at best only partially real.

For nature preservation attitudes to have arisen in ancient Greece, Greek philosophers would have needed to develop a basic set of metaphysical assumptions very different from the ones outlined in this chapter. Essentially, nature had to be more permanent than the fleeting reality attributed to the world of experience and much less permanent than the unchanging and indestructible reality of the forms or material substance. For efforts to preserve natural objects to make sense, first of all, those objects have to be reasonably permanent under some set of normal conditions. Second, they have to be impermanent enough that they can be damaged. Third, it has to be possible for human action and inaction to affect the continued existence of those objects in a significant way. Aristotle came close to developing such a position in his geological writings but was prevented from doing so by his own acceptance of the general Greek belief in the indestructibility of ultimate reality. The proper conception of nature did not appear until the end of the eighteenth century with the establishment of uniformitarianism in geology, when it was finally realized that although nature changed slowly in accordance with physical and chemical processes, humans, acting as geological agents, for example, comparable in scale to glaciers, earthquakes, and volcanoes, could accelerate such change, with catastrophic effect.

MODERN PHILOSOPHY

Although Greek philosophy is the primary source of the philosophical perspectives that have historically inhibited the development of appropriate environmental and preservationist attitudes, a second period in the history of philosophy has also played a similar role. This is the modern period, which begins in the early seventeenth century and includes most of the twentieth century. This period may be broken down into three subperiods: the early modern period, which is characterized by two philosophical movements, rationalism and empiricism; nineteenth-century philosophy; and twentieth-century or contemporary philosophy. For our purposes, it will not be necessary to examine each of these in any detail. Despite the fact that the philosophical approaches in each subperiod are markedly different, the features of the modern period that are important environmentally are common to all three.

Because these features developed in part in reaction to the philosophical perspectives of the medieval period that preceded it, some discussion of the relationship of the two periods is required. The medieval period was really more a religious than a philosophical period. Medieval philosophy remained almost entirely within a Christian religious framework. In the early Middle Ages, the connection with Greek philosophy was broken and the primary task of philosophers in the middle and late Middle Ages was the reintroduction and assimilation of Greek philosophy, specifically the writings of Plato and Aristotle, into a fully Christian context. Because from a Christian standpoint, God existed beyond rather than in the world, in a relationship that was similar to the relationship between the world and Plato's forms, the general features of early Christian philosophy tended to be Platonic, and much time and effort was devoted to the problem of the existence of universals, essentially Platonic forms. In the late Middle Ages, after nearly all of Aristotle's writings had been reintroduced, Aristotelian-style philosophy gradually overshadowed the earlier Platonism. Because Aristotle was so important at the end of the medieval period, early modern philosophers reacted against his writings specifically, overlooking his contributions, for example, to science, and adopted a philosophical perspective that was in spirit Platonic and Pythagorean. This perspective was then consciously used as the foundation for the development of modern science as we know it, with unfortunate results from an environmental standpoint, as we have already seen.

One of the little-recognized but, for our purposes, critical differences between the medieval and early modern periods was the general approach to *thinking* in each period. During the Middle Ages, it was customary to think symbolically. A medieval Christian, when confronted with natural objects or images of natural objects, for example, pictures of fish, birds, and trees, automatically tried to find Christian religious significance in them by associating them with parables and key remarks in the Bible. In the early modern period, in contrast, it became customary to think representationally. Instead of associating images as symbols with biblical stories and sayings, people thought of the images as representations of natural objects. If they saw a picture of a fish or a bird, they thought about real fish and birds in the world. The emergence of the representational perspective is most obvious in painting, which became increasingly realistic over the next two centuries, but it is equally important in modern philosophy, which became obsessed with the analysis of the relationship of mental images created out of sensory experience and physical objects in the external world.[31]

The key philosopher in the early modern period, and indeed the entire modern period, was René Descartes. It was his philosophy that created the representational puzzle that gave modern philosophy its characteristic form. Even though all philosophers since Descartes have been critical of his philosophy, all have worked within a philosophical framework that is entirely Cartesian. Because Descartes' influence is primarily in terms of his general approach to philosophy, independent of the conclusions he reached, he is not, strictly speaking, the father of modern philosophy but is more accurately the father of modern philosophical problems. It is in terms of these problems—the existence of the external world, the nature of natural science, and the objectivity of value—that modern philosophy achieved its characteristic antienvironmental bias.

Descartes, Cartesianism, and the Existence of the Natural World

Philosophically, Descartes was a rationalist, like most other philosophers of his time. He looked to Plato and Pythagoras rather than Aristotle for inspiration and was therefore distrustful of sensation, relying instead on the use of reason to gain knowledge. At the beginning of his most important book, *Meditations on First Philosophy*, he set about doubting everything that was not completely certain, seeking at the same time for some statement or principle that was self-evidently true. According to Descartes, *cogito, ergo sum* ("I think, therefore I am") was just such a statement. Descartes believed that at the moment when he thought those words, he was in a position to be absolutely certain intuitively that he existed. Using this knowledge of his own existence as a first principle or premise, he then tried to show by logical argument and the light of reason that God, other human beings, and the material world all existed as well.

Unfortunately, Descartes' whole enterprise depended heavily on his two proofs of God and in turn on God's goodness as a guarantee of the truth of our commonsense belief in the existence of other people and the world. When Descartes' critics rejected these proofs as inconclusive, the whole chain of argument collapsed. All that remained was the method of philosophical doubt, in the first meditation, and the proof of personal existence, in the second, and neither was very satisfactory. Philosophical doubt, first of all, did not provide knowledge; it was a method of undermining belief, and it did so very effectively, undermining all the things that Descartes was trying to prove: the existence of God, other people, and the external world. Second, the proof of personal existence was a proof only from the point of view of the person doing the thinking, and it established a person's existence only as a mental entity, not as a material being.

Although Descartes' philosophical and theological colleagues did not accept his proofs of God, they did accept many of his basic assumptions and all of his basic problems. Adopting self-evident knowledge of personal existence as their starting point, they launched philosophy on a three hundred–year quest for proofs of the existence of God, other minds, and the physical world. Because it was not possible to produce such proofs, this Cartesian enterprise marked the beginning of a period of profound skepticism, with regard not only to the existence of God but also to the existence of the external world.

In terms of the basic Cartesian framework, the problem of the existence of the external world was an epistemological problem rather than a metaphysical one. The question was not whether the world existed but whether it was possible to *know* that the world existed. In trying to answer this question, philosophers were attempting to do metaphysics through epistemology. Starting with knowledge of self as a mental entity, the next step for them was an examination of the ideas that were in the mind of that mental entity. This was the representational problem. The Cartesians wanted to know whether these ideas, as mental substance, represented physical objects, as material substance, and if so, whether the properties of these objects, as they appeared in the mind, were represented accurately.

Descartes' conception of matter was somewhat different from that of the Greeks. There were two basic kinds of matter or substance: corporeal, or physical, substance and incorporeal, or mental, substance. Both were *created* substances created by God, an *uncreated* substance. These created substances differed from Greek matter in two very significant ways: First, created substance was not permanent and indestructible; rather it was maintained from moment to moment through the power of God, requiring, Descartes believed, the same amount of power for each moment that was required at the time of the original creation. Second, the two kinds of created substance were incapable of interacting with each other. In order for there to be two kinds of substance, it was necessary, Descartes and the early Cartesians maintained, that the substances have no common properties, and since, as a result, they had nothing in common, they could not interact. This situation thus forced God not only to maintain the world from moment to moment but also to solve the problem of the interaction between the two kinds of substances in a very practical way. When human beings decided to move their fingers, God had to do it for them.

Although this conception of God's function in the world suited an age that was deeply religious, since it guaranteed an extremely intimate relationship between each human and God, it created complications with regard to the representation of the properties of physical objects in the mind. Applying a distinction originally made by Galileo, [32] Descartes identified two kinds of properties in mental representations: primary and secondary. The primary properties were all examples of extension; the three dimensions—length, width, depth—were properties that could be measured geometrically and quantified. The secondary properties were colors, tastes, smells, and other qualities that could not be quantified and were perceived differently by different people and by the same people at different times. Because of these disagreements about secondary properties, Descartes argued that they were subjective, dependent on the perception of the individual human, and did not represent actual properties in external objects. He concluded that the primary properties were objective and did accurately represent the extension of external objects in space. In reaching this conclusion, however, Descartes created a new problem for his philosophical system, for if extension existed both in objects in the external world and in representations of those objects in the mind, extension was something common to his two kinds of substance, which, by definition, were not supposed to have anything in common. Thus the representation of extension in human minds required additional assistance and intervention by God.

Despite many differences with Greek theory, the Cartesian theory of matter, as Descartes originally proposed it, also solved the problem of the existence of the natural world in such a way that preservationist concern could not arise. Following the Greek and Christian model, human souls were once again permanent and indestructible. Unlike the Greek conception, physical matter was not permanent and indestructible, and it popped into and out of existence as God sustained it from moment to moment; however, since the existence of physical matter was directly dependent on the exercise of the power of God, there was still no appropriate context for human involvement and concern. Changes in nature, good or bad, were simply God's will and thus beyond human control.

Because of the many problems with Descartes' system, his conception of matter was eventually abandoned as too complicated and too dependent on divine involvement. While in theory the abandonment of Descartes' theory of matter ought to have provided circumstances in which concern for the preservation of nature could develop, in practice this was not the case, for the general Cartesian approach to the problem of matter, in terms of the philosophical doubt employed in the first meditation, made belief in the existence of the physical world appear to be so questionable that most philosophers dropped it from their philosophical systems. The empiricists were the first to do so. Berkeley's arguments that physical matter was an unnecessary hypothesis and that primary properties were just as subjective as secondary properties were followed by Hume's arguments that, strictly speaking, all that we could know was that sensations or impressions existed. Although Kant tried to preserve a conception of the physical world (as the unknowable noumenal world) in his answer to Hume, philosophers in the nineteenth century influenced by Kant dropped reference to the external world from their own philosophies. Thus Kant's philosophy, against his wishes, produced a century of idealism, in which most philosophers and philosophies held that existence was mental only and that the external world did not exist.

This lunacy was finally put effectively to rest at the end of the nineteenth century when G. E. Moore courageously led a rebellion against the philosophies of Kant and Hegel at Cambridge University, which brought about the end of idealism as mainstream philosophy and permitted the rehabilitation of the external world.[33] By that time, however, philosophy, by default, had already missed its opportunity to participate in the creation of modern environmental thought.

Modern Science and Environmental Thought

From a twentieth-century perspective, it is obvious that science has played a fundamental role in shaping the way we think about the environment. Environmentalism, for example, is so closely associated with the science of ecology that the environmental and ecological perspectives are virtually synonymous. This strong and close association, nevertheless, tends to hide the fact that historically, environmental thought developed in a scientific context that was not generally favorable to it. As we shall see in Chapter 3, geology and biology both played significant roles in the creation of the environmental perspective long before anyone knew what ecology or even evolution was. In those days, however, these environmental sciences, then called natural history sciences, were not considered to be a part of mainstream science and frequently were not considered to be part of science at all. This association with the "wrong" kind of science further inhibited the emergence of the environmental perspective in a way that fit together with and complemented the epistemological and metaphysical difficulties with professional philosophy that we have just examined. Although we are now dealing with early modern scientific attitudes, the origins of these attitudes are once again philosophical, and the key figure involved is still René Descartes.

As noted, early modern philosophers, as rationalists, looked to Plato and Pythagoras as their spiritual leaders and reacted against the philosophy of Aristotle. This general orientation also characterized early modern science in the same way and made modern science curiously antiobservational. Although today we think of science as being based on observation, this was not the case in the seventeenth century. Since early modern philosopher-scientists, like Descartes and Galileo, followed the mainstream Greek position, concluding that sensation interfered with the study of nature, they too tried to look beyond the world of experience to find principles that applied to ultimate reality in its most fundamental form. Observation did not make its appearance in modern science until empiricism, more than a century later, had made it more fashionable and Hume's analysis of causation had revealed the need for experimentation with controls.

The method of early modern science was the application of reason alone and was often referred to as the "geometrical method." The point of this method was to emphasize physical measurement in terms of extension and to eliminate reference to time. Time was initially deemed unnecessary because the knowledge that these scientists were seeking was supposed to be, in accordance with Greek tradition, necessary, permanent, universal, and eternal, and therefore timeless. As Hanson has pointed out, both Galileo and Descartes were held up several decades in their efforts to discover the formula for the acceleration of falling bodies by their (unconscious) unwillingness to consider time as a key factor. The correct formulation was finally found when Galileo realized that he had to replace distance squared, the geometrically correct measurement, with time squared.[34]

The geometrical method also brought with it Greek philosophy's aesthetic preference for idealized, general, simple, perfect geometric figures. This preference likewise had some inhibiting influence. Kepler, for example, was delayed in his discovery of the shape of the orbits of the planets by his belief that the ellipse was not a perfect figure.[35] Despite such problems, the tendency to characterize nature in a geometrically simple and perfect way continues in modern science even today, especially in research at the atomic and subatomic levels in physics and chemistry.

The primary and most influential aspect of the early modern scientific method, however, has been its reductionist character. The reductionist method, explicitly formulated by Descartes in his *Discourse on Method*, involved the reduction of complex ideas into their simple parts, followed by their reconstruction through reason.[36] It worked well in physics and chemistry because scientists were able to isolate key factors as they reduced them to their simple parts. Technological manipulation was achieved through the handling of these simple parts in isolation. This approach has been so successful over the past three centuries that it is still routinely employed today in all scientific research, whether its ultimate orientation is reductionist or holistic.

Because early modern science was fundamentally antiobservational, geometrical, and reductionistic, natural history science did not fit the model of what science was supposed to be. First of all, geologists and biologists studied nature at the level at which it is encountered in experience. As a result, their approach was not rationalistic in any significant way. They spent their time making observations and collecting data, using their senses, not formulating models and hypotheses in accordance with pure reason.

Second, time gradually came to play an inordinate and very ungeometric role in natural history science. Though originally history in the sense in which Aristotle used the term, as inquiry, natural history science evolved into sciences that dealt with history in the sense in which it is used when speaking of human history, as a description of past events. For the most part, time was kept under control in physics and chemistry, playing a role in physical reactions that usually lasted only a few seconds and therefore did not in any important way affect the necessary and universal character of the research being done. In natural history science, however, time expanded so that human history was eventually only a very tiny part of the history of the world as a whole, and in this context, the results of this research were historical statements that were singular rather than universal, contingent rather than necessary, historical rather than eternal and timeless, and therefore, from a mainstream perspective, not very scientific.

Third, because the reductionist method worked less well in the study of the complex geological and biological relationships that make up natural systems and since environmental factors could not usually be manipulated in isolation, natural history scientists and their work were routinely treated with contempt by their fellow scientists and by philosophers, who did not bother to take them into account in the development of a major field within philosophy, philosophy of science. Only late in this century are efforts to examine the philosophy of geology, biology, and ecology finally under way.

Especially troublesome and embarrassing for natural history scientists was the primary/secondary property distinction. Because physicists limited their observations to primary properties, which according to Galileo and Descartes were supposed to represent physical objects objectively, their observations were acceptably scientific. In contrast, the observations made by geologists and biologists focused on secondary properties—colors, tastes, smells, sounds—that were believed to be apprehended subjectively rather than objectively. The researchers' interest in shapes, moreover, was not primarily for the purpose of precise measurement and hardly ever geometric, since natural objects rarely appear as simple and perfect geometric forms. This focus on secondary properties, as we shall see in Chapter 3, meant that natural history scientists often had more in common with poets and painters than they did with physicists and chemists.

Since modern science through the natural history sciences has had a profound effect on environmental thought, it is unfair to treat modern science as a whole as antienvironmental. However, it is important to realize (1) that the positive influence on environmental thought came out of sciences that did not fit the preferred model of what science should be and (2) that the orientation of the preferred model was completely incompatible with an environmental perspective. As already noted, the preferred model for scientific inquiry encouraged scientists not to think about the environment as it is encountered in experience. This significantly inhibited environmental concern. Scientists who directly studied living and nonliving nature as biological or geological phenomena often expressed concern about the natural objects they studied. Scientists who studied nature at the atomic level in terms of physical or chemical hypotheses about an indestructible material substratum did not. Moreover, the preferred method encouraged mainstream scientists to narrow their focus to very simple, maximally isolated physical and chemical events of very short duration in experiments in a laboratory setting. As a result, this type of scientific research failed to provide a context in which damage to the environment could be identified or assessed. Finally, the emphasis on scientific objectivity reduced the scientist's domain to the collection and analysis of facts as something distinct from values, making concern about nature unscientific and therefore in principle inappropriate.

The Triumph of Fact over Value

Over the past three centuries, value has gradually become less and less important to philosophers and scientists. This change began with the primary/secondary property distinction, gained speed with the *is/ought* or fact/value distinction of Hume, and culminated with the logical positivists' rejection of ethical and value statements as meaningless in the early twentieth century.

Early modern philosophers and scientists were concerned about finding ways to study nature that were objective. They wanted to deal with facts that were independent of the subjective elements of judgment and perception. It was for this reason that Galileo and Descartes developed the primary/secondary property distinction in the first place. Because primary properties were supposed to be objective, they became the focus of scientific study. Secondary properties, because they were considered subjective, were ignored.

This distinction in turn led directly to a dichotomy between fact and value. Although the idea that facts and values are incompatible was probably not original wth Hume, he made it explicit in his *Treatise* in a passage just preceding his discussion of *is* and *ought*, in which he makes specific reference to primary and secondary properties as a precedent:

> Vice and virtue . . . may be compar'd to sounds, colours, heat and cold, which, according to modern philosophy, are not qualities in objects, but perceptions in the mind: And this discovery in morals, like the other in physics, is to be regarded as a considerable advancement of the speculative sciences.[37]

Even though Hume went on to insist that values (for him, sentiments) were nevertheless extremely important ("Nothing can be more real, or concern us more"), his distinction came to be the basis on which the sciences and the humanities were differentiated and separated. From that time on, it was generally held that scientists dealt with facts and humanists with values.

Although this division had little effect on the humanities and humanities scholars, it encouraged major changes in the way that scientists looked at the world and the manner in which they were educated. Feeling that value considerations adversely influenced their objectivity, scientists began avoiding humanities training in values and adopted a doctrine of moral neutrality with regard to their work. The result was an estrangement of the sciences from the humanities such that scientists generally lost the desire and the ability to communicate with nonscientific scholars. After these attitudes were defended by logical positivists in the early twentieth century, the gap grew to the point that many scientists were no longer willing to accept that the work of humanists had any meaning at all. According to the positivists, statements about values are scientifically (or factually) unverifiable and are therefore nonsense; talk about values is just the expression of emotion and has no objective significance.[38] By the middle of the twentieth century, the sciences and the humanities were generally considered to be so different from each other that they could appropriately be characterized as two different cultures.[39]

To see the effect of the scientific fascination with fact on the humanistic values of scientists, we must return to the nineteenth century, a time when scientists still received training in the humanities. In his autobiography, for example, Charles Darwin writes:

> Up to the age of thirty, or beyond it, poetry of many kinds, such as the work of Milton, Gray, Byron, Wordsworth, Coleridge, and Shelley, gave me great pleasure, and even as a schoolboy I took intense delight in Shakespeare, especially in the historical plays. I have also said that formerly pictures gave me considerable, and music very great delight. But now for many years I cannot endure to read a line of poetry; I have tried lately to read Shakespeare, and have found it so intolerably dull that it nauseated me. I have also lost my taste for pictures and music. . . . I retain some taste for fine scenery, but it does not cause me the exquisite delight which it formerly did.[40]

In the next paragraph Darwin continues:

> My mind seems to have become a kind of machine, for grinding general laws out of large collections of facts, but why this should have caused the atrophy of that part of the brain alone, on which the higher tastes depend, I cannot conceive. A man with a mind more highly organized or better constituted than mine, would not, I suppose, have thus suffered; and if I had to live my life again, I would have made a rule to read some poetry and listen to some music at least once every week; for perhaps parts of my brain now atrophied would thus have been kept active through use. The loss of these tastes is a loss of happiness, and may be injurious to the intellect, and more probably to the moral character, by enfeebling the emotional part of our nature.[41]

Though this loss of taste is a mystery to Darwin, it need be no mystery to us. It is a natural consequence of his attempt to be scientific, to deal with the facts alone. This experience is uncommon today only because scientists are now usually so little exposed to the humanities in their education that they are unable to note, let alone lament, their insensitivity and even aversion to literature, poetry, art, philosophy, music, religion, and ethics.

Darwin expresses concern that his moral character may have been affected. Although he gives no example in his autobiography, a comparison of his account of his travels on the *Beagle* with his later writings suggests that his concern on this point was justified. The journal is filled with many strong expressions of concern for the welfare of primitive peoples. Speaking of the war of extermination in Bahía Blanca, for example, he writes: "Who would believe that in this age such atrocities could be committed in a Christian civilised country?" After a few paragraphs of description he adds: "It is melancholy to trace how the Indians have given way before the Spanish invaders."[42] In *The Descent of Man,* however, the emotional and moral tone has vanished. "At some future period," he writes, "not very distant as measured by centuries, the civilised races of man will almost certainly exterminate, replace the savage races throughout the world. At the same time the anthropomorphous apes . . . will no doubt be exterminated." Here the extermination of human beings is nothing more than the natural order of things in accordance with the principles of evolution: "it is the same problem as that presented by the extinction of the higher animals—of the fossil horse, for instance."[43] For Darwin, primitive peoples have become facts to be worked into theories: objects of scientific interest, not moral concern. Scientific detachment and objectivity have resulted in the suspension of moral concern.

Because the natural world confronted natural history scientists in their daily work, it was hard for them to follow the mainstream trend and dismiss the beauty of nature. As Darwin notes, he retained "some taste for fine scenery," although it ceased producing "the exquisite delight which it formerly did." Aesthetics as a philosophical discipline was nevertheless significantly influenced. Although aesthetics in the late seventeenth century literally began with an examination of the sublime, the terrifying in nature, in contrast to the beautiful, it gradually lost interest in nature and natural beauty, leaving the growing movement in natural appreciation with little theoretical support. The subsequent discussion of natural beauty over the next two centuries, under the heading of philosophical criticism, focused on aesthetic taste in picturesque beauty in natural scenery and is not generally regarded as part of the history of philosophy today. Except for passing reference to Burke's and Kant's discussions of the sublime, aesthetics as taught in the twentieth century usually ignores nature and natural beauty. The subject has even been redefined as the study of art, rather than beauty, thereby eliminating the context in which natural beauty can be discussed. By the nineteenth century, when the preservation of natural beauty had become both an ethical and political issue in Western civilization, most philosophers had already lost interest and were thus not able or willing to contribute to the environmental debate.

PHILOSOPHY AND ENVIRONMENTAL THOUGHT

Because most academic and scientific disciplines have come directly out of philosophy—for example, history, mathematics, astronomy, physics, sociology, psychology, political science, economics, and linguistics—professional philosophers can take a great deal of pride in their role in the shaping of Western civilization. Some suggestion of the historical importance of philosophy is retained even today in academic education with the Ph.D., which is a degree in philosophy whether any courses in philosophy have been taken or not. It was, however, much more obvious in the last century, when scientists were still called, and thought of themselves, as natural philosophers.[44]

As should be clear from my brief discussions of the Greek and early modern periods, philosophy was especially important to the development of modern science. Greek speculations about nature established the context in which modern science would develop, and early modern philosophers working with, and indeed as, scientists charted the course that science would take throughout the modern period. Although philosophy has, of course, made many contributions to Western civilization, this is probably its greatest triumph.

Despite philosophy's many monumental achievements, however, it has consistently failed to provide a foundation for environmental thought throughout the course of Western civilization. This failure has been widespread throughout its major divisions: metaphysics, epistemology, ethics, social and political philosophy, philosophy of science, and, of course, aesthetics. In particular, the notions of permanence and indestructibility attributed to physical matter in Greek metaphysics made it difficult right into this century for many Westerners to think in environmental terms. The skepticism about the existence of the world in epistemology in modern philosophy over the past three centuries likewise made philosophy irrelevant to the historical development of environmental thought, especially in the nineteenth century. Both periods inhibited the development of a theory of natural beauty, and modern philosophy seriously undermined the foundations of ethics and value theory in general. Finally, philosophy of science has consistently undercut the legitimacy of the environmental or natural history sciences, further compounding the problem, and as we shall see in the next chapter, even social and political philosophy has ignored the environment, for example, in developing our modern theory of property.

Nevertheless, even though these negative influences on environmental thought are easy to locate—indeed, they are often the main features of the history of philosophy—there is a tendency among Western philosophers today to deny all the points made in this chapter, categorically and without any argument, as if they can simply refuse to believe in the damage that traditional Western philosophy has done environmentally in the same way that their predecessors refused to believe that the external world exists. According to these philosophers, philosophy did not and does not inhibit environmental thought; environmental thought just happens to be incompatible with Western thought, traditions, and civilization.

This attitude among professional philosophers is especially unfortunate, for it serves no constructive purpose and indeed perpetuates the very problems that are being denied. The environmental crisis is certainly the most serious problem confronting Western civilization today, and it is only fitting and proper that philosophy and philosophers should play a key role in solving it. Refusing to participate—that is, refusing to help with the establishment at long last of proper intellectual foundations for environmental thought—does not protect the integrity of the history of philosophy but instead defames it. It runs counter to the spirit of philosophy, which is supposed to be a search for truth, not a defense of traditional principles, right or wrong, as if they are the dogmatic beliefs of a primitive tribe, unable to accept criticism of their beliefs or change in the world.

While it is true that environmental ethics is fundamentally in conflict with many traditional assumptions in the history of philosophy, this fact does not make environmental ethics unphilosophical. Such conflicts constitute most of what counts as the history of philosophy today. If criticism of traditional philosophy is now declared unphilosophical, contemporary mainstream philosophy, by discouraging critical inquiry and debate, has made itself unphilosophical.

Environmental ethics is philosophy's opportunity to rectify its greatest error, the rejection of the natural world as it is experienced concretely in real life. Not to do so, moreover, would be to deny its own past, to give up its historic intellectual role in Western society, and to allow the study of philosophy to become archaic, irrelevant, and silly.

At the beginning of this century, Nathaniel Southgate Shaler, a Harvard geologist, wrote a book called *Man and the Earth* in which he attempted to deal comprehensively with the scientific, ethical, and aesthetic issues in the nature preservation and conservation movements of his time. Aware that traditional philosophy had little to offer as a philosophy of nature and that all the possible positions were "ancient and rather out of date," he tried to find a school of philosophy that could plausibly be twisted into providing some support for an environmental ethic. Choosing solipsism, a radical philosophical position that absolutely denies the existence of the external world and other minds, he argued that some protection for nature could be justified even in terms of it if we are willing to accept that "the universe is an extention of man."[45] Let us hope that nature preservationists and conservationists at the beginning of the next century will have a better selection of mainstream philosophical theories available to them so that they will not feel forced, as Shaler was, to select as the foundation of their environmental philosophy a position that denies the very existence of what they are trying to protect.

NOTES

1. Aldo Leopold, "The Land Ethic," in *A Sand County Almanac, and Sketches Here and There* (New York: Oxford University Press, 1949), pp. 209–210; *A Sand County Almanac: With Essays on Conservation from Round River* (New York: Ballantine Books, 1970), p. 246.
2. Genesis 1:26, 28.
3. John Passmore, *Man's Responsibility for Nature: Ecological Problems and Western Traditions* (London: Duckworth, 1974), p. 7n.
4. Ibid.
5. Aristotle, *Politics* 1256b20; J. Donald Hughes, "Ecology in Ancient Greece," *Inquiry* 18 (1975): 124.
6. John Locke, *The Second Treatise of Government*, ch. 5.
7. Milton C. Nahm, ed., *Selections from Early Greek Philosophy*, 4th ed. (Englewood Cliffs, N.J.: Prentice-Hall, 1964), p. 42.
8. Ibid., pp. 123–124.

9. Ibid., pp. 38–39.
10. Aristotle, *De Anima* 405a19; 411a7
11. Nahm, *Early Greek Philosophy*, pp. 39–40.
12. Ibid., pp. 93–94.
13. Plato, *Phaedo* 78b–84b.
14. For a concise account of the importance of these kinds of relationships, see Aristotle, *Nicomachean Ethics* 1139b18–35.
15. Aristotle, *De Partibus Animalium* 640b18–29.
16. Aristotle, *Meteorology* 351a19–353a26.
17. Ibid., 352b25–30.
18. Aristotle, *Politics* 1256b7–22.
19. Hughes, "Ecology in Ancient Greece," pp. 122–124.
20. See Henry Rushton Fairclough, *Love of Nature among the Greeks and Romans* (White Plains, N.Y.: Longman, 1930).
21. Plato, *Phaedrus* 227a–230e.
22. Plato, *Parmenides* 130c–e.
23. Plato, *Phaedo* 109e–110b.
24. Marjorie Hope Nicolson, *Mountain Gloom and Mountain Glory: The Development of the Aesthetic of the Infinite* (New York: Norton, 1963), pp. 207–217.
25. Plato, *Republic* 600e–607c.
26. Plato, *Critias* 111a–d.
27. Aristotle, *Meteorology* 352a16–30.
28. Ibid., bk. 1, ch. 14.
29. Aristotle, *Metaphysics* 1034b15–19.
30. Aristotle, *Nicomachean Ethics* 1097b9–15.
31. The best discussion of symbolism in the Middle Ages as a way of thinking can be found in J. Huizinga, *The Waning of the Middle Ages: A Study of the Forms of Life, Thought and Art in France and the Netherlands in the XIVth and XVth Centuries* (New York: St. Martin's Press, 1924), pp. 182–194. As Huizinga notes, although it is hard for us today not to view symbolism as "a short-circuit of thought," it is possible to view it "in a more favorable light by abandoning for a while the point of view of modern science" and taking "into account the fact that it is indissolubly linked up with the conception of the world which was called Realism in the Middle Ages, and which modern philosophy prefers to call, though less corrrectly, Platonic Idealism" (pp. 184–185). For an excellent discussion of the change from symbolism to representation in painting, see Kenneth Clark, *Landscape into Art* (New York: Harper & Row, 1976), esp. ch. 1–2.
32. Galileo, "The Assayer," in *Discoveries and Opinions of Galileo*, trans. Stillman Drake (Garden City, N.Y.: Doubleday/Anchor Books, 1957), p. 274. Descartes introduces the distinction implicitly in his discussion of a piece of wax in his second meditation and explicitly in the third. It is regularly discussed in his replies to the objections of his critics.
33. G. E. Moore's attack on idealism began with "The Nature of Judgment," *Mind* 8 (1899): 176–193. It was followed by "The Refutation of Idealism," *Mind* 12 (1903): 433–453. Moore is best known for two later papers on the subject, "A Defense of Common Sense," published in 1925, and "Proof of the External World," published in 1939, both of which can be found in G. E. Moore, *Philosophical Papers* (London: George Allen & Unwin, 1959), pp. 32–59, 127–150.
34 Norwood Russell Hanson, *Patterns of Discovery* (Cambridge: Cambridge University Press, 1965), pp. 37–49.
35. Ibid., pp. 70–83.

36. René Descartes, *Discourse on Method*, pt. 2.

37. David Hume, *A Treatise on Human Nature*, bk. 3, sec. 1.

38. See A. J. Ayer, "Critique of Ethics and Theology," in *Language, Truth and Logic* (New York: Dover Publications, 1950), pp. 102–120.

39. C. P. Snow, *The Two Cultures and the Scientific Revolution* (New York: Cambridge University Press, 1961). See also C. P. Snow, "The Moral Unneutrality of Science," in C. P. Snow, *Public Affairs* (New York: Scribner, 1971), pp. 187–198.

40. Francis Darwin, ed., *The Autobiography of Charles Darwin and Selected Letters* (New York: Dover Publications, 1958), pp. 53–54.

41. Ibid., p. 54.

42. Charles Darwin, *The Voyage of the Beagle* (New York: Bantam Books, 1958), pp. 88–89.

43. Charles Darwin, *The Origin of Species* and *The Descent of Man* (New York: Modern Library, n.d.) pp. 521, 550.

44. The term *scientist* was invented by a British philosopher named William Whewell in 1840 because he felt that there were beginning to be too many people claiming to be philosophers who by training were not.

45. Nathaniel Southgate Shaler, *Man and the Earth* (New York: Duffield & Company, 1917), pp. 228–229.

CHAPTER TWO
LAND USE ATTITUDES

Such protected areas as Yosemite, Yellowstone, and the Grand Canyon are often cited as great successes of the environmental movement in nature preservation and conservation. Yet not all natural objects and areas worthy of special protection or management are of such national significance and these must be dealt with at state, regional, or local levels. In such cases, environmentalists almost always plead their cause before a county court, a local administrative political body, usually consisting of three judges elected by the rural community, who may or may not have legal backgrounds.

Here the environmentalists are probably in for a great shock. Inevitably, some rural landowner will defend his special property rights to the land in question. He will ask the court rhetorically, "What right do these outsiders, these so-called environmentalists, have to come in here and try to tell me what to do with my land?" and answering his own question, he will continue, "They don't have any right. I worked that land; it's my property, and no one has the right to tell me what to do with it!" The environmentalists may be surprised that the farmer does not bother to reply to any of their carefully made points, but the real shock comes at the end, when the county court dismisses the environmental issues, ruling in the favor of the landowner.

While the environmentalists may suspect corruption (and such dealings are not unlikely), usually both the judges and the landowner are honestly convinced that they have all acted properly. The property rights argument recited by the rural landowner is a very powerful defense, particularly when presented at this level of government. The argument is grounded in a political philosophy almost three centuries old as well as in land use practices that go back at least to Saxon and perhaps even to Celtic times in Europe and England. When the argument is presented to county court judges who share these beliefs and land use traditions, the outcome of the court decision is rarely in doubt. On the other hand, the tradition that natural objects and areas of special beauty or interest ought to be protected from landowners claiming special property rights and from the practice of landowning in general is of very recent origin and without comparable historical and emotional foundations.

For several decades in the late nineteenth century, the rural landowner's theory of property and land use rights was the primary basis for arguments opposing the preservation of Yellowstone as a national park. During the floor debate on the Yellowstone bill in 1872, for example, Senator Cole of California stated:

> The geysers will remain no matter where the ownership of the land may be, and I do not know why settlers should be excluded from a tract of land forty miles square, as I understand this to be in the Rocky Mountains or any other place. . . . There are some places, perhaps this is one, where persons can and would go and settle and improve and cultivate the grounds, if there be ground fit for cultivation.

When Senator Edmunds of Vermont reminded Cole that, according to reports, the land could not be cultivated, Cole replied, "The Senator is probably mistaken in that. Ground of a greater height than that has been cultivated and occupied," and he continued:

> But if it cannot be occupied and cultivated, why should we make a public park of it? If it cannot be occupied by men, why protect it from occupation: I see no reason in that. If nature has excluded men from its occupation, why set it apart and exclude persons from it? If there is any sound reason for the passage of the bill, of course, I would not oppose it; but really I do not see any myself.[1]

Similarly, during the floor debate in 1883 in which the Senate considered for the first time whether Congress ought to appropriate money for maintaining the roads of the park and for the salary of the superintendent, until then an unpaid position, Senator Ingalls of Kansas rose to inform his colleagues that "the best thing that the Government could do with Yellowstone National Park is to survey it and sell it as other public lands are sold." Returning to this point after a lengthy digression, Ingalls concluded:

> I do not understand myself what the necessity is for Government entering into the show business in Yellowstone National Park. I should be very glad myself to see an amendment to this bill to authorize that that portion of the public domain to be surveyed and sold, leaving it to private enterprise, which is the surest guarantee for proper protection for such objects of care as the great natural curiosities in that region.[2]

Although no comparable debates have been recorded over Yosemite, which received park status about eight years before Yellowstone, judging by J.D. Whitney's comments in *The Yosemite Book,* published in 1868, the situation was in fact more perilous than at Yellowstone. Apparently, the State of California seriously considered permitting two individuals to preempt the valley floor—a procedure predating but similar to homesteading in which the landholder demanded special rates for purchase of the land he had illegally occupied or asked for financial compensation for the "improvements" he had made. Preemption would have left only the walls of the valley in public hands, and, as Whitney puts it, paraphrasing Keats, "the Yosemite Valley instead of being 'a joy forever' will become, like Niagara Falls, a gigantic institution for fleecing the public."[3]

To environmentalists, the attitudes of Cole, Ingalls, and the landholders in Yosemite seem as unenlightened as those of the rural landowner in the county court today, but at the time of the Yellowstone National Park bill, a mere ten years after the passage of the immensely popular Homestead Act, they were probably a more accurate representation of public attitudes toward western lands than those of the supporters of either park. Most people in those days believed that western lands should be distributed free, and freely, to unpropertied Americans willing to work and improve the land over a short period of time. Because the Yellowstone bill called for an enormous tract of land to be "reserved and withdrawn from settlement, occupancy, or sale under the laws of the United States, and dedicated and set apart as a public park or pleasuring-ground for the benefit and enjoyment of the people,"[4] many Americans naturally felt that the bill must be the first step in a political scheme to rob deserving Americans of their natural right to western land.

Anticipating this kind of opposition, park supporters claimed that the land was not suitable for farming or mining. The report of the Committee on Public Lands contained the following remarks:

> We have already shown that no portion of this tract can ever be made available for agriculture or mining purposes. Even if the altitude and climate would permit the country to be made available, not over fifty square miles of the entire area could ever be settled. The valleys are all narrow, hemmed in by high volcanic mountains like gigantic walls.

> The withdrawal of this tract, therefore, from sale or settlement takes nothing from the value of the public domain, and is no pecuniary loss to the government, but will be regarded by the entire civilized world as a step of progress and honor to Congress and the nation.[5]

These were the statements that Senator Edmunds was referring to when he told the disbelieving Cole that the land was not fit for cultivation.

Although these remarks may make sense to people who place high value on land in a natural and unused state, Cole, with his strong concern for the rights of potential homesteaders, believed them to be bordering on the irrational and the absurd. From his point of view, the claims of the park supporters were contradictory. The land was said to be both worthless and valuable beyond compare. In addition, he was being asked to help protect the land from use and at the same time being told that the land could not be used. Cole could conclude only that these claims were very suspicious and that the Yellowstone bill must somehow be a threat to the land use philosophy that he supported as a fundamental part of the American heritage.

The incongruity in the park supporters' position producing these seeming paradoxes was the claim that Yellowstone had no use. It was introduced only because it was an expedient way for park supporters to achieve their objective with minimum opposition. Because the claim could be taken to imply approval of the homestead land use philosophy, it created the illusion that no great issue was at stake. However, as everyone knew, the uselessness of Yellowstone for agricultural or mining purposes had had nothing at all to do with the mounting interest in preserving the area. Most likely, some attempt would have been made to preserve Yellowstone even if it had turned out to contain prime agricultural land or valuable minerals. Thus the Yellowstone bill, far from being compatible with land use attitudes embodied in the Homestead Act of 1862, really was a threat to them.

As support increased in early nineteenth-century America for homesteading and for recognition of the natural and absolute rights of Americans to western land as private property, opposition to this viewpoint also grew among eastern intellectuals who were finding aesthetic and scientific value in land independent of its commercial use. This new attitude toward land is reflected in Thoreau's remark in his essay "Walking" that "the best part of the land is not private property; the landscape is not owned" and in similar remarks by Emerson in *Nature,* where he writes, "The charming landscape which I saw this morning is indubitably made up of some twenty or thirty farms. Miller owns this field, Locke that, and Manning the woodland beyond. But none of them owns the landscape." The members of the 1870 Washburn expedition to Yellowstone, who first called public attention to the wonders of that area, were themselves acting in accordance with this new land value attitude when, after much discussion, all but one of them abandoned plans to preempt Yellowstone for their own personal gain, having decided that it was too extraordinary a place to be privately owned by a few individuals.[6]

How this new viewpoint developed is the subject of the next chapter. My present purpose is to examine traditional land use attitudes. First, I examine the ancient land use practices that gave rise to these attitudes; second, the political activities and views of Thomas Jefferson, who secured a place for them in American political and legal thought; and finally, the political philosophy of John Locke, who provided them with a philosophical foundation.

LANDHOLDING AMONG EARLY GERMAN AND SAXON FREEMEN

About two thousand years ago, most of Europe was occupied by tribes of peoples known collectively today as the Celts. At about that time, these peoples came under considerable pressure from the Romans moving up from the south and from Germanic tribes entering central Europe from the east. Five hundred years later, the Celts had either been subjugated by the German and Roman invaders or pushed back into Ireland and fringe areas of England. The Roman Empire, too, after asserting its presence as far north as England, was in decay. Roman influence would continue in the south, but in northern and central Europe as well as in most of England, German influence would prevail.

The Germanic tribes that displaced the Celts and defeated the Romans were composed of four classes: a few nobles or earls, a very large class of freemen, a smaller class of slaves, and a very small class of semifree men or serfs. Freemen were the most common people in early German society. They recognized no religious or political authority over their own activities, except to a very limited degree. As *free* men, they could, if they desired, settle their accounts with their neighbors and move to another geographic location. Each freeman occupied a large amount of land, his freehold farmstead, on which he grazed animals and, with the help of his slaves, grew crops. When necessary, he joined together with other freemen for defense or, more often, for the conquest of new territories.[7]

Freemen were the key to German expansion. When overcrowding occurred in clan villages and little unoccupied land remained, freemen moved to the border and with other freemen defeated and drove away the neighboring people. Here they established for themselves their own freehold farmsteads. Their descendants then multiplied and occupied the vacant land between the original freehold estates. When land was no longer available, clan villages began to form again, and many freemen moved on once more to the new borders to start new freehold farmsteads. In this way, the Germans slowly but surely moved across northern and central Europe with freemen leading the way until no more land was available.

Strictly speaking, a freeman did not own his land. The idea of landownership in the modern sense was still many centuries away. In England, for example, landowning did not become a political and legal reality until 1660, when feudal dues were finally abolished once and for all. Freemen, however, lived in prefeudal times. They usually made a yearly offering to the local noble or earl, but technically this offering was a gift rather than a feudal payment and had nothing to do with their right to their land. As the term *freehold* suggests, a freeman held his land freely without any forced obligations to an overlord or to his neighbors.

In early times, when land was readily available, each freeman occupied as much land as he needed. There was no set amount that a freeman ought to have and no limit on his holdings, except that he could not hold more land than he could use. Thus, in effect, his personal dominion was restricted only by the number of animals that he needed to graze and the number of slaves he had for agricultural labor. Sometimes, when the land began to lose its fertility, he would abandon his holdings and move to some other unoccupied location nearby. The exact location of each holding was only vaguely determined, and when disputes arose about boundaries, they were settled with the help of the testimony of neighbors or, when that failed, by armed combat between the parties involved.

Much of the unoccupied land was held in common with other freemen in accordance with various local arrangements. Sometimes the use was regulated by establishing the number of cattle that each freeman could place on the land. In other cases, plots were used by different freemen every year on a rotational basis.

When unoccupied border lands were no longer available for new freemen to settle, the way of life of the freemen began to change. The primary problem was one of inheritance. In the beginning, land had never been divided; rather, it had always been "multiplied" as sons moved to adjacent areas and established new freehold farmsteads. Eventually, however, it became necessary for the sons to divide the land that had been held by their father. A serious problem then developed, for if division took place too many times, the holdings became so small that they had little economic value, and the family as a whole slipped into poverty.

The solution was *entail,* inheritance along selected family lines. The most common form of entail was *primogeniture,* according to which the eldest son inherited everything and the others little or nothing. In this way, the family head remained powerful by keeping his landholdings intact, but most of his brothers were condemned to the semifree and poverty-stricken life of serfdom. As a result of these new inheritance practices, the number of freemen became an increasingly smaller portion of the society as a whole as most of the rest of the population, relatives included, rapidly sank to the level of serfs.

Another problem affecting freemen was taxation. The custom of giving an offering to the local noble was gradually replaced by a tax, and once established, taxes often became large burdens on many of the poorer freemen, who in many instances paid taxes while other richer landholders were exempted. In such circumstances, freemen often gave up their status and their lands to persons exempted from the taxes and paid a smaller sum in rent as tenants.

Germans thus made a transition from prefeudal to feudal conditions, and freemen ceased to be an important element in the community as a whole. Though freemen never disappeared altogether, most lost the economic freedom that they formerly had. Although theoretically free to move about as they pleased, they often lacked the economic means of settling their accounts and so in most cases were little better off than the serfs.

These feudal conditions did not appear in England until long after they were firmly established on the European continent. At the time of the invasion of England by William the Conqueror, most Englishmen were freemen. Thus in England, unlike Germanic Europe, prefeudal conditions did not slip away gradually but were abruptly replaced by a feudal system imposed on much of the native population by the victorious Normans. Under such circumstances, freemen declined in numbers but struggled as best they could to maintain their freeman status in opposition to Norman rule and as a part of their Saxon heritage. As a result, freemen managed to maintain a presence in England no longer conceivable on the continent. Through them, memories of the heyday of the flamboyant Saxon freemen remained to shade political thought and to shape land use attitudes for centuries after the conquest. Ironically, the conquest drew attention to a class status that might otherwise have quietly passed away.

There were four major political divisions in Saxon England: the kingdom, the shire (called the *county* after the arrival of the Normans), the hundred, and the township, the last two being subdivisions of the shire or county. Throughout English history, the exact nature of the government of the kingdom fluctuated, sometimes very radically. Changes occurred in the hundreds and the townships as the courts at these levels were gradually replaced by those of the local nobility, probably with the support of the government of the kingdom. The shire or county and its court or moot, however, persisted unchanged and continued to be one of the most important political units from the earliest Saxon times in England to the present day in both England and the United States.

The county court met to deal with cases not already handled by the hundred moots and with other business of common importance to the community. The meetings were conducted by three men: the alderman, representing the shire, the sheriff, representing the king; and the bishop, representing the church. All freemen in the county had the right to attend the court and participate in the decision process. Most of them, of course, were usually too busy to come except when personal interests were at stake.

There are only small differences between the county courts of Saxon and Norman times and those of modern rural America. The three judges, alderman, sheriff, and bishop, have been replaced by elected judges. Court procedure in most of these courts, however, remains as informal today as it was in pre-Norman England. In many, no record is kept by the court of its decisions, and except for word of mouth and intermittent coverage by the news media, little is known of what goes on there. Court judges are primarily concerned with keeping the local landowners contented by resolving local differences and by providing the few community services under the administrative jurisdiction of the court, such as maintaining dirt or gravel roads. This casual form of government is replaced only when the county becomes urbanized, thereby enabling residents to incorporate it and enjoy extensive new administrative and legal powers and, of course, responsibilities.

The special considerations given to the local landowner by the modern rural county court reflects the relationship of Saxon freemen to the court at the time when such courts first came into existence. The court evolved out of the freeman's custom of consulting with his neighbors during local disputes as an alternative to physical combat between the parties involved. Thus, rather than being something imposed on the freemen from above, the court was created by them for their own convenience. Since the freemen gave up little or none of their personal power, the power of the court to enforce its decisions was really nothing more than the collective power of the freemen ultimately comprising the membership of the court. From the earliest times, freemen had had absolute control over all matters pertaining to their own landholdings. When county courts were formed, freemen retained this authority over what they considered to be their own personal affairs. This limitation on the power of the court was maintained for more than a thousand years as part of the traditional conception of a county court and its function. Today, when a landowner demands to know what right the court or anyone else has to tell him what to do with his own land, he is referring to the original limitations set on the authority of the county court and is appealing to the rights that he has informally inherited from his political ancestors, Saxon or German freemen—specifically, the right to do as he pleases without considering any interests except his own.

A modern landowner's argument that he has the right to do as he wishes is normally composed of a set series of claims given in a specific order. First, he points out that he or his father or grandfather worked the land in question. Second, he asserts that his ownership of the land is based on the work or labor put into it. Finally, he proclaims the right of uncontrolled use as a result of his ownership claim. Not all of this argument is derived directly from the freeman's world view. As mentioned, the modern concept of ownership was unknown to freemen, who were engaged in landholding rather than landowning. In other respects, however, there are strong similarities between the views of modern landowners and those of the freemen.

Landholding among German freemen was based on work. A freeman, like the nineteenth-century American homesteader, took possession of a tract of land by clearing it, building a house and barns, and dividing the land into fields for the grazing of animals and the growing of crops. His initial work established his claim to continued use.

This emphasis on work as the basis for landholding is especially clear in connection with inheritance. When plenty of vacant land was available, landholdings were never divided among the sons, but, as described earlier, the sons moved to unoccupied land nearby and started their own freehold farmsteads. Thus inheritance in those early times was not the acquisition of land itself but rather the transferal of the right to acquire land through work. This distinction is reflected in the early German word for inheritance, *Arbi* in Gothic and *Erbi* in Old High German, both of which have the same root as the modern High German word, *Arbeit,* meaning work.[8]

Thus freemen were interested in land use rather than landownership. The right to land was determined by their social status as freemen and not by the fact that they or their fathers had occupied or possessed a particular piece of ground. The specific landholdings were thus not of major importance to the early freemen. Conceivably, they might move several times to new landholdings, abandoning the old without the size of their landholdings being affected in any way. As mentioned, it was their ability to use their holdings, the number of grazing animals, and slave workers they owned, not some form of ownership, that determined the size of their landholdings at any particular time in their lives.

Of course, once unoccupied land ceased to be readily available, freemen started paying much more attention to their land as property, encouraging the development of the idea of landownership in the modern sense. When the inheritance of sons became only the right to work a portion of their father's holdings, the transition from landholding to landowning was well on its way.

Until the time when there were no more unoccupied lands to move to, there was really no reason for freemen to be concerned with proper use or management of their land or for them to worry about possible long-term problems for themselves or their neighbors resulting from misuse and abuse of particular pieces of land. When a freeman lost his mobility, however, he did start trying to take somewhat better care of his land, occasionally practicing crop rotation and planting trees to replace those he cut down, but apparently these new necessities had little influence on his general conviction that as a freeman he had the right to use and even abuse his land as he saw fit.

Today's rural landowner finds himself in a situation not unlike that of freemen in the days when inheritance became the division of land rather than the multiplication of it. In the late eighteenth century and during most of the nineteenth, American rural landowners led a way of life much like that of prefeudal German freemen; now modern landowners face the same limitations their freeman ancestors did as feudal conditions began to develop. Although willing to take some steps toward good land management, especially ones that provide obvious short-term benefit, when faced with broader issues involving the welfare of their neighbors and the local community and the protection and the preservation of the environment as a whole, they claim ancient rights that have come down to them from German freemen and take advantage of their special influence with the local county court, a political institution as eager to please them today as it was more than a thousand years ago.

THOMAS JEFFERSON AND THE ALLODIAL RIGHTS OF AMERICAN FARMERS

When British colonists arrived in North America, they brought with them the land laws and land practices that were current in England at that time. These included entail, primogeniture, and most other aspects of the feudal tenure system that had taken hold in England after the Norman Conquest. The American Revolution called into question the right of the king of England to lands in North America, which in turn led to attempts to bring about major land reform—specifically, efforts to remove all elements of the feudal system from American law and practice and replace them with the older Saxon freehold tenure system. At the forefront of this movement was a young Virginian lawyer named Thomas Jefferson. According to Jefferson's biographer, Merrill D. Peterson, although social and economic forces may have already made the success of the land reform movement inevitable, Jefferson's efforts "capped the development and exalted the principle of freehold tenure."[9] Whether or not Jefferson caused the land reform, he did manage to identify himself with the effort to such a degree that his statements on the subject could later be used with great authority to justify additional reform, leading eventually to the Homestead Act of 1862. So great was Jefferson's influence on these later reforms that they are usually erroneously viewed as the fulfillment of a Jeffersonian dream arising out of new democratic principles rather than as the achievement of the much older dream of economically disadvantaged Saxon freemen dating back to the Norman Conquest.

From the first moment that Jefferson began airing his land tenure opinions, however, he made it completely clear that they were based entirely on Saxon, not Norman, common law. Thus he consistently spoke of allodial rights, *allodial* referring to *allodium,* an estate held in absolute dominion without obligation to a superior—the early Germany and Saxon freehold farmstead.

Jefferson's attitudes toward the disposition of land developed naturally out of his early studies of the origins of the British legal system, as he himself notes in a letter written some years later:

> The opinion that our lands were allodial possessions is one which I have very long held, and had in my eye during a pretty considerable part of my law reading which I found alwais strengthened it.[10]

As a law apprentice to George Wythe of the law firm Small, Wythe, and Fauquier, Jefferson first read Sir Edward Coke's *Institutes of the Laws of England,* a work that championed common-law English rights, tracing them back to the time of the Magna Charta. Then he continued his readings with the work of Henry Bracton and a digest of King Alfred's laws, both of which deal with Saxon law before the coming of the Normans. These readings convinced Jefferson that Coke's thesis was false and that English common law was actually based on Saxon foundations perverted by later Norman influence. Thereafter Jefferson sought to purge American law of this Norman corruption by using the original Saxon common law as his model.[11]

Jefferson's first public expression of his position came in a political pamphlet titled *A Summary View of the Rights of British America,* published in Williamsburg, Philadelphia, and London in 1774. In the second paragraph, Jefferson claims that all British citizens came to America with the rights of Saxon freemen:

> Our ancestors, before their emigration to America, were the free inhabitants of the British dominions in Europe, and possessed a right, which nature has given to men, of departing from the country in which chance, not choice has placed them, of going in quest of new habitations, and of there establishing new societies, under such laws and regulations as to them shall seem most likely to promote public happiness. That their Saxon ancestors had under this universal law, in like manner, left their native wilds and woods in the North of Europe, had possessed themselves of the island of Britain then less charged with inhabitants, and had established there that system of laws which has so long been the glory and protection of that country. Nor was ever any claim of superiority or dependence asserted over them by that mother country from

> which they had migrated: and were such a claim made it is believed his majesty's subjects in Great Britain have too firm a feeling of the rights derived to them from their ancestors to bow down the sovereignty of their state before such visionary pretensions. And it is thought that no circumstance has occurred to distinguish materially the British from the Saxon emigration. America was conquered, and her settlements made and firmly established, at the expense of individuals, and not of the British public. Their own blood was spilt in acquiring lands for their settlement, their own fortunes expended in making that settlement effectual. For themselves they fought, for themselves they conquered, and for themselves alone they have right to hold.

Noting the right of a Saxon freeman to settle his accounts and move to another realm at his own pleasure without obligation to the lord of his previous domain, Jefferson argues that this is also the case with the British citizens who moved to North America. According to this analogy, England has no more claim over residents of America than Germany has over residents of England. In accordance with Saxon tradition, the lands of North America belong to the people living there and not to the king of England.[12]

Later in the pamphlet, Jefferson expands on this point, arguing that the belief that the king owns North America is based on the erroneous claim that feudal law rather than Saxon law applies in British America:

> The introduction of the Feudal tenures into the kingdom of England, though antient, is well enough understood to set this matter in a proper light. In the earlier ages of the Saxon settlement feudal holdings were certainly altogether unknown, and very few, if any, had been introduced at the time of the Norman conquest. Our Saxon ancestors held their lands, as they did their personal property, in absolute dominion, disencumbered with any superior, answering nearly to the nature of those possessions which the Feudalists term Allodial: William the Norman first introduced that system generally.

According to Jefferson, William the Conqueror confiscated the lands of those who fell at the Battle of Hastings and these lands legally became subject to feudal duties, "but still much was left in the hands of his Saxon subjects, held of no superior, and not subject to feudal conditions." Later, Norman lawyers found ways to impose feudal burdens on the holders of these lands, "but still they had not been surrendered to the king, they were not derived from his grant, and therefore they were not holden of him." Of this great swindle, Jefferson writes:

> A general principle indeed was introduced that 'all lands in England were held either mediately or immediately of the crown': but this was borrowed from those holdings which were truly feudal, and only applied to others for the purposes of illustration. Feudal holdings were therefore but exceptions out of the Saxon laws of possession, under which all lands were held in absolute right. These therefore still form the basis or groundwork of the Common law, to prevail wheresoever the exceptions have not taken place.

Jefferson goes on to claim that this same deception is also being perpetrated on the citizens of British America:

> America was not conquered by William the Norman, nor it's [sic] lands surrendered to him or any of his successors. Possessions there are undoubtedly of the Allodial nature. Our ancestors however, who migrated hither, were laborers, not lawyers. The fictitious principle that all lands belong originally to the king, they were early persuaded to believe real.

It is not the king, Jefferson declares, but the individual members of a society collectively or their legislature that determine the legal status of land, and, if they fail to act, then, in accordance with the traditions of Saxon freemen, "each individual of the society may appropriate to himself such lands as he finds vacant, and occupancy will give him title."[13]

Jefferson was addressing issues of great importance in the history of British legal and political philosophy. William the Conqueror had claimed title to all Anglo-Saxon estates, but the claim had never been fully accepted by the defeated Saxons, who had continued to view themselves as freemen without any legitimate legal obligation to their Norman rulers beyond what their German heritage had always required. The controversy was still adequately alive in the mid-seventeenth century for Thomas Hobbes, a major British political philosopher, to take up the issue on behalf of the crown. Hobbes writes in *Leviathan:*

> the First Law, is for Division of the Land it selfe: wherein the Soveraign assigneth to every man a portion, according as he, and not according as any Subject, or any number of them, shall judge agreeable to Equity, and the Common Good.

After a long discussion of the ancient Jewish conquest of Israel, Hobbes continues with the specific claim that Jefferson is disputing:

> though a People coming into possession of a Land by warre, do not alwais exterminate the antient inhabitants . . . , but leave to many, or most, or all of them their Estates; yet it is manifest they hold them afterwards, as of the Victors distribution; as the people of *England* held all theirs of *William* the *Conquerour*[14]

Jefferson, of course, did not succeed in refuting the claim of the king of England to all land in British America, but by arguing in terms of this old dispute, he gives his position a legal basis that would have strong appeal among Englishmen with Saxon backgrounds, assuring some political support of the American cause in England.

In 1776, Jefferson got the opportunity to try to turn his theory into practice. Although Jefferson is most famous for writing the Declaration of Independence, most of his time that year was spent working on his draft of the Virginia constitution and on the reform of various Virginia laws, including the land reform laws. In his draft constitution, Jefferson included a provision that gave every person of full age the right to fifty acres of land "in full and absolute dominion." In addition, lands previously "holden of the crown in feesimple" and all other lands appropriated in the future were to be "holden in full and absolute dominion, of no superior whatever."[15] Although these provisions were deleted, and similar bills submitted to the legislature failed to pass, Jefferson did succeed in getting the legislature to abolish the feudal inheritance laws, entail and primogeniture.

In a series of letters exchanged with Edmund Pendleton, the speaker of the House of Delegates, during the summer of 1776, Jefferson expresses his desire to reestablish ancient Saxon law in Virginia. In one letter, after insisting that unoccupied land should neither be rented nor given away in return for military service, Jefferson continues:

> Has it not been the practice of all other nations to hold their lands as their personal estate in absolute dominion? Are we not the better for what we have hitherto abolished of the feudal system? Has not every restitution of the antient Saxon laws had happy effects? Is it not now better that we return at once to that happy system of our ancestors, the wisest and most perfect ever yet devised by the wit of man, as it stood before the 8th century?

As for the government selling the land, Jefferson was completely opposed. "I am against selling the land at all," he writes to Pendleton. "By selling the lands to them, you will disgust them, and cause an avulsion of them from the common union. They will settle the lands in spite of every body."[16] This prediction proved to be remarkably correct as evidenced by the fact that the next eighty years of American history was cluttered with squatters illegally occupying government land and then demanding compensation for their "improvements" through special preemption laws.

In 1784, when he was appointed to head the land committee in the Congress of the Confederation, Jefferson had a second opportunity to reestablish the Saxon landholding system. Whether Jefferson tried to take advantage of this opportunity is not known because the report of the committee, called the Ordinance of 1784, contains nothing about allodial rights to land. In addition, it even contains recommendations for the selling of western lands as a source of revenue for the government. It should be noted, however, that in one respect at least the document still has a very definite Saxon ring to it. Jefferson managed to include in his report a recommendation that settlers be permitted to organize themselves into new states on an equal footing with the original colonies. This recommendation, which was retained in the Ordinance of 1787, a revised version of the earlier ordinance, not only created the political structure necessary to turn the thirteen colonies into a much larger union of states but also provided future generations of Americans with an independence and mobility similar to that enjoyed by the early Saxon and German freemen. In his *Sum-*

mary View of 1774, Jefferson had argued that just as the Saxons invading England had had the right to set up an independent government, so British Americans had the right to an independent government in North America. The Ordinances of 1784 and 1787 extended this right to movement and self-determination of American settlers leaving the jurisdiction of established states and moving into the interior of the continent. In large measure, it is thanks to this provision that Americans today are able to move from state to state without any governmental control in the form of visas, passports, immigration quotas, or the like, as unrestrained by such details as the early German freemen.

The absence of any provisions specifically granting landowners full and absolute dominion over their land, however, does not mean that Jefferson abandoned this conception of landholding or ownership. Privately and in his published writings, he continued to champion the right of Americans to small freehold farmsteads. The only major change seems to be that he stopped trying to justify his position in terms of historical precedents and instead began speaking in moral terms, claiming that small, independent landholders were the most virtuous citizens any state could ever hope to have. In a letter to John Jay in 1785, Jefferson writes:

> Cultivators of the earth are the most valuable citizens. They are the most vigorous, the most independent, the most virtuous, and they are tied to their country and wedded to it's liberty and interests by the most lasting bands.[17]

In a letter to James Madison the same year, he adds:

> Whenever there is in any country, uncultivated lands and unemployed poor, it is clear that the laws of property have been so far extended as to violate natural right. The earth is given as a common stock for man to labour and live on. If, for the encouragement of industry we allow it to be appropriated, we must take care that other employment be furnished to those excluded from that appropriation. If we do not the fundamental right to labour the earth returns to the unemployed. It is too soon yet in our country to say that every man who cannot find employment but who can find uncultivated land, shall be at liberty to cultivate it, paying a moderate rent. But it is not too soon to provide by every possible means that as few as possible shall be without a little portion of land. The small landholders are the most precious part of the state.[18]

In *Notes on the State of Virginia,* published in 1787, Jefferson continues in much the same vein:

> Those who labour in the earth are the chosen people of God, if ever he had a chosen people, whose breasts he has made his peculiar deposit for substantial and genuine virtue. It is the focus in which he keeps alive that sacred fire,

> which otherwise might escape from the face of the earth. Corruption of morals in the mass of cultivators is a phaenomenon of which no age nor nation has furnished an example. It is the mark set on those, who not looking up to heaven, to their own soil and industry, as does the husbandman, for their subsistance, depend for it on the casualties and caprice of customers. Dependance begets subservience and venality, suffocates the germ of virtue, and prepares fit tools for the designs of ambition. This, the natural progress and consequence of the arts, has sometimes perhaps been retarded by accidental circumstances: but, generally speaking, the proportion which the aggregate of the other classes of citizens bears in any state to that of its husbandman, is the proportion of its unsound to its healthy parts, and is a good-enough barometer whereby to measure its degree of corruption. While we have land to labour then, let us never wish to see our citizens occupied at a work-bench, or twirling a distaff.[19]

It is in the context of these remarks that Senator Cole and Senator Ingalls felt the need to convince their colleagues in Congress of the necessity of surveying Yellowstone into lots and opening it to settlement. From their point of view, the moral character of the American people as a whole was at stake. These remarks are probably also the basis for the position of rural landowners today when faced with environmental issues. They are defending the American moral virtues that they have always been told their style of life and independence represents.

Had Jefferson been alive in the late nineteenth century when his views were being cited in opposition to the preservation of Yellowstone or were he alive today to see his Saxon freemen busily sabotaging county planning and zoning, he might have become disillusioned with his faith in the virtues of independent rural landowners. After all, as a result of his purchase of the Natural Bridge, perhaps the first major act of nature preservation in North America, Jefferson ranks as a very important figure in the history of the nature preservation movement. Unfortunately, however, Jefferson's homesteaders and their modern-day descendants did not always retain his aesthetic interest in nature or his respect for sound agricultural management, which he interwove with his Saxon land use attitudes to form a balanced land use philosophy.

In part, the callousness and indifference of most rural landowners to environmental matters reflects the insensitivity of ancient Saxon freemen, who viewed land as something to be used for personal benefit and who, being seminomadic, were unconcerned about whether that use would result in irreparable damage to the particular piece of land that they held at any given point in their lives. In addition, however, it can also be traced back to the political philosophy and theory of property of John Locke, a seventeenth-century British philosopher, who had a major impact on the political views of Jefferson and most other American statesmen during the American Revolution and afterward.

JOHN LOCKE'S THEORY OF PROPERTY

As noted, German and Saxon freemen did not have a concept of landownership, only of landholding. As long as there was plenty of land for everyone's use, they did not concern themselves with exact boundaries. Disputes arose only when two freemen wanted to use the same land at the same time. By the end of the Middle Ages, however, with land in short supply, landholders began enclosing their landholdings to help ensure exclusive use. Enclosure kept the grazing animals of others away and also provided a sign of the landholder's presence and authority. Although enclosure was only a small step toward the concept of landownership, it proved useful as a pseudoproperty concept in early seventeenth-century New England, where Puritans were able to justify their occupation of Indian lands on the grounds that the lack of enclosures demonstrated that the lands were vacant. Landownership became an official legal distinction in England after 1660 with the abolishment of feudal dues. The concept of landownership was introduced into British social and political philosophy thirty years later as part of John Locke's theory of property. This theory was presented in detail in Locke's *Two Treatises of Government,* a major work in political philosophy first published in 1690.[20]

Jefferson had immense respect and admiration for Locke and his philosophical writings. On one occasion, he wrote to a friend that Locke was one of the three greatest men that had ever lived (Bacon and Newton being the other two). Jefferson's justification of the American Revolution in the Declaration of Independence was borrowed directly from Locke's second treatise. Many of Jefferson's statements in the document are almost identical to remarks made by Locke. For example, when Jefferson speaks of "life, liberty, and the pursuit of happiness," he is closely paraphrasing Locke's own views. His version differs from Locke's in only one minor respect: Jefferson substitutes for Locke's "enjoyment of property" the more general phrase "the pursuit of happiness," a slight change made to recognize other enjoyments in addition to those derived from the ownership of property. Years later, when Jefferson was accused by John Adams and others of having stolen most of his ideas from Locke's writings, he simply acknowledged his debt, pointing out that he had been asked to write a defense of the American Revolution in 1776, not to create an entirely new and original political philosophy. He added that he had not referred to Locke's writings when writing the Declaration of Independence or consciously tried to paraphrase Locke's remarks. Locke's influence on him, however, had been so strong that without his being fully aware of it, bits and pieces of Locke's own words had found their way into the document.[21]

Although Locke's political philosophy proved to be tailor-made for the American Revolution, it was actually the partisan product of a somewhat earlier period of political turmoil in English history. Locke's *Two Treatises* was written and published near the end of a century characterized by major changes in the British political system. The power of the king and the aristocracy was beginning to give way to the kind of party system that still dominates British and American politics today. Locke had been a theological student at Oxford during Cromwell's dictatorship. During the last part of the reign of Charles II and all of the reign of James II he was in exile in France and Holland, returning to England during the Glorious Revolution of 1688 with the new rulers, William and Mary. Locke wrote his *Two Treatises* for political purposes. He hoped to justify the revolution settlement and also to help create a political climate favorable to the political party of his late friend, Lord Shaftesbury. This party was an alliance of a few liberal aristocrats with the discontented rich of London and other major towns.

A new theory of property ownership was important to these people. Previously, property rights had been tied to inheritance and to the divine rights of kings. A person owned property because his father and his father's father had owned it and also because at some point, at least theoretically, the property had been given to his family by the king. The king's right to bestow property was based on certain agreements made between God and Adam, and later Noah, in which He gave the entire earth to the children of God. The king, as a descendant of Adam and as God's designated agent, served more or less as an executor for the estate. Since the doctrine of the divine rights of the king was being rescinded by act of Parliament, a new theory of property was needed to justify private ownership.

The divine rights of kings had been defended by Robert Filmer in a book titled *Patriarcha,* published posthumously in 1680.[22] The first treatise is a direct and all-out attack on Filmer's arguments. The second treatise develops Locke's own position. It is this position which I am primarily concerned with here.

In the second treatise, Locke bases property rights on the labor of the individual:

> Though the Earth, and all inferior Creatures be common to all Men, yet, every Man has a *Property* in his own *Person.* This no Body has any Right to but himself. The *Labour* of his Body, and the *Work* of his Hands, we may say, are properly his. Whatsoever then he removes out of the State that Nature hath provided, and left in, he hath mixed his *Labour* with, and joyned to it something that is his own, and thereby makes it his *Property.*[23]

This theory of property served Locke's friends well since it made their property rights completely independent of all outside interest. According to Locke, property rights are established without reference to kings, governments, or even the collective rights of other people. If a man mixes his labor with a natural object, the product is his.

The relevance of Locke's labor theory to the American homestead land use philosophy becomes especially clear when he turns to the subject of land as property:

> But the *chief matter of Property* being now not the Fruits of the Earth, and the Beasts that subsist on it, but the Earth *it self* as that which takes in and carries with it all the rest; I think it is plain, that *Property* in that too is acquired as the former. *As much land* as a Man Tills, Plants, Improves, Cultivates, and can use the Product of, so much is his *Property.* He by his Labour does, as it were, inclose it from the Common. . . . God, when He gave the World in common to all Mankind, commanded Man also to labour, and the penury of his Condition required it of him. God and his Reason commanded him to subdue the Earth, *i.e.* improve it for the benefit of Life, and therein lay out something upon it that was his own, his labour. He that in Obedience to this Command of God, subdued, tilled, sowed any part of it, thereby annexed to it something that was his *Property,* which another had no Title to, nor could without injury take from him.[24]

In this passage, the right of use and ownership is determined by the farmer's labor. When he mixes his labor with the land, the results are *improvements,* the key term in homesteading days and even today in rural America, where the presence of such improvements may qualify landowners for exemption from planning and zoning under a grandfather clause. Since property rights are established on an individual basis independent of a social context, Locke's theory of property also provides the foundation for the landowner's claim that society has little or no role in the management of his land, that nobody has the right to tell him what to do with his property.

Locke reinforces the property owner's independence from societal restraints with an account of the origins of society in which property rights are supposedly more fundamental than society itself. According to Locke, the right to the enjoyment of property is a presocietal *natural right.* It is a natural right because it is a right that a person would have in a state of nature. Locke claims that there was once, at some time in the distant past, a true state of nature in which people possessed property as a result of their labor but did not yet have societal relations with one another. This state of nature disappeared when these ancient people decided to form a society, thereby giving up some of their previous powers and rights. They did not, however, Locke emphatically insists, relinquish any of their natural rights to their own property, and the original social contract establishing the society did not give society any authority at all over personal property. In fact, the main reason that society was formed, according to Locke's account, was to make it possible for individuals to enjoy their own property rights more safely and securely. Thus society's primary task was and allegedly still is to protect private property rights, not to infringe on them. A government that attempts to interfere with an individual's natural and uncontrolled right to the enjoyment of his property, moreover, deserves to be overthrown, and the citizens of the society are free to do so at their pleasure. In effect, Locke is arguing along lines completely compatible with the early Saxon (and later Jeffersonian) doctrine that a landowner holds his property in full and absolute dominion without any obligation to a superior.

The similarity of Locke's position to this doctrine invites the conclusion that Locke was drawing inspiration from Saxon common law and that Locke's social contract was actually the establishment of the shire or county court by Saxon freemen. Curiously, however, Locke makes no mention of the Saxons in these contexts, and even more curiously, no political philosopher seems to have considered the possibility that Locke might have been referring to this period of English history. Yet in his chapter on conquest, Locke does demonstrate (1) that he knew what a freeman was, (2) that he was aware of the legal conflicts resulting from the Norman Conquest, and (3) that he sided with the Saxons in that controversy. In the one paragraph where he mentions the Saxons by name, he flippantly remarks that even if they did lose their rights as freemen at the time of the conquest, as a result of the subsequent six centuries of intermarriage all Englishmen of Locke's day could claim freeman status through some Norman ancestor and it would "be very hard to prove the contrary."[25] Locke may have chosen not to mention the specifics of Saxon history for fear that if he did so, his political philosophy might have been treated as nothing more than another call for a return to Saxon legal precedents. It is hard to imagine, nonetheless, that Locke's readers in the seventeenth century were not aware of these unstated connections, considering the ease with which Jefferson saw them eighty years later in colonial North America. It is also possible, of course, that Locke may have been ignorant of the details of Saxon common law and may have simply relied on the popular land use attitudes of his day without being aware of their Saxon origin. At any rate, however, the ultimate result would be the same—a political philosophy that provides philosophical foundations for the ancient Saxon land use attitudes and traditions.

Whether Jefferson derived his own land use philosophy from both Locke and Saxon common law from the very beginning or turned to Locke for additional support after arguing first on Saxon precedent alone is difficult to determine. Jefferson's claim in his *Summary View* that "each individual of the society may appropriate to himself such lands as he finds vacant, and occupancy will give him title" is generally taken to be a sign of Locke's influence, though it comes at the end of a long discussion of Saxon law. In any case, Locke's presence is indisputable in the passages from various letters and in *Notes on the State of Virginia* written in the 1780s, some of which I quoted in connection with the moral overtones of Jefferson's position. In all of these, Jefferson speaks repeatedly of the right to "labour the earth" and of the property rights derived from this labor. The introduction of a Christian context in which "those who labour in the earth are the chosen people of God" may also be an indication of Locke's influence, though, of course, the ultimate source in this case is probably the passage in Genesis where God commands His people to multiply and to subdue the Earth.[26]

Not everyone in the first half of the nineteenth century shared Jefferson's enthusiasm for land reform based on Saxon common law modified by Locke's theory of property, and for a time the idea of landholding independent of landowning continued to be influential in American political and legal thought. Early versions of the homestead bill before the beginning of the Civil War, for example, often contained inalienability and reversion clauses. According to these, a homesteader had the right to use the land but could not subdivide it, sell it, or pass it on to his children after his death. These limitations, however, were not compatible with the wishes of potential homesteaders who wanted to be landowners, not just landholders, and as a result, they were not included in the Homestead Act of 1862. It is unlikely that homesteading based entirely on Saxon common law ever had much chance of passing Congress because early nineteenth-century settlers squatting illegally on western lands and demanding the enactment of special preemption laws had always had landownership as their primary objective.[27]

Because it was probably Locke's theory of property as much as Saxon common law that encouraged American citizens and immigrants to move westward, both should be given a share of the credit for the rapid settlement of the American West, which ultimately established a national claim to all the lands west of the Appalachians as far as the Pacific. This past benefit to the American people should not be the only standard for evaluating this doctrine's continuing value, however. We must still ask just how well the position is suited to conditions in twentieth-century America.

MODERN DIFFICULTIES WITH LOCKE'S POSITION

One obvious problem with Locke's theory today is his claim that there is enough land for everyone.[28] This premise is of fundamental importance to Locke's argument because if a present or future shortage of land can be established, any appropriation of land past or present under the procedure Locke recommends, enclosure from the common through labor, is an injustice to those who must remain unpropertied. By Locke's own estimates, there was twice as much land at the end of the seventeenth century as all the inhabitants of the Earth could use. To support these calculations,

Locke pointed to the "in-land, vacant places of America"—places that are now occupied.[29] Since his argument depends on a premise that is now false, Locke would have great difficulty advancing and justifying his position today.

Another problem is Locke's general attitude toward uncultivated land. Locke places almost no value on such land before it is improved, and after improvement he says the labor is still the chief factor in any value assessment:

> When any one hath computed, he will then see, how much *labour makes the far greatest part of the value* of things we enjoy in this World: And the ground which produces the materials, is scarce to be reckon'd in, as any, or at most, but a very small part of it; So little, that even amongst us, Land that is left wholly to Nature, that hath no improvement of Pasturage, Tillage, or Planting, is called, as indeed it is, *waste* and we shall find the benefit of it amount to little more than nothing.[30]

According to Locke's calculations, 99 to 99.9 percent of the value of land even after it is improved still results from the labor and not the land. Although these absurdly high figures helped strengthen Locke's claim that labor establishes property rights over land by making it seem that it is primarily the individual's labor mixed with the land rather than the land itself that is owned, such estimates, if presented today, would be considered scientifically false and contrary to common sense.

Locke's land value attitudes reflect a general desire prevalent in his time as well as today for maximum agricultural productivity. From Locke's point of view, it was inefficient to permit plants and animals to grow naturally on uncultivated land:

> I aske whether in the wild woods and uncultivated waste of America left to Nature, without any improvement, tillage, or husbandry, a thousand acres will yield the needy and wretched inhabitants as many conveniences of life as ten acres of equally fertile land doe in Devonshire where they are well cultivated?

The problem, however, is not just productivity and efficiency but also a general contempt for the quality of the natural products of the earth. Locke writes with great conviction that "*Bread* is more worth than Acorns, *Wine* than Water, and *Cloth* or *Silk* than Leaves, Skins or Moss."[31]

Even though we might be inclined to agree with Locke's pronouncements in certain contexts, more than two hundred years of the American experience have provided us with new attitudes incompatible with those of Locke and his contemporaries, and apparently completely unknown to them, that place high value on trees, water, animals, and even land itself in a wholly natural and unimproved condition. Unlike Locke, we do not always consider wilderness land or uncultivated land synonymous with waste.

At the very core of Locke's land value attitudes is his belief that "the Earth, and all that is therein, is given to Men for the Support and Comfort of their being."[32] In one sense, this view is very old, derived from the biblical and Aristotelian claims that the Earth exists for the benefit and use of human beings. At the same time, it is very modern because of Locke's twin emphases on labor and consumption. Both of these activities are of central importance in communistic and capitalistic political systems, and they became so important precisely because the founders and ideologists of each system originally took their ideas about labor and consumption from Locke's philosophy. In accordance with these ideas, the Earth is nothing more than raw materials waiting to be transformed by labor into consumable products. The Greeks and Romans would have objected to this view on the grounds that labor and consumption are too low and demeaning to be regarded as primary human activities.[33] From a twentieth-century standpoint, given the current emphasis on consumption, the neglect of the aesthetic and scientific (ecological) value of nature seems to be a more fundamental and serious objection to this exploitative view.

The worst result of Locke's property theory is the amoral or asocial attitude that has evolved out of it. Locke's arguments have encouraged landowners to behave in an antisocial manner and to claim that they have no moral obligation to the land itself or even to the other people in the community who may be affected by what they do with their land. This amoral attitude, which has been noted with dismay by Aldo Leopold, Garrett Hardin, and others, can be traced directly to Locke's political philosophy, even though Locke himself may not have intended to create this effect. The reasons why this moral apathy developed are complex.

First, the divine rights of kings had just been abolished. In accordance with this doctrine, the king had had *ultimate* and *absolute* property rights over all the land in his dominion. He could do whatever he wanted with this land—give it away, take it back, use it himself, or even destroy it as he saw fit. Locke's new theory of property stripped the king of this power and authority and transferred these *ultimate* and *absolute* rights to each and every ordinary property owner. This transfer has been a moral disaster in large part because the king's rights involved moral elements that did not carry over to the new rights of the private landowner. As God's agent on Earth, the king was morally obligated to adhere to the highest standards of right and wrong. Furthermore, as the ruler of the land, the king had a moral and political obligation to consider the general welfare of his entire kingdom whenever he acted. Of course, kings did not always behave as they should have, but both kings and subjects did recognize standards of proper and moral kingly behavior. Private landowners, however, did not inherit these obligations. Because they were not instruments of church or state, the idea that they should have moral obligations limiting their actions with regard to their own property does not seem to have come up. The standard that landowners adopted to guide their actions was a purely selfish and egotistical one. Because it involved nothing more than the economic interest of the individual, it was devoid of moral obligation or moral responsibility.

If Locke had been writing in a more politically stable period of English history, it is possible that he might not have developed these views. As mentioned earlier, one of the primary reasons that Locke developed his theory of property was to help protect personal property from arbitrary governmental interference. Locke had grown up during the reign of Charles I, whose behavior had brought about a civil war and the establishment of the commonwealth under Cromwell. Afterward, Locke had lived through much of the reigns of Charles II and James II in exile. Thus with good reason for fearing the uncontrolled power of English kings, Locke sought to put as much power into the hands of the people as he could. The result was a weakening of governmental power without a comparable lessening of governmental responsibility.

This difficulty is revealed momentarily in the first treatise, where Locke argues that property owners have the right to destroy their property if they can derive an advantage from doing so. Locke apparently feels compelled to acknowledge the right of property owners to destroy *in general* in order to justify the killing of animals for food, but, obviously uneasy about the point he has just made, he adds that the government has the responsibility of making sure that this destruction does not adversely affect the property of others:

> Property, whose Original is the Right a Man has to use any of the Inferior Creatures, for Subsistence and Comfort of his life, is for the benefit and sole Advantage of the Proprietor, so that he may even destroy the thing, that he has Property in by his use of it, where need requires; but Government being for the Preservation of every Man's Right and Property, by preserving him from the Violence or Injury of others, is for the good of the Governed.[34]

Ironically, the very rights to property that the government is supposed to protect hinder or even prevent the government from carrying out this responsibility.

Theoretically, Locke's qualification of the right to destroy property is compatible with the American conception of checks and balances, and it might have provided a *political* solution to the problem, though not a moral one. Unfortunately, however, it has not been carried over into our political and legal system as successfully as the right to destroy. A man certainly has a right in the United States to sue for damages in court after the fact if the actions of others have clearly injured him or his property, but the right of the government to take preventive action before the damage is done has not been effectively established. It is this preventive action that private landowners are assailing when they assert their right to use and even destroy their land as they see fit without any outside interference. The success of landowners in this area is amply demonstrated by the great reluctance of most state legislatures to place on small private *landowners* waste management restrictions that have long governed the activities of rural land *developers.*

Government regulation of individual private landowners has been ineffective historically because from the very beginnings of American government, representation at the state and federal levels has nearly always been based on landownership, an approach that has usually assured rural control of the legislature even when most of the citizens in the state lived in urban population centers. Government leaders intent on acting primarily in the interests of landowners could hardly have been expected to play the preventive role that Locke recommends. The unwillingness of legislators to act in this way in the nineteenth century and most of the twentieth further contributed to the amoral belief of rural landowners that they can do whatever they want without being concerned about the welfare or rights of others.

When Jefferson attempted to build American society on a Lockeian foundation of small landowners, he did so in large measure because he believed that small landowners would make the most virtuous citizens. He failed to foresee, however, that the independence provided by Locke's presocietal natural rights would discourage rather than encourage social responsibility and would therefore contribute little to the development of moral character in American landowners. Since social responsibility is basic to our conception of morality today, the claim of landowners that their special rights relieve them of any obligation or responsibility to the community can be regarded only as both socially and morally reprehensible. The position of such rural landowners is analogous to that of a tyrannical king. When it is justified at all, tyranny is always justified by a claim that the tyrant has the *right* to do as he pleases regardless of the consequences. In practice, however, the impact of rural landowners more closely approaches anarchy than tyranny, but only because landowners, though sharing a common desire to preserve their special rights, do not always have common economic interests. As a result, landowners are usually more willing to promote the theoretical rights of their fellow property owners than their specific land use and development projects, which as members of society they may find objectionable or even despicable—in spite of their Saxon and Lockeian heritage rather than because of it.

A landowner cannot justify his position morally except with the extravagant claim that his actions are completely independent and beyond any standard of right and wrong—a claim that Locke, Jefferson, and even Saxon freemen would probably have hesitated to make. Actually, there is only one precedent for such a claim. During the Middle Ages, church philosophers concluded that God was independent of all moral standards.

They felt compelled to take this position because moral limitations on God's actions would have conflicted with His omnipotence. Therefore, they reasoned that God's actions created and defined moral law and that theoretically, moral law could be radically changed at any moment. Descartes held this position in the seventeenth century, and in the nineteenth and twentieth centuries some atheistic existential philosophers have argued that because God is dead, each man is now forced to create his own values through individual actions. Although this position could be adopted as a defense of the landowner's extraordinary amoral rights, it would probably be distasteful to most landowners. Without it, this aspect of the rural landowners' position may be indefensible.[35]

Today, of course, whenever Locke's theory of property and the heritage of the ancient Saxon freeman surface in county courts, at planning and zoning meetings, and at state and federal hearings on conservation and land management, they still remain a formidable obstacle to constructive political action. As they are normally presented, however, they are certainly not an all-purpose answer to our environmental problems or even a marginally adequate reply to environmental criticism. When a landowner voices a Lockeian argument he is consciously or unconsciously trying to evade the land management issues at hand and to shift attention instead to the dogmatic recitation of his special rights as a property owner.

As I noted, some of Locke's fundamental assumptions and attitudes are either demonstrably false or no longer generally held even among landowners. These difficulties need to be ironed out before the landowners can claim that they are really answering their environmental critics. Furthermore, it is likely that even if the position should be modernized, the moral issues will remain unresolved.

As it stands, the force of the rural landowners' arguments depends on their historical associations—their biblical trappings, the echoes of Locke's political philosophy, the Saxon common-law tradition, the feudal doctrine of the divine rights of kings, and the spirit of the nineteenth-century American land laws. Can they be modernized? That remains to be seen. Until they are, however, landowners, environmentalists, politicians, and ordinary citizens should regard them with some suspicion.

NOTES

1. U.S. Congress, Senate, *Congressional Globe,* 42d Cong., 2d Sess., 1 (January 30, 1872), p. 697.

2. U.S. Congress, Senate, *Congressional Record,* 47th Cong., 2d Sess., 14 (March 1, 1883), p. 3488.

3. J. D. Whitney, *The Yosemite Book: A Description of the Yosemite Valley and Adjacent Regions of the Sierra Nevada and the Big Trees of California* (New York: Julius Bien and State of California, 1868), p. 20.

4. U.S. Congress, Senate, *Congressional Globe,* 42d Cong., 2d Sess., 1 (January 30, 1872), p. 697.

5. Report written by F. V. Hayden at the request of the Committee on Public Lands and quoted in *The Yellowstone National Park and the Mountain Regions of Portions of Idaho, Nevada, Colorado and Utah,* described by F. V. Hayden, illustrated by Thomas Moran (Boston: L. Prang and Company, 1876), p. 12. This rare book is included in the Thomas Moran papers at the Jefferson National Expansion Memorial, St. Louis.

6. Henry David Thoreau, "Walking" (1862), in *The Portable Thoreau,* ed. Carl Bode, 1st rev. ed. (New York: Viking Press, 1975), p. 602; Ralph Waldo Emerson, *Nature* (1836), sec. 1, in *The Selected Writings of Ralph Waldo Emerson,* ed. Brooks Atkinson (New York: Modern Library, 1950), p. 5; Nathaniel Pitt Langford, *The Discovery of Yellowstone Park: Journal of the Washburn Expedition to the Yellowstone and Firehole Rivers in the Year 1870,* with a foreword by Aubrey L. Haines (Lincoln: University of Nebraska Press, 1972), pp. 117–119.

7. The account given here is based on Denman W. Ross, *The Early History of Land-holding among the Germans* (Boston: Soule and Burgbee, 1883), and Walter Phelps Hall, Robert Greenhalgh Albion, and Jennie Barnes Pope, *A History of England and the Empire-Commonwealth,* 4th ed. (Lexington, Mass.: Ginn, 1961).

8. Ross, *Land-holding,* p. 24.

9. Merrill D. Peterson, *Thomas Jefferson and the New Nation: A Biography* (New York: Oxford University Press, 1970), p. 113.

10. Jefferson to Edmund Pendleton, August 13, 1776, in *Papers of Thomas Jefferson,* ed. Julian P. Boyd et al., 17 vols (Princeton, N.J.: Princeton University Press, 1950), 1: 491.

11. Peterson, *Jefferson and the New Nation,* pp. 16–18.

12. Thomas Jefferson, *A Summary View of the Rights of British America,* in *The Portable Thomas Jefferson,* ed. Merrill D. Peterson (New York: Viking Press, 1975), pp. 4–5.

13. Ibid., pp. 17–19.

14. Thomas Hobbes, *Leviathan,* ed. C. B. MacPherson (Harmondsworth, England: Penguin Books, 1968), pt. 1, ch. 24.

15. Thomas Jefferson, "Draft Constitution for Virginia," in *Portable Jefferson,* p. 248.

16. Jefferson to Edmund Pendleton, August 13, 1776, in *Papers of Thomas Jefferson,* 1: 492.

17. Jefferson to John Jay, August 23, 1785, in *Portable Jefferson,* p. 384.

18. Jefferson to James Madison, October 28, 1785, ibid., p. 397.

19. Thomas Jefferson, *Notes on the State of Virginia,* ibid., p. 217.

20. John Locke, *Two Treatises of Government,* ed. Thomas I. Cook (New York: Hafner Press, 1947).

21. Jefferson to John Trumbull, February 15, 1789, in *Portable Jefferson,* pp. 434–435; Locke, "Second Treatise," sec. 6, in *Two Treatises;* Carl Becker, *The Declaration of Independence: A Study in the History of Political Ideas* (New York: Knopf, 1960), pp. 24–28.

22. Robert Filmer, *Patriarcha or the Natural Power of Kings,* in Locke, *Two Treatises,* pp. 249–310.

23. Locke, "Second Treatise," sec. 27, ibid.

24. Ibid., sec. 32.

25. Ibid., sec. 177.

26. Jefferson, *Summary View,* in *Portable Jefferson,* p. 19; letters, ibid., p. 384; Jefferson, *Notes on Virginia,* ibid., p. 217; Locke, "Second Treatise," secs. 25–26, in *Two Treatises;* Genesis 1:28.

27. Paul W. Gates, *History of Public Land Law Development* (Washington, D.C.: Public Land Law Commission, 1968), pp. 390–393.

28. Locke, "Second Treatise," sec. 33, in *Two Treatises.*

29. Ibid., sec. 36.

30. Ibid., secs. 42–43.

31. Ibid., secs. 37, 42.

32. Ibid., sec. 26.

33. For a full discussion of labor and consumption, see Hannah Arendt, *The Human Condition* (Chicago: University of Chicago Press, 1958), ch. 3.

34. Locke, "First Treatise," sec. 92, in *Two Treatises;* Locke also addresses this point to some degree in the second treatise, sec. 31, where he writes that "nothing was made by God for Man to spoil or destroy." Here Locke emphasizes the abundance of the natural things supplied by God and states that human beings who set limits on themselves with their reason will not claim more than their fair share.

35. Jean-Paul Sartre, *Existentialism and Human Emotions,* (New York: Philosophical Library, 1957), pp. 13–18.

Part II
The Environmental Position

CHAPTER THREE
AESTHETIC AND SCIENTIFIC ATTITUDES

For many years now, environmentalists have been calling for a new ethic that will help protect the natural environment from destruction. According to John Passmore, however, there is no basis in the history of Western civilization for such an idea. He argues that preservationist-oriented environmentalists are nothing more than antiscientific nature mystics who have abandoned the "analytical, critical approach," which has always been the "peculiar glory" of Western civilization, and have frivolously justified their irrational positions in terms of strange Oriental religions. Preservationist attitudes and actions, in addition, are entirely inconsistent with man's fundamental mission on Earth—civilizing the world—and if they are permitted to flourish, it may well mean the end of Western civilization and the end of man. There is only one good way to relate to nature—in terms of its possible usefulness to human beings in terms of economic utilitarianism. Of course, Passmore admits, various arguments can be given for protecting and preserving the environment. "But they are none of them 'knock-down' arguments; they allow that economic considerations, in a broad sense of that phrase, might under certain circumstances outweigh the case for preservation." Passmore scorns the aesthetic argument and similar appeals for preserving nature on the grounds that "they rest on the presumption that our descendants will still delight in what now delights only some of us and did not delight our predecessors."[1]

In this chapter I argue that modern environmental attitudes are the product of several centuries of changing attitudes toward nature and are most closely associated with nineteenth-century developments in the natural history sciences of botany, biology, and geology and in the arts, particularly poetry and American landscape painting. Unlike Passmore, I claim that the perception of the world of modern ecologists and environmentalists is little different from and is directly traceable to the *aesthetic* perceptions of early botanists, biologists, and geologists and is therefore, in this sense, compatible with at least one important component of science and with Western civilization and man.

In large measure, my views are in agreement with many of Whitehead's major themes in *Science and the Modern World,* especially those that deal with a romantic reaction to science.[2] One major difference, however, is that by separating the natural history sciences from the physical sciences—a distinction that Whitehead does not seem to make—I am able to claim that even though the romantic reaction was most certainly opposed to some aspects of physical science, it was nonetheless in tune with the natural history sciences, which were strongly value-oriented from the very beginning. In the seventeenth and eighteenth centuries particularly, the physical and natural history sciences could be distinguished from each other in terms of their reliance on primary and secondary properties. While early physicists dealt exclusively with primary properties (measurable and quantifiable properties like extension, figure, motion, and number), natural history scientists were forced by the nature of their subject matter to classify the objects they studied in terms of secondary properties (nonquantifiable properties like color, smell, taste, and sound). It was this focus on secondary properties that not only sharply separated natural history science from physics but also provided it with important links with poetry, painting, and gardening, aesthetic disciplines also grounded in secondary properties.

In addition, my analysis has some bearing on the *is/ought* controversy. Holmes Rolston, III, for example, has pointed out that environmentalists often present their arguments for preserving nature in such a way that the "sharp is/ought dichotomy" seems to disappear. He writes:

> What is ethically puzzling, and exciting, in the marriage and mutual transformation of ecological description and evaluation is that here an "ought" is not so much derived from an "is" as discovered simultaneously with it.

Rolston is puzzled because he has a feeling that ecology, which he rightly recognizes as a science, *ought,* like more traditional branches of science, to concern itself with facts and leave problems of value alone. Yet he is excited because he suspects that it might be possible to justify this new disregard of the *is/ought* distinction by means of a close examination of "existing ethical sentiments that are subecological, that is, [that] anticipate the ecological conscience, and on which we can build."[3] I present some of the developments that historically have led to this special relationship between fact and value.

My account differs from Passmore's in two important respects. (1) I argue that the aesthetic attitudes toward nature that have developed in the West during the past three centuries are too well grounded in Western culture and science to be passed off as a fad or as an Oriental intrusion. (2) I allow for a greater degree of diversity in aesthetic tastes in Western civilization than Passmore. For example, William Wordsworth's call for "a national property" in England's Lake District, which was contemporary with George Catlin's call for "a nation's Park" in the American West, suggests a similarity between preservationist attitudes in the United States and England in the early nineteenth century.[4] That these attitudes prospered in the United States and failed to do so in England does not demonstrate that one country or the other now has aesthetic attitudes more properly in line with some standard of Western civilization. It merely indicates that for various social, political, and geographic reasons, certain attitudes were appropriate in one country and not in the other. Furthermore, while it may be impractical or inappropriate for American environmental attitudes to be exported to other countries, this does not mean that they are any less Western or any less deserving of being perpetuated, at least in their own cultural niche in Western civilization.

INTRINSIC AND INSTRUMENTAL VALUE

Passmore is especially critical on historical and utilitarian grounds of the environmentalist claim that natural objects and species have a right to exist. While he is correct in asserting that there is no Western tradition supporting such rights, he nevertheless overlooks the fact that until very recently there was not much support in one part of the West—the United States—for the economic utilitarianism that he espouses either. Passmore's utilitarianism was introduced into American environmental issues by Gifford Pinchot, who picked it up in Europe near the end of the nineteenth century while studying forestry. Pinchot's teachers urged him to demonstrate as soon as he returned home that forests could be grown and cut economically. It was advice that Pinchot never forgot, and it became the basis for his conception of the U.S. Forest Service and later, after Pinchot established himself as an environmental adviser to Teddy Roosevelt, the basis for the American conservation movement as well, defined narrowly as the rational management and use of natural resources for present and future generations.[5]

Although Pinchot totally abhorred the preservationist tradition and considered Yellowstone and the Adirondacks Forest Reserve to be wastes of good lumber, early preservationist efforts were not opposed by those who held his brand of economic utilitarianism, nor in fact by any advocates of utilitarianism, but rather by those who held land use doctrines framed in terms of John Locke's theory of property. Many people who believed that land was imperfect and in need of improvement through human labor wished to divide up America's first parks into homesteads and sell them to farmers. To them land had little or no value until someone had worked it, thereby putting value into it. In this context, preservationist arguments approached utilitarianism very closely, since preservationists were able to claim that they were protecting these wilderness areas from the few for the many. Their position differed from most forms of utilitarianism in that they held that the good of the many, primarily aesthetic beauty and scientific interest, was intrinsic, not instrumental.

By the end of the nineteenth century, however, as a result of Pinchot's influence, arguments involving intrinsic value were displaced by appeals employing *use* terminology. The aesthetic value of a wilderness area became a use measured by the aesthetic delight triggered in tourists by natural objects. Unfortunately, aesthetic value, in this formulation no longer regarded as an intrinsic (or higher) good, did not fare well in competition with its instrumental and economic counterparts. The aesthetic value of a forest seemed petty in comparison with its value as building material, paper pulp, and fuel.[6] Beginning in the early twentieth century, nevertheless, foresters and naturalists working within a Pinchot-style framework began a slow movement back in the direction of intrinsic value, first through a doctrine of multiuse and then with claims that natural objects and species have rights to exist.

Although Passmore's attack on such rights may be justifiable in accordance with his historical approach, it does not touch on the issues that prompted environmentalists to assert them; nor does it demonstrate that there is no Western tradition that supports the general preservationist viewpoint. Intrinsic value arguments, though seldom used today by environmentalists, were employed by early environmentalists in the nineteenth century, and since they can rightfully claim a conceptual heritage extending back to the beginnings of Western thought and philosophy, they cannot be refuted by Passmore's historical criticism as easily. Thus a reexamination of the place of intrinsic value in environmentalist arguments may be the best way to answer critics like Passmore.

THE AESTHETIC AND SCIENTIFIC TRADITIONS

Passmore presents an account of the general development of modern attitudes toward nature that is in disagreement with that of many scholars, critics, and scientists. Myra Reynolds' timetable is a characteristic scholarly account. According to Reynolds, attitudes appreciative of nature first appeared in poetry and landscape gardening between 1725 and 1730 and about thirty years later in landscape painting, fiction, and travel literature.[7] Passmore disregards all of these except landscape gardening. He discounts poetry on the grounds that although "eighteenth- and nineteenth-century romanticism, with its nature-mysticism, was responsible for a transvaluation of values. . . . That it will persist into the twenty-first century, however, can certainly not be taken for granted."[8] As for painting, fiction, and travel literature, he makes no mention of them at all. Instead, Passmore makes the incredible claim that the proper and enduring changes in nature attitudes began and *ended* with landscape gardening—specifically, in the transition from the formal to the nonformal garden.[9] In addition, Passmore appears to be unaware of the claim of nineteenth-century natural history scientists both in America and in Europe that science, and not art and literature, created the conditions permitting the development of attitudes appreciative of nature. For example, Sir Archibald Geike in England and William H. Brewer in America both maintained that H. B. de Saussure's interest in mountains in the eighteenth century led to an aesthetic appreciation of mountains and nature in general.[10] Although I do not claim that either science or the arts alone brought about this transformation in attitude, I make the weaker claim that it resulted from an interplay between them.

Passmore believes that there are three possible stages of development in the aesthetic appreciation of nature: (1) appreciation of formal landscape gardens in which plants are clipped, cut, and planted in geometric forms and patterns, (2) appreciation of nonformal gardens in which "the gardener was to take his materials from nature, to treat them reverently, but to arrange them in a better composition," thus, "improving" rather than "imposing" form, and (3) appreciation of unimproved, and indeed untouched, wilderness. He recognizes that the first is unsatisfactory and completely deplores the third but is happy with the second, which he considers an excellent example of what he means by "the civilising of nature." Passmore defends his preference for the nonformal garden as follows:

> It converts nature into something at once more agreeable and more intelligible than wilderness; man understands domesticated nature, because he has helped to make it. He arranges nature in such a way that he "can enter her world and enjoy our origins." From the wilderness he is always in some measure alienated; it stands in a relationship to him of pure externality. Yet at

> the same time the civilised garden does not involve the mutilation of nature, at least in the topiarist's manner. Its trees are still recognisably elms and limes and oaks, but by skilful placing and pruning they have been brought to a perfection of shape they rarely achieve in the forest.[11]

Actually, in some respects Passmore's position is not significantly different from that of American environmentalists, who, like Passmore, also want to enjoy, understand, and commune with nature. They differ irreconcilably only over the value of wilderness. According to Passmore, Western man is alienated by wilderness—"it stands in a relationship to him of pure externality"—and he strongly desires to make plants more perfect and enjoyable by trimming them and planting them in places where they would not ordinarily grow. Environmentalists, by contrast, are not alienated by wilderness; they feel a kind of spiritual unity or harmony with it, and they are able to appreciate plants as they are without "skilful placing and pruning."

Passmore's position would be strengthened if it could be argued as a psychological thesis about a fixed human nature; historically, however, such an approach has little foundation. Most nineteenth-century scholars and lovers of nature, for example, would have considered Passmore's disagreements with environmentalists nothing more than a matter of taste. Since many of them could remember a time when nature was rarely appreciated at all, they would scarcely have ventured to claim that an appreciation of nonformal gardens or wildernesses had anything to do with man's nature but rather would have considered it a cultural change brought about in part by education. While Passmore's talk of the alienation of man by wilderness sounds plausible, removed as we are now from firsthand knowledge of a time when most people were completely indifferent to nature, a claim that the appreciation of wilderness is contrary to human nature still appears to be difficult to establish and is probably contrary to fact. Perhaps Passmore is alienated by wilderness, but this condition is not universally shared by all human beings. In the United States, in particular, wilderness has been a matter of national pride for at least a century and a half, and wildness has been regarded as the special characteristic that sets the natural beauty of American scenery apart from that of Europe.[12]

Passmore's belief that the nonformal landscape garden is the ultimate expression of man's relationship with nature is also difficult to defend. Passmore quite simply fails to see that the historical factors that produced the nonformal landscape garden also made it a transitional phenomenon leading toward an appreciation of wilderness. It is important to realize that nonformal gardens became popular at the same time that horticultural societies began to be organized in Europe and America. These societies sent agents to all parts of the world to bring back seeds and plants. The landscape garden naturally became the showplace for these botanical exhibits, and the introduction of these new plants into them produced a more relaxed attitude toward nature by forcing garden enthusiasts to accept new and wilder standards of beauty. Since almost no one associated with these gardens—except perhaps the horticultural agent, probably already off again to some strange country—even knew for sure what the plants looked like in a natural state, and indeed no one at all knew whether they would grow in their new environments, the prudent improvement of these plants by judicious trimming was suddenly completely out of the question. Nor was the formal placement of the foreign plants in relation to native ones of any consequence. The visitor to the garden no longer admired the formal geometric patterns that plants formed as a group, nor did he marvel at the excellent manner in which they had been trimmed into unnatural shapes. The latter might even have greatly angered him. In fact, the visitor was not much concerned at all with the internal relations of plants *within* the garden. Since each individual plant was an emissary, so to speak, from some mysterious and bizarre corner of the Earth, the thoughts of the garden enthusiast inevitably turned to the contemplation of the natural and alien environment, *outside* and far away from the garden, that the plant represented. In this way, an interest in wilderness areas arose that helped prepare the way for their direct appreciation later, both scientifically and aesthetically.

The most significant factor, however, was more immediate and fundamental. When looking at plants in the nonformal landscape garden, both scientific and nonscientific admirers of nature shared a common object orientation that was unprecedented. In the formal landscape garden, plants had been regarded as indifferent blobs of *matter* to be shaped into whatever forms the gardeners chose, and attention was directed toward these artificial and indeed superficial shapes and not toward the properties of the plants themselves. In the nonformal garden, by contrast, the natural qualities and characteristics of the plants became matters of great interest, and the plants were elevated to the status of self-contained and self-organizing entities worthy of admiration and study for their own sake. This transformation was paralleled by a similar development then taking place in botany and in the other natural history sciences. Scientists working within the tradition of seventeenth-century rationalist philosophy had used observation primarily as a means to speculation about unseen, hypothetical entities. Since these entities were not experienced by the senses, they had no aesthetic properties, and it was thus difficult for an aesthetic value orientation to develop. Natural history scientists, however, had to deal with objects that were directly perceived and encountered in ordinary experience and that at this level possessed aesthetic properties—at least in the broadest sense of the word. Not surprisingly, these scientists came to focus some of their attention on the aesthetic aspects of the natural objects and other phenomena they studied. When writing in their field notebooks, most of them matter-of-factly jotted down their aesthetic judgments alongside their factual descriptions. In this way, they began to attend to values as well as to facts, just at the time when nonscientific garden enthusiasts were expanding their interests in the direction of botanical science. This change in attitude toward perceived objects in both botany and gardening provided the foundations for a broader association of science and art later in the nineteenth century.

Although farther removed from personal contact with scientists than landscape gardeners, nature poets were also making their contribution to the reconciliation of the aesthetic and the scientific viewpoints. In fact, the British nature poets of the eighteenth and nineteenth centuries were as much involved in detailed observation of the natural environment as the natural history scientists. Marjorie Hope Nicolson makes this point in her book *Mountain Gloom and Mountain Glory*, where she writes: "Wordsworth's Nature descriptions were written with the eye on the object. Pope's 'Nature tame and Nature methodized' was culled from books."[13] Many years earlier, Myra Reynolds emphasized even more pointedly that "the new feeling toward Nature, as exemplified in the early nineteenth-century poets, especially Wordsworth, . . . is marked by full and first-hand observation." Romantic poets are given little credit for their observational prowess because, as Reynolds notes:

> what the eighteenth-century poets did was to give truthful expression to very many facts of a kind fairly obvious to an age well versed in the lore of field and wood; but new to an age just emerged from the gates of a park.[14]

To a very great extent, in fact, many of these observations can be regarded as scientific. Nicolson, for one, has shown that James Thomson, England's first major nature poet, placed great emphasis on geology in his major work *The Seasons*, published in 1726.[15] This trend was to continue in America in the poetry and writings of Bryant, Emerson, and Thoreau and is particularly striking in American landscape painting, itself heavily influenced by poets. It was a very small step from the romantic and often poetically inspired landscapes of Thomas Cole to the scientific landscapes of Frederick Edwin Church, Cole's pupil.

In landscape painting in the nineteenth century, there is again the close working relationship between science and art that had developed earlier in the nonformal landscape garden. The need for visual documentation in the natural history sciences encouraged and speeded the transition from a purely scientific point of view to a more aesthetic one in the sciences, and vice versa in art. Lacking cameras, scientists had either to develop artistic abilities themselves or to bring artists with them into the field. The resulting interplay between naturalists, geologists, and artists led to a common perception of the natural world, shared by both groups, that placed emphasis on both fact and value. This new world view was passed on to the general public through popularized travel accounts of scientific expeditions, through engravings, woodcuts, and landscape paintings, and, after 1860, through landscape photographs.

Examples of the interrelationships between artists and scientists are not difficult to find. Charles Willson Peale of Philadelphia is probably the most outstanding example from the beginning of the nineteenth century. Peale was a major artist, a lecturer on natural history, and the founder of America's first natural history museum. Two of Peale's sons, Rembrandt and Titian, also shared this dual interest in science and art. Rembrandt Peale became a leading portrait painter like his father and, in addition, founded his own natural history museum in Baltimore. Titian Peale became a biologist and accompanied the Long expedition to the Rocky Mountains in 1819 as a naturalist. Eventually leaving biology to take up a career as a scientific illustrator, he served in that capacity in the first American expedition to the Antarctic.

With the popular success of Frederick Edwin Church's painting *The Heart of the Andes* in 1859, science and art also became intricately intertwined in mainstream landscape painting. After reading John Ruskin's *Modern Painters,* a multivolume book of art criticism that stresses the importance of scientific knowledge and accuracy to "truth in art"–style landscape painting, and Humboldt's *Cosmos,* which contains a chapter on the importance of landscape painting in the study of natural history, Church left for Ecuador to retrace Humboldt's steps and to paint the natural history of South America.[16] *The Heart of the Andes* was one of the products of Church's journey. By the early 1860s, scientific accuracy had become so important to art criticism that James Jackson Jarves was able to write of Albert Bierstadt, not known today for scientific detail, that "he seeks to depict the absolute qualities and forms of things. The botanist and geologist can find work in his rocks and vegetation. He seizes upon natural phenomena with naturalistic eyes."[17]

Throughout much of the nineteenth century, the movement between artistic and scientific circles continued. William H. Holmes, best known for his detailed drawings of the entire length of the Grand Canyon, gave up a promising career as a painter to work as scientific illustrator for F. V. Hayden's geological survey. After a year with Hayden, Holmes was promoted to geologist, the first of his several related careers, including archeologist, anthropologist, and ethnologist, before he returned to art as the curator of the National Gallery of Art in Washington. An even more interesting example is Clarence King, the first head of the U.S. Geological Survey. King became interested in geology after reading Ruskin's *Modern Painters,* and he went to California to work for the newly formed state geological survey in large measure because of a romantic and scientific interest in Mount Shasta, which King thought of as the Cotopaxi of California—Cotopaxi being a volcano in Ecuador made famous by the paintings of Church. At first King's superiors did not think he would be successful as a geologist because of his obsessive interest in climbing mountains to watch sunsets; however, within a few years, King was the head of his own survey. Throughout his career King never waivered in his interest in art, and as a geologist he encouraged pioneer work in landscape photography, which is considered art today.

Both poetry and art had great influence on the travel accounts of the nineteenth century, most of which, in America at least, were also scientific journals. The trend is already clear in the journals of Lewis and Clark, where Meriwether Lewis, attempting to describe the Great Falls of the Missouri, becomes disgusted with the results and laments that he does not have "the pen of Thomson," who was, as already mentioned, England's first major nature poet, or the "pencil of Salvator Rosa," an Italian painter known for his depiction of the sublime, and, along with Claude Lorraine, the model for early nineteenth-century landscape painting.[18] Lewis' remark shows that he went west intent on viewing what he found not only from a scientific point of view but also from an aesthetic one in line with the most advanced thinking in the poetry and art of his time.

In general, both scientific and nonscientific travelers had difficulty expressing their feelings about the landscapes they visited, and so they frequently quoted appropriate lines of poetry to fill the voids in their travel accounts. In this way, poetry guided the traveler's perception and helped create the vocabulary needed to describe nature without merely labeling it "beautiful," "sublime," or "picturesque." Like poetry, landscape paintings also influenced written descriptions. In most cases, written accounts of particular places were composed as verbal pictures. One can feel the eye of the author moving across the scenery in an organized manner, much as it would across the canvas of a landscape painting. This organization was not accidental. The author of the description normally moved to a vantage point where he commanded a view of the scenery comparable to one that would be painted by a landscape artist. As interest in paintings moved from the picturesque to the panoramic and sublime, the vantage point of these descriptions shifted from the floors of river valleys to mountaintops.[19]

THE BEAUTIFUL, THE PICTURESQUE, AND THE SUBLIME

In the nineteenth century, the concept of beauty gradually expanded to the point that nothing was considered ugly. British landscape painter John Constable, for example, on hearing a lady call an engraving ugly, rebuked her saying, "No, madam, there is nothing ugly; *I never saw an ugly thing in my life.*" Emerson wrote in *Nature* that "there is no object so foul that intense light will not make beautiful. . . . Even the corpse has its own beauty." John Muir, following Emerson but also extending the idea into an environmental context, remarked in an article titled "The Wild Parks and Forest Reservations of the West" that "none of Nature's landscapes are ugly so long as they are wild."[20] This new aesthetic stance was the inevitable result of the developments just discussed.

At first the transformation of the standards of beauty centered around two aesthetic categories: the *picturesque,* actually a subcategory of the beautiful, and the *sublime.* With the picturesque, natural rather than artificial or improved objects were given preference. The new taste for the natural included an appreciation and even a love of wild things. A wide range of objects became interesting for their own sake rather than as elements in aesthetic patterns or as aesthetically indifferent instruments or raw materials. A recognition that the world was "God's work" prepared the way for the aesthetic enjoyment of nature analogous to the enjoyment of art created by human beings. New criteria replaced old: balance rather than harmony, asymmetry rather than symmetry, irregular and curved lines rather than straight ones, rough surfaces rather than smooth ones, complexity rather than simplicity, and diversity, variety, and individuality rather than sameness.

With the rise in popularity of the sublime came an aesthetic appreciation of the harmful as well as the pleasing. People began to be impressed with vastness, massiveness, chaos, and disharmony. Since sublime nature was often considered incomplete and unfinished, the analogy with works of art, possible with the picturesque, broke down, but objects were nevertheless evaluated even more broadly on their own terms and without the earlier desire to improve them. The sublime required a change in attitude toward God and a reappraisal of man's importance and position in the world. As Nicolson points out, attributes that had previously been reserved for God were now being applied to sublime objects.[21] In addition, a person who appreciated the sublime could not look at the world as a place created solely for human use or perhaps even for human purposes at all. In this sense, the sublime signified the end of the age in which natural objects were evaluated exclusively in terms of human uses and needs. With the sublime, we at last reach objects that Passmore might consider alienating to man. These objects were not, however, whole wildernesses, only small parts of them. Although it was admittedly difficult to love sublime landscapes, one could enjoy them, and the fears of past generations could be replaced by a kind of respect.

Some, but not all, of the new standards associated with the picturesque and the sublime were derived from the natural history sciences. The complexity, diversity, and variety of nature, and the individuality of plants, animals, and natural objects became apparent to amateur and professional botanists and naturalists in the eighteenth century as they attempted to classify plant and animal life and to learn something of the rock structure of the Earth. Even more important was the discovery of geologic time, which arose out of geology and, to a lesser degree, biology. In the late seventeenth century, ruined castles and towers were popularly regarded as signs of the antiquity of man. The realization that ruins were the product of weathering, erosion, and decay over long periods of time led to the conclusion that the rest of the landscape was also changing in time in the same way. Weathered rock, folded layers of sediment, and other formations could by analogy be called ruins and in this sense were taken as remnants of the biblical Deluge. This breakthrough, however, did not produce the idea of geologic time, since natural ruins and human ruins were viewed as contemporary and were believed to have originated within the limits of human history. Beginning with Hutton and Lyell and culminating with the geological sections of Darwin's *Origin of Species*, however, the need for truly immense periods of time to account for alterations in the face of the Earth gradually dawned on the scientific community. Human history began to shrink in relation to geologic time, becoming only an infinitesimal part of an incredibly expanded geological history that was almost entirely prehuman. While the earlier conception of time in terms of human history was picturesque, geologic time was sublime. Not only were the time scales of geologic time mind-boggling, but, more importantly they offered to human imagination ages and worlds that were prehuman and indeed nonhuman.

Complexity, diversity, variety, individuality, and geologic time have found their way into environmental arguments. The first four usually appear in reference to the uniqueness of particular objects to support their worthiness for protection and preservation. Geologic time appears in appeals to reverence for the age of natural objects and also in claims that the time required to replace them under natural conditions is so long as to make them in effect irreplaceable. The terms *picturesque* and *sublime,* in contrast, are never found in modern arguments and only rarely in nineteenth-century arguments. They may be absent in part because, as mentioned earlier, as descriptive powers and vocabularies increased, they dropped out in favor of fuller, more individualized descriptions; however, the main reason seems to be that they were transitional categories that were replaced by an expanded conception of beauty encompassing much of what they had originally stood for and also by a new aesthetic or quasi-aesthetic category arising out of the natural history sciences—the *interesting.*

THE INTERESTING

In the early nineteenth century beauty and interest were occasionally mentioned side by side. What interest meant in these cases, however, was far from clear. Traditionally it has been held that interest is subservient to beauty, an element which has to be present in a beautiful object, but which is never considered an aesthetic category in its own right. The following comment by Duke Paul of Württemburg written in 1822 after looking at the American prairie for the first time is a good example of the traditional use of the term: "It appeared picturesquely beautiful when it presented itself to the eye for the first time, but loses much of its interest, for its monotony wearies the senses." In this excerpt from Fielding B. Meek's 1849 field notebook, however, beauty and interest seem to have an almost equal status:

> Dr. Shinnard & Mr. Patten returned from the Wisconsin this morning at 11 o'clk. Their representations of the great beauty of the country—especially of some of the scenery not far from the Dallas of that stream, and on the Baraboo near the Devils Lake, where there is an extensive exposure of quartzite—as well as the geological interest of the country generally made me regret exceeding[ly] that I had not been able to take sketches & study the geology of this interesting region.[22]

Meek has two grounds for wishing to see the Wisconsin river area: its beauty and its interest. In this case, the interest is clearly scientific and distinct from the beauty of the area; that is, the interest would remain whether the area was considered beautiful or not.

How interest reached its new and elevated position is difficult to uncover; however, Prince Maximilian of Neu-Wied's experiences on the Upper Missouri between 1832 and 1834 may provide some clues. In the early part of his travel account dealing with the eastern United States, Prince Maximilian displays both a romantic and a scientific interest in nature and is at home with the picturesque and to some degree with the sublime. Curiously, though, while Maximilian reveled in the scenery, his traveling companion, Swiss artist Karl Bodmer, expressed his dissatisfaction with these same landscapes, which to him were little different from those found in Europe. On the Upper Missouri, however, the situation was reversed. There Bodmer finally found strange new scenery to paint, while Maximilian, who could find nothing beautiful about the country, was at a loss for words, later apologizing in his book for dwelling on subjects that would have been left out if there had been something of beauty to describe. Although it is not possible to tell from his manuscript, it seems likely that Maximilian, unable to speak of beauty, spoke instead with those he met of the interest of the country. Judging by this account of Maximilian's journey written by Kenneth McKenzie, a fur trader, the word *interest* came to Maximilian's lips quite often:

> He has made a valuable & interesting collection of objects in Natural history & Mr. Bodmer has been very industrious in making drawings of the peculiarly interesting scenery of the upper country with a great number of Indian portraits. The Baron expresses himself as greatly *interested* with his voyage. . . .

The second use of the term—"the peculiarly *interesting* country"—is definitely in an aesthetic sense. The underlining of the third occurrence probably was intended to indicate McKenzie's perplexity over Maximilian's excessive "interest" in a region that McKenzie himself considered an "inhospitable clime."[23]

Perhaps the best illustrations of the evolution of *interest* as an aesthetic term, and of the influence of the natural history sciences on the aesthetic perception of the natural world, can be found in the journals and letters of William H. Brewer. Brewer was a professor of botany and agriculture at Yale before 1860, spent four years as the assistant director of the newly formed California Survey before returning to teaching at Yale, and taught three years at the Yale School of Forestry just before his retirement in 1904. As a student at Yale in 1848, Brewer looked at a special exhibit of Pratt's *Garden of Eden,* a painting based on Milton's descriptions in *Paradise Lost,* and wrote in his diary that "the painting was a very fine one indeed. Very interesting in a botanical sense as well as others."[24] In another diary, written in 1852, Brewer tells of using scientific material to aid in his aesthetic appreciation of Niagara Falls:

> The view from the Ferry, and the bank on the Canadian side was all very fine indeed. Stopped and viewed it from many points, sat a long time on Table rock. Notwithstanding the many drawings and cuts I had seen, taken from different points, the geological diagrams I had studied, and the many descriptions I had read, I still had formed but a very imperfect conception of the scene.[25]

Later, again visiting Niagara Falls, he writes:

> Goat Island, what an interesting spot, not to be surpassed by any on earth. Surrounded by such rapids, in such a river, dividing Niagara Falls, the greatest of cateracts. Interesting alike to the painter, poet and man of science. But comment is needless.[26]

Traveling through New York in August 1853, he writes:

> The wild and romantic scenery of the road between Albany & Springfield delighted the senses, and had their effect heightened by the length of time that the mind has been compelled to dwell upon the lovely but gentle scenery of New York. The complicated Geology of this region gave it an additional charm and I saw many fine species of plants strangers to me.[27]

In California, this mixture of science and aesthetics was to become even more pronounced.

As a member of the California Geological Survey, Brewer explored areas with landscapes far different from those he had seen and loved in the eastern United States and in Europe. Like Prince Maximilian on the Upper Missouri, Brewer recognized that these landscapes were not beautiful in any accepted sense, but unlike Maximilian, he was very strongly moved by them aesthetically, and he sought in his journals to describe his feelings about them in aesthetic terms. At first, Brewer took refuge in the sublime, writing in one instance that the "Alps are beautifully grand, Mt. Shasta sublimely desolate;"[28] however, he soon gave up referring to California's desolation as sublime and began looking for more appropriate words. Viewing Lake Tahoe for the first time in 1863, he took another step forward, abandoning for good his European aesthetic standards:

> Its beautiful waters, the rugged mountains rising around it, spotted with snow perhaps which has lain for centuries, all conspire to form an enchanting picture. It lacks many of the elements of beauty of the Swiss lakes, of lake Geneva, it lacks the grassy, green sloping hills, the white-walled town, the castles with their stories and histories, the chalets of herders—in fact, it lacks *all* the elements that give their peculiar charm to the Swiss scenery, its beauty is its own, is truly Californian.[29]

Returning to the Lake Tahoe area more than a year later, Brewer comes back to the same problem but this time introduces a more specific category—interest:

> The landscape is of an uniformly grey-brown color, no forests, no pastures, no green, but little water, nothing apparently to cheer the eye, or revive the spirits of a passing traveller. So it seems—but at sunset & sunrise the most beautiful tints rest on the mountains, and the landscape has a peculiar beauty of its own, or perhaps a peculiar *interest* rather than beauty.[30]

Here at last interest has finally achieved full aesthetic status, not by default as in the case of Maximilian's experiences on the Upper Missouri where beauty seemed to be lacking, but rather, much like the picturesque when first introduced, positively, to describe aesthetic perceptions that, though powerful, fall outside the realm of conventional standards of beauty.

Today environmentalists usually present the beauty of a natural object as grounds for its preservation in preference to its interest, but when beauty is lacking, the appeal then centers on interest. By the 1870s, if not before, this sort of interrelationship between beauty and interest had already been established. The Earl of Dunraven provides an example in his book *The Great Divide,* a travel account of a visit to Yellowstone National Park undertaken in 1874. Upon reaching Mammoth Hot Springs, this English nobleman immediately launches into a lengthy discussion of the relative beauty of these springs in comparison with those of New Zealand and Iceland. Discarding Iceland's springs at once, he narrows the contenders down to a spring in New Zealand and the Mammoth Hot Springs in Yellowstone and after much deliberation concludes that the one in New Zealand "excels that rival in beauty, though not in general interest."[31] Here interest appears as a separate category distinct from beauty in the modern environmentalist sense. The close relationship of beauty and interest is highlighted by the fact that there is a significant overlap in the criteria used to evaluate the beauty and interest of the Yellowstone springs.

IMPACT ON ENVIRONMENTAL THOUGHT

That these interrelationships between science and art did have a major impact on environmental thinking can be demonstrated easily by referring to the reasons given for the establishment of Yosemite in the 1860s and Yellowstone in the 1870s.[32] Although the original idea for the creation of each can be traced to representatives of two transportation companies, one a steamboat company in California and the other a railroad based in New York, there is no evidence that the financial motives of these companies played a major role. Indeed, it is not even clear that the steamboat company had a financial motive at all.

Three primary justifications were given for making Yellowstone a national park: its geological interest, its aesthetic interest, and its usefulness as a preserve for wild animals. Its geological value was forcefully called to the attention of Congress by F. V. Hayden, head of the territorial geological survey that had explored the area the year before. Hayden lobbied for the park and wrote articles on it for professional and popular magazines. The aesthetic value of Yellowstone was amply documented by the photographs of W. H. Jackson, Hayden's landscape photographer, and by the sketches and watercolors of Thomas Moran, a major artist who visited Yellowstone with Hayden. Knowledge that Moran was nearing completion of what was believed to be his most important painting, *The Grand Canyon of the Yellowstone,* may have also influenced the federal legislators. Although no one seems specifically to have called for the preservation of Yellowstone's animal populations, Congress on its own initiative chose to prohibit all hunting, except for a small amount by park personnel for food when working in remote areas of the park, thus adding a biological justification. This action may have been intended to satisfy the civilian and military naturalists, biologists, and western travelers, who, for over fifty years in their official reports and popular accounts had been pleading for legal protection for western wild animal populations.

Although the information available on the establishment of Yosemite is very limited, it is clear that the justifications for this park were very similar to those given for Yellowstone—in this case, botanical, aesthetic, and geological interest. Botanical interest focused on the giant sequoias and was in fact the chief reason for the establishment of the park. Botanists had discovered and called attention to the giant sequoias by the early 1850s. A traveling exhibit of a large section of bark from one of these trees not only familiarized easterners with them but soon brought accusations from outraged Americans that the exhibitors were tree murderers. It was hoped that the park would help preserve some of these trees from similar exploitation and abuse. Stories were circulating of giant trees being burned, dynamited, and made into fence posts. The Yosemite valley itself, which did not contain any of these trees, was included in the federal legislation primarily for aesthetic reasons but also for its geological interest. Congress and the California legislature were made aware of the beauties and sublimities of the valley with visual documentation similar to that later presented on behalf of Yellowstone. This probably included the landscape photographs of C. E. Watkins, who was soon to win a gold medal with them at a Paris exposition, and perhaps some paintings by Albert Bierstadt, who was then beginning to acquire his reputation as America's foremost western artist largely on the strength of his Rocky Mountain and Yosemite paintings.

The importance of science and art to the Yosemite preservation effort is well noted in landscape architect Frederick Law Olmsted's report to the California legislature, which Olmsted wrote in 1865 as the head of a commission studying the value of Yosemite as a park. In the report, Olmsted stressed that Yosemite ought "to be considered as a field of study for science and art," and he added that "already students of science and artists have been attracted to it from the Atlantic states and a number of artists have at heavy expense spent the summer in sketching the scenery." Olmsted even recommended that four of the eight park commissioners be "students of natural science or landscape artists."[33]

An examination of the scientific and aesthetic orientations of key environmentalists and scientists also provides abundant evidence of the close relationship between science, art, and nature protection. Consider, for example, the lives of John Muir, a major nineteenth-century preservationist, and Clarence King, a major nineteenth-century geologist. Although Muir did not share King's extensive interest in landscape painting, he did have some influence over landscape painter William Keith, and like professional naturalists, Muir made sketches of what he saw in the wilds. King, on the other hand, did not share Muir's intensive interest in transcendental philosophy; yet he was deeply involved in the spiritual aspects of nature. Unlike Muir, King was not a prolific writer on the subject of nature, yet his book *Mountaineering in the Sierra Nevada* is still regarded as a first-rate example of nature literature today. Moreover, Muir and King *did* share a common interest in geology, and both men were known for their geological interpretations in opposition to the theories of J. D. Whitney, particularly on the subject of glaciers and glacial action in California's mountains. In fact, since Muir's interest extended to botanical collecting and some biological studies, he probably had much wider interests as a naturalist than King, who remained narrowly focused on geology and geological theory. What separated these men on environmental issues could not have been anything fundamental such as a difference in scientific or aesthetic viewpoint, since basically their viewpoints were about the same. Most probably the difference was simply that King, unlike Muir, was not located at the center of early preservationist activity in California except for a very short period of his life, and, as head of the Fortieth Parallel Survey and the U.S. Geological Survey, he did not have the time to become involved in preservationist efforts.[34] As a matter of fact, it was quite easy for scientists to become involved if they could find the time for it. For example, William H. Brewer, King's supervisor in California, an associate of Muir on a government forestry commission, and a friend of both men, frequently became involved in nature preservation, both willingly and unwillingly. Since Brewer was well known in connection with his writings on the sequoias for the California Geological Survey, he was on occasion swamped with letters from people concerned about the welfare of these trees, and in lieu of answering their letters individually, he was forced to make public statements on the subject. In addition, Brewer followed preservationist activity in Connecticut very closely and was active in the effort to establish East Rock Park in New Haven.

IMPACT ON PASSMORE'S POSITION

Because Passmore is seemingly unaware of these sorts of relationships, he not only falsely classifies environmentalists as antiscientific nature mystics but also distorts their most basic arguments. At one point in his book, for example, Passmore suggests that preservationists might sometime wish to protect the yellow fever germ on the grounds that it is "an organism, no doubt, of considerable interest and beauty."[35] Though it is not inconceivable that preservationists and other environmentalists might decide that the yellow fever germ ought to be protected in some sense and for some reason, if my historical analysis of beauty and interest is correct, they would never make such an argument. Since the yellow fever organism is far too small to be experienced aesthetically (except perhaps by microscope), it is absurd to think that anyone could speak of the beauty of such an entity in a general sense for public appreciation, and if, as I have claimed, interest is also a general aesthetic term, it is just as unlikely in the case of interest. Of course, it is not beyond the realm of possibility that at some time in the future environmentalists might seek to preserve something like the yellow fever germ as a *means* to preserving or protecting something else. For example, when Leopold discusses the relationship of Spessart oak and certain microscopic flora and fauna in Germany, he is arguing in this manner;[36] however, although arguments along these lines do involve ecological relationships and the fulfillment of human needs and objectives (in this case, the making of high-quality cabinets) and are consistent with the seventeenth- and eighteenth-century land use doctrines that Passmore invokes, they have nothing to do with interest arguments as they are used by environmentalists.

Passmore's most treasured land use attitudes are on shaky ground even when applied to nineteenth-century American science. A commitment on the part of scientists and the general public in America to land use did not preclude or interfere with the development of an appreciation and love for nature or with a preservationist sympathy for wilderness. Of course, Passmore's conservative land use attitudes may be quite acceptable in a country like England. British conservationist L. Dudley Stamp, for example, once estimated that despite the British preoccupation since ancient times with converting waste into useful land, the British have actually been using their land to the full extent of the agricultural technology available since the fourteenth century and that as a result, "very little indeed of the scenery, even in the wildest and least touched parts of our islands, can truthfully be described as natural."[37] With such a long history of land use practice, it is quite understandable that Englishmen today would be almost exclusively dedicated to land use and would find discordant American views incomprehensible. In America, however, there was no similar use tradition, and thus nothing comparable to the intensive British commitment to land use developed. Throughout the nineteenth century, very large areas of the United States remained wild and almost completely untouched by man, even in the East. Thus while Americans did adopt Locke's view that land exists for man to improve it and to give it value, familiarity with natural areas that were not needed at the time permitted the emergence of a separate tradition that placed a high value on land in a natural and unused state. This alternative view of land influenced scientists and ordinary Americans alike. Lewis and Clark, for instance, were given detailed instructions to look for every possible use for the lands they explored;[38] yet they did not fail to see and note its beauty and interest as well.

During the era of exploration following the Lewis and Clark expedition, scientists were often plagued by conflicts between use, on the one hand, and aesthetic and scientific interest, on the other. J. D. Whitney's struggles with the California legislature over what the geological survey was supposed to be doing is perhaps one of the best examples. Whitney wanted to study the geology of California systematically *for its own sake* without stressing application, whereas the legislature wanted the survey to concentrate on helping miners find gold. When Whitney's work in paleontology was criticized for being impractical, Whitney did not even point out that it was needed to help pinpoint gold-bearing layers of rock, apparently fearing that he and the survey might then be seen as bowing to the economic interests of politicians.[39] Although in most cases the conflict was not so great as in California, scientists continued to balance the two points of view, sometimes noting the economic value of particular areas or objects in their notebooks but nearly as often praising their value just as they were in a natural state.

Despite Passmore's claim that American environmentalists oppose all use, this balance of instrumental and intrinsic value remains part of the environmentalist viewpoint even today. Passmore is shown to be in error by the writings of Aldo Leopold, one of Passmore's chief targets. In the essay "The Land Ethic," Leopold writes:

> A land ethic of course cannot prevent the alteration, management, and use of these "resources," but it does affirm their right to continued existence, and, at least in spots, their continued existence in a natural state.[40]

No matter how one feels about Leopold's endorsement of the right of natural objects and species to exist, no one can truthfully say that he rejects land use. In fact, land use played a major role in Leopold's thinking long before—and after—he ever considered more radical environmental ideas. As Susan Flader shows in her intellectual biography of Leopold's career, Leopold began as a naturalist and forester (that is, as a natural history scientist) working initially within the context of Pinchot's land use ideas and economic utilitarianism; only gradually, as a result of the specific problems Leopold faced in his career, did he move toward a preservationist position.[41]

Of course, Passmore might want to claim that the natural history sciences are not part of the Western scientific tradition. I confess that I do not know how he could make such a claim nor whether he could argue for it successfully, but even if he could, there would still remain the fact that arguments involving intrinsic value, common in the early nineteenth-century preservationist tradition, share a philosophical heritage extending continuously back to Greek philosophy. Thomas Cole, for instance, once remarked in his preservationist-oriented "Essay on American Scenery" that "there is in the human mind an almost inseparable connexion between the beautiful and the good, so that if we contemplate the one the other seems present."[42] Emerson wrote in his influential essay *Nature:*

> A nobler want to man is served by nature, namely the love of Beauty.
> The ancient Greeks called the world *kosmos,* beauty. Such is the constitution of all things, or such the plastic power of the human eye, that the primary forms, as the sky, the mountain, the tree, the animal, *give us a delight in and for themselves.*[43]

That these remarks, all modern forms of Greek ethical and aesthetic ideas, are far from isolated cases is amply demonstrated by the fact that romantic nature poetry, especially the works of Wordsworth, express similar thoughts and ideas, either broadly Greek or Platonic in origin.

LOVE FOR MATERIAL OBJECTS

What may be new is the application of these aesthetic and ethical concepts to natural objects, since Greek philosophers admittedly associated beauty with objects of thought and not with material objects. Consider, for example, the following advice to young artists offered in an editorial of the artist magazine *The Crayon:*

> Let it be remembered that the subject of the picture—the material object or objects from which it is constructed—[is] the essential parts of it. If you have no love for them, you can have no genuine feeling for the picture which represents them. You may have a kind of admiration for the masterly treatment, and remarkable technical qualities, but that does not constitute love for Art—it is only an intellectual perception of power. We *love* Nature and Beauty—we admire the artist who renders them in his works.[44]

Though widely held in nineteenth-century America, this viewpoint would have seemed strange to Greek philosophers and indeed to modern European existential philosophers as well, who, like Sartre, have shown no love for physical objects. Yet it would have been in harmony with the art and literature of ancient Greece, which, unlike Greek philosophy, manifested a love for nature.[45] Thus to this extent it may still be said to be consistent with Western thought and may even represent some resolution of an old conflict between Greek philosophy and Greek art and literature.

Even though the American love for natural objects was compatible with and flourished in the natural history sciences, it was exhibited in American art, literature, and philosophy long before they became fully scientific and may therefore best be accounted for as initially arising out of a primitive love for natural objects among ordinary people—perhaps also the source of nature love in ancient Greece.

Landscape painter Thomas Cole's experiences in the 1820s when landscape paintings were beginning to become popular illustrate just how powerful and influential this primitive love for nature was. American painters, at that time seeking subject matter that would assure them of a ready income in a country without art patrons, eventually found that landscapes depicting wildernesses sold very well. The difficulty with landscape paintings, however, was that public tastes for them did not always coincide with the artistic sensitivities of artists like Cole. Cole preferred to compose his paintings out of rocks and trees that he had found here and there, and, moreover, he preferred to paint from memory so that—in line with the distinction between mind and matter—he would be painting thoughts (his memories) rather than things or physical objects. Much to his disgust, American buyers wanted paintings that represented real places, and they wanted so much detail that close observation was required, forcing Cole to paint things rather than thoughts. In addition, art patrons usually wanted to know the name and location of the place painted, and they made trips there to stand where the artist had stood to compare the painting with the original. Cole, who very much wanted to paint religious allegories, thought that the poor taste of Americans in these matters kept him from becoming a better painter; nevertheless, the paintings that he despised and painted only for money are those for which he is still best known and which had the most influence on his contemporaries. Because of them, Cole was acclaimed the founder of the Hudson River School, the most important school of painting in the United States in the nineteenth century.[46]

The American fascination with natural objects and their accurate representation in landscape painting can hardly be said to have been a passing fad since it can be traced from Cole's work to the Hudson River School, American impressionism, and finally abstract expressionism. As Robert Rosenblum puts it in an essay titled "The Primal American Scene":

> It would seem that for American artists, elemental nature is still a source of myth and energy. Were this view of "the natural paradise" to extend into the generation that followed the Abstract Expressionists, it would have to leave behind the realm of paint and canvas and move to the land itself, and precisely to what is left of those remote, still pristine regions of Nevada, Arizona, Utah, or California, which for the 1960s and 1970s are the equivalent of the unspoiled American wildernesses that inspired a Cole or Church.[47]

Rosenblum is wrong in only one respect. The move to the land itself was taken long ago by environmentalists and other lovers of nature. Yosemite and Yellowstone were the first results.

Since the 1950s a major reevaluation of mid-nineteenth-century landscape painting has been under way. Both Barbara Novak and John Baur point out that American landscape painting can be characterized best in terms of light reflecting off material objects.[48] The American artists of this time—now grouped together as luminists—were, it seems, involved in the same experiments with light that were commanding the attention of the Europeans then moving toward impressionism; however, while in European paintings the light *became* the picture and the objects dropped out, in luminism the light remained *within* the picture in association with solid objects. This object orientation was so persistent that impressionism was very slow in coming to the United States, and even when it finally triumphed, the integrity of the objects was usually retained. If the art enthusiast stood back far enough, the American impressionist painting often took on the characteristic photographic realism of the luminist school.

Despite their object orientation and emphasis on accurate and factual representation, luminists introduced moral and religious value into landscape painting. In one of his letters of advice to young landscape painters, for instance, Asher Durand wrote, "The poet sees in nature more than mere matter of fact, yet he does not see more than is there, nor what another may not see when *he* points it out."[49] The extra something that was there beyond the facts was moral and religious value. One way in which painters introduced moral value into a painting was to place a solitary tree in the foreground. A tree of this sort, knotted, bent, broken, and decaying, often symbolized admirable American character traits, including self-reliance, perseverance, and freedom. Rocks scarred by time sometimes produced similar effects. The primary way in which value was introduced, however, was through the use of the same light effects that were already highlighting the material reality of the objects represented in the painting. In religious paintings earlier in the century, and indeed in paintings long before that in Europe, strong, intense light emanating from the heavens had been considered to have moral and religious significance. Beams of light piercing through clouds and reflecting off water, when introduced into American landscape painting, thus suggested such values in these otherwise secular paintings.

TRANSCENDENTAL PHILOSOPHY

There was also some influence from American transcendental philosophy, which possesses an object orientation similar to that just discussed in American landscape painting. Whereas European idealists tended to consider nature as *human nature,* American idealists more often thought of it as rocks, trees, flowers, rivers, and mountains. Furthermore, though Emerson's suggestion that there is "an occult relation between man and the vegetable" may not adequately express the American idealist's view of the relationship of man and nature, his general philosophical viewpoint does. According to Emerson, as an idealist, it is possible to become "a transparent eyeball" in which the self and nature almost become one. As he puts it in his essay "The American Scholar," one comes to see that "nature is the opposite of the soul, answering to it part for part. One is seal and one is print. Its beauty is the beauty of his own mind." This viewpoint permitted the transcendentalist to humanize the wilderness by taking it into his own mind and self, accepting it as the mirror image of his own soul.[50] Seen in this way, it was difficult for the transcendentalist to feel alienated, estranged, or separated from nature, and because of this transcendental relationship between the world and man, it was easy to find moral as well as aesthetic value in the contemplation of nature.

The radical difference between Transcendentalists and even modern European idealists can be seen by comparing Thoreau's vision of nature at the top of Mount Katahdin with Sartre's vision in the novel *Nausea,* where Sartre's main character sees raw nature revealed for the first time in a city park. Both Thoreau and Sartre's character are writing within the idealist tradition; each finds himself confronting the matter underlying his sensations of the world, and each has to struggle to maintain his identity in the face of nature revealed. Yet there are more differences than similarities. Sartre's character does not focus his attention on nature as objects but rather as matter. He writes:

> Existence had suddenly unveiled itself. It had lost the harmless look of an abstract category: it was the very paste of things, this root was kneaded into existence. Or rather the root, the park gates, the bench, the sparse grass, all that had vanished: the diversity of things, their individuality, were only an appearance, a veneer. This veneer had melted, leaving soft, monstrous masses, all in disorder—naked, in a frightful, obscene nakedness.[51]

Thoreau writes:

> Talk of mysteries!—Think of our life in nature,—daily to be shown matter, to come in contact with it,—rocks, trees, wind on our cheeks! the *solid* earth! the *actual* world! the *common sense!* Contact! *Who* are we? where are we?[52]

Although Thoreau, like Sartre, considers the objects to be derived from some underlying source, for him objects do not lose their individuality or fade away as an illusion or veneer. They remain rocks, trees, and wind. Also, unlike Sartre's character, who is caught by surprise by the underlying "soft, monstrous masses," Thoreau is actively seeking nature on its own terms so that he can learn how to "conceive of a region not inhabited by man."[53] Thoreau is afraid of what he sees, but he expected to be, and rather than run from it in terror and nausea, he takes pleasure from the sight of it in accordance with the sublime and tries to embrace it emotionally and intellectually through aesthetic evaluation and scientific inquiry. Although wild nature proves more stupendous and overwhelming than he anticipated, he does not delve below it as Sartre does and so is not repulsed by nature as Sartre's character is; nor is he so frightened that he cannot take time out to taste some wild blueberries growing near the summit. If Thoreau were alive today, he would probably think the Sartrean fear silly, just as most Americans do today if they read *Nausea,* however much they might tremble looking over the edge of the Grand Canyon of the Yellowstone.

ONTOLOGICAL CONSIDERATIONS

The American interest in material objects encouraged attitudes favoring nature preservation because it was an interest in *existent* objects. Wordsworth, a first-rate modern preservationist in his own right in view of his efforts in 1844 to save the Lake District from the Kendal and Windermere

Railway, seems to have become a preservationist as a result of this kind of thinking.[54] In his *Guide to the Lakes,* written in 1835, Wordsworth quotes the following lines from the poet Gray on the Vale of Grasmere:

> Not a single red tile, no flaring gentleman's house or garden-wall, breaks in upon the repose of this little unsuspected paradise; but all is peace, rusticity, and happy poverty, in its neatest and most becoming attire.

Then Wordsworth adds:

> It is well for the undisturbed pleasure of the Poet that he had no forebodings of the change which was soon to take place; and it might have been hoped that these words, indicating how much of the charm of what *was* depended upon what was *not* would have preserved the ancient franchises of this and other kindred mountain retirements from trespass; or (shall I dare to say?) would have secured scenes so consecrated from profanation.[55]

In America, George Catlin, known for his portraits of Indians on the Upper Missouri, voiced similar sentiments at about the same time, as the following remarks, part of the justification for Catlin's seminal call for the establishment of a national park, indicate:

> Many are the rudenesses and wilds in Nature's works, which are destined to fall before the deadly axe and desolating hands of cultivating man; and so amongst her ranks of *living*, of beast and human, we often find noble stamps, or beautiful colours, to which our admiration clings; and even in the overwhelming march of civilized improvements and refinements do we love to cherish their existence, and lend our efforts to preserve them in their primitive rudeness. Such of Nature's works are always worthy of our preservation and protection; and the further we become separated (and the face of the country) from that pristine wilderness and beauty, the more pleasure does the mind of enlightened man feel in recurring to those scenes, when he can have them preserved for his eyes and his mind to dwell upon.[56]

Catlin, as he puts it, loves to cherish the *existence* of nature's works, and his desire to preserve them both for the mind and the eye is based on their value both as objects of thought and as existent entities. Once it is realized that Catlin's viewpoint is basically the same as the one that caused the landscape-buying public of the time to prefer paintings of real places that they could visit and see for themselves, it is not difficult to imagine how it could have blossomed into widespread sympathy for nature preservation.

Although no philosopher has tried to develop a preservationist philosophy as such, many of the elements of one can be found in the philosophy of G. E. Moore. Not only does Moore take a commonsense view toward existent objects compatible with the views of nineteenth-century Americans, but he also displays a preference in *Principia Ethica* for paintings of real places and real objects rather than composed scenes. Speaking of the relationship of paintings to existent landscapes, Moore writes:

> I think that the additional presence of a belief in the reality of the objects makes the total state much better, if the belief is true; and worse, if the belief is false. In short, where there is belief, in the sense in which we *do* believe in the existence of Nature and horses, and do *not* believe in the existence of an ideal landscape and unicorns, the *truth* of what is believed does make a great difference to the value of the organic whole.

A few lines later he continues:

> We do think that the emotional contemplation of a natural scene, supposing its qualities equally beautiful, is in some way a better state of things than that of a painted landscape: we think that the world would be improved if we could substitute for the best works of representative art *real* objects equally beautiful.[57]

Moore's aesthetic position follows from his general ethical position that questions about what is good also involve the question "What ought to be?"[58] In making this claim, Moore is drawing not only on Greek sources but on medieval and early modern ones as well. He thus presents a curious ontological argument in which preference is given to existent objects on the grounds that their existence adds to their aesthetic (and perhaps also moral) value. Since his position reflects the same naive realist bias that prompted American art patrons to prefer paintings representing real places and objects to imaginary ones, it provides a good historical and philosophical basis for preservationist arguments, as we shall see in some detail in Chapter 6.

NATURE PRESERVATION AND WESTERN CIVILIZATION

Although Moore's philosophy is most closely related to the nineteenth-century developments discussed in this chapter, other philosophers have also taken relevant positions on nature protection, especially William James and Alfred North Whitehead. In his essay "On a Certain Blindness in Human Beings," for example, James makes some attempt to defend the new attitudes toward nature and wilderness. In one anecdote, he remarks that after looking on the "unmitigated squalor" created by the "improvements" of settlers at the turn of the century, he felt compelled to defend the preservation of the forests of North Carolina on the grounds that "the beauties and commodities gained by the centuries are sacred. They are our heritage and birthright."[59] Despite Passmore's claim that the word *sacred* indicates dangerous and corrupting Oriental influence, there is every reason to believe that James' remarks are of purely Western origin and sentiment.

In Whitehead's *Science and the Modern World* there is an even stronger and more spirited environmentalist-style position than James'. Whitehead's aim is to combat science's and philosophy's "assumption of the bare valuelessness of mere matter [which] led to a lack of reverence in the treatment of natural or artistic beauty" and brought about two evils: "one, the ignoration of the true relation of each organism to its environment; and the other, the habit of ignoring the intrinsic worth of the environment which must be allowed its weight in any consideration of final ends."[60] Indisputably, this is also an environmentalist aim. Most interesting of all is the similarity of some of Whitehead's comments and those of environmentalist Aldo Leopold. Long passages in the last chapter of *Science and the Modern World,* for instance, could easily have served as the source of some of Leopold's ideas and suggest that Leopold's notion of community could be derived from Whitehead's theory of organism without much difficulty. In one place especially, Whitehead speaks of "associations of different species which mutually cooperate," and he refers to the forest environment as "the triumph of the organization of mutually dependent species." A few lines later he adds that "every organism requires an environment of friends, partly to shield it from violent changes, and partly to supply it with its wants."[61] It is a small step from Whitehead's "environment of friends" to Leopold's "biotic community," one that requires no detours into Oriental philosophy or religion.

Of course, neither the views of these philosophers nor the various points discussed here prove that the environment ought to be preserved and protected; however, they do show how shallowly based are Passmore's historical analyses and his speculations that man may return to the aesthetic values of the nonformal garden in the twenty-first century. The developments that have occurred in the past century and a half in art, literature, and the natural history sciences, and are themselves part of a broader evolution of man's attitude toward nature over the past three centuries, cannot be accounted for, as Passmore claims, simply as romantic or Oriental drivel, and even though man's views toward nature in the twenty-first century may be different from what they are today and may even be nonpreservationist, there is no reason to think that they will regress to those of the eighteenth-century garden enthusiast. In large measure, the attitudes of future generations will depend on future conditions. If all natural areas are destroyed in the name of economic utilitarianism and human beings are no longer able to experience wilderness, it is possible that preservationist attitudes may disappear. If, however, some areas are retained in their natural condition and the contrast between them and populated areas sharpens, future generations may be even more radically preservationist than today's.

The central issue is not whether or not there is any basis in Western civilization for nature preservation, since clearly there is, but rather whether there are any grounds for defending natural objects and species from economic exploitation. Passmore is dedicated to the idea that there will always be economic considerations that will override the preservation of anything. If this idea is ultimately triumphant, there can never be an environmental ethic of any sort, and the environment can never be given any permanent protection. The correct approach seems to be to return to the notion of higher and lower goods. Even the most utilitarian philosophers of the nineteenth century always held that some things are of such great value intrinsically that they are exempt from calculations based on instrumental and economic good. In this context, the idea that *some* natural objects and *some* representatives of nearly all species ought to be preserved because of their intrinsic beauty and interest can, I believe, be defended as a reasonable and conservatively Western idea. It does not mean the end of Western civilization or the end of man since it does not by any means completely oppose the economic use of the Earth for human purposes. In addition, it does not involve an intrusion of any Oriental influences, merely the return to a more balanced Western value system.

NOTES

1. John Passmore, *Man's Responsibility for Nature: Ecological Problems and Western Traditions* (London: Duckworth, 1974), pp. 3, 101, 124–125, 110; see also pp. 36–40, 173–181.
2. Alfred North Whitehead, *Science and the Modern World: Lowell Lectures, 1925* (New York: Free Press, 1967), pp. 75–94, 193–208.
3. Holmes Rolston III, "Is There an Ecological Ethic?" *Ethics* 85 (1975): 101–103.
4. *William Wordsworth's Guide to the Lakes,* 5th ed. (1835) (Oxford: Oxford University Press, 1970), pp. 91–92; George Catlin, *Letters and Notes on the Manners, Customs, and Conditions of the North American Indians: Written during Eight Years' Travel (1832–1839) amongst the Wildest Tribes of Indians in North America* (New York: Dover Publications, 1973), vol. 1, p. 262.
5. See Pinchot's own autobiography for the best account of this man's life and thinking: Gifford Pinchot, *Breaking New Ground* (Orlando, Fla.: Harcourt Brace Jovanovich, 1947).
6. These changes are most evident in the writings of John Muir during his association with Pinchot. For a short but good account of the relationship of these two men, their conflict, and its impact on their environmental positions, see Roderick Nash, *Wilderness and the American Mind,* rev. ed. (New Haven: Yale University Press, 1973), pp. 129–140.
7. Myra Reynolds, *The Treatment of Nature in English Poetry* (New York: Gordian Press, 1966), pp. 327–332.
8. Passmore, *Man's Responsibility,* p. 109.
9. Ibid., pp. 36–40.
10. Sir Archibald Geike, *Founders of Geology,* 2nd ed. (New York: Dover Publications, 1962), pp. 181–182; William H. Brewer Papers, Yale Historical Man-

uscript Collection: "Forest Physiography" Lecture 24 (March 24, 1904) in Box 40/Folder 203, and draft of address, "The Debt of This Century to Learned Societies," delivered at the Centennial Anniversary of the Connecticut Academy of Arts and Sciences, October 11, 1899, in Box 42/Folder 231. An edited version of this address appeared in *Transactions of the Connecticut Academy of Arts and Sciences* 9 (1901–1902): xlvi-liii.

11. Passmore, *Man's Responsibility,* pp. 36–37.

12. For a discussion of this point, see Nash, *Wilderness,* pp. 67–83.

13. Marjorie Hope Nicolson, *Mountain Gloom and Mountain Glory: The Development of the Aesthetic of the Infinite* (New York: Norton, 1963), pp. 20–21.

14. Reynolds, *Treatment of Nature,* pp. 327, 335.

15. Nicolson, *Mountain Gloom,* pp. 347–348.

16. John Ruskin, *Modern Painters,* 5 vols. (Boston: Dana Estes & Company, n.d.); Alexander von Humboldt, *Cosmos: A Sketch of a Physical Description of the Universe,* trans. E. C. Otte, vol. 2 (New York: Harper & Row, 1852), pp. 82–105.

17. James Jackson Jarves, *The Art-Idea,* ed. Benjamin Rowland, Jr. (Cambridge: Belnap Press of Harvard University Press, 1960), p. 192.

18. Reuben Gold Thwaites, ed., *Original Journals of Lewis and Clark Expedition,* (New York: Dodd, Mead, 1904), p. 149. The remark was written on June 13, 1805.

19. Emerson's claim that "the eye is the best of artists" probably encouraged this trend; see Emerson, *Nature,* sec. 3, in *Selected Writings of Ralph Waldo Emerson,* ed. Brooks Atkinson (New York: Random House, 1940), p. 9.

20. John Constable, *The Crayon* 3 (1856): 99; Emerson, *Nature,* sec. 3, in *Selected Writings,* p. 9; John Muir, *Our National Parks* (Boston: Houghton Mifflin, 1901), p. 4.

21. Nicolson, *Mountain Gloom,* pp. 71, 143, 215.

22. Paul Wilhelm, Duke of Württemberg, *Travels in North America, 1822–1824,* trans. W. Robert Nitske, ed. Savoie Lottinville (Norman: University of Oklahoma Press, 1973), p. 260; Fielding B. Meek Papers, Smithsonian Institution, Box 10, Owen Survey, 1849, p. 3, September 16.

23. Prince Maximilian of Neu-Wied, *Travels in the Interior of North America* (1843), in *Early Western Travels, 1748–1864,* ed. Reuben Gold Thwaites (Cleveland: Arthur H. Clark Co. 1904–1906), vol. 22, pp. 52, 26–28; letter from Kenneth McKenzie to Joshua Pilcher, dated December 16, 1833, and letter from Kenneth McKenzie to Baron de Braunsberg (Prince Maximilian), dated March 20, 1834, both in Fort Union letterbook, Chouteau Papers, Missouri Historical Society, St. Louis.

24. 1848 Diary, p. 15, in Box 8/Folder 208, William H. Brewer Papers, Yale Historical Manuscripts Collection.

25. 1851–1852 Diary, p. 6, in Box 8/Folder 208, Brewer Papers.

26. Ibid., p. 13.

27. 1853 Diary, p. 109, in Box 8/Folder 208, Brewer Papers.

28. Typescript, p. 412, in Box 8/Folder 211, and also in *Up and Down California in 1860–1864: The Journal of William H. Brewer,* ed. Francis P. Farquhar (Berkeley: University of California Press, 1966), p. 318.

29. Typescript, p. 551, in Box 8/Folder 211, Brewer Papers; *Up and Down California,* p. 443.

30. Typescript, p. 682, in Box 8/Folder 211, Brewer Papers; omitted in *Up and Down California.*

31. Earl of Dunraven, *The Great Divide: Travels in the Upper Yellowstone in the Summer of 1874,* Bison Books (Lincoln: University of Nebraska Press, 1967), p. 207; see also pp. 287–288.

32. For comprehensive discussions on the establishment of these parks, see Hans Huth, "Yosemite: The Story of an Idea," *Sierra Club Bulletin* 30 (1948): 47–78,

and Aubrey L. Haines, *Yellowstone National Park: Its Exploration and Establishment* (Washington, D.C.: U.S. Government Printing Office, 1974).

33. Frederick Law Olmstead, "The Yosemite Valley and the Mariposa Big Trees," *Landscape Architecture* 43 (1952): 24–25.

34. See note 26 in Chapter 5 for still another possibility.

35. Passmore, *Man's Responsibility,* p. 123.

36. Aldo Leopold, *A Sand County Almanac: With Essays on Conservation from Round River* (New York: Ballantine Books, 1970), pp. 190–191, and Aldo Leopold, *Round River: From the Journals of Aldo Leopold,* ed. Luna B. Leopold (New York: Oxford University Press, 1953), p. 147.

37. L. Dudley Stamp, *Man and the Land: The New Naturalist* (London: Collins, 1955), pp. 95, xiii.

38. Donald Jackson, ed., *The Letters of the Lewis and Clark Expedition* (Urbana: University of Illinois Press, 1962), pp. 61–66.

39. William H. Goetzmann, *Exploration and Empire: The Explorer and the Scientist in the Winning of the American West* (New York: Knopf, 1966), pp. 372–373.

40. Aldo Leopold, *A Sand County Almanac, and Sketches Here and There* (New York: Oxford University Press, 1949), p. 204; Leopold, *Sand County Almanac: With Essays on Conservation from Round River,* p. 240.

41. Susan L. Flader, *Thinking like a Mountain: Aldo Leopold and the Evolution of an Ecological Attitude toward Deer, Wolves, and Forests* (Columbia: University of Missouri Press, 1974).

42. Thomas Cole, "Essay on American Scenery," *American Monthly Magazine* 1 (1836): 2, in John W. McCoubrey, ed., *American Art, 1700–1969: Sources and Documents* (Englewood Cliffs: Prentice-Hall, 1965), p. 99.

43. Emerson, *Nature,* sec. 3, in *Selected Writings,* p. 9.

44. "Common Sense in Art," *The Crayon* 1 (1855): 81.

45. See Henry Ruston Fairclough, *Love of Nature among the Greeks and Romans* (White Plains, N.Y.: Longman, 1930).

46. Cole's difficulties and the metaphysical background of luminism and American landscape painting as a whole are discussed very fully in Barbara Novak, *American Painting of the Nineteenth Century: Realism, Idealism, and the American Experience* (New York: Praeger, 1969).

47. Robert Rosenblum, "The Primal American Scene," in *The Natural Paradise: Painting in America, 1800–1950,* ed. Kynaston McShine (New York: Museum of Modern Art, 1976), p. 37. There appears to be a direct correlation between places painted in the nineteenth century and places preserved. By painting particular places, artists often established them in the minds of the general public as places of beauty especially worthy of preservation. This was the case in Yosemite and Yellowstone, the Adirondacks, and many other lesser-known sites. Some places that were not painted by a major artist—for example, the Great Falls of the Missouri—did not survive to the end of the century.

48. Novak, *American Painting,* p. 96; John I. H. Baur, "American Luminism," *Perspectives USA,* 9 (Autumn 1954): 90–98.

49. Asher B. Durand, "On Landscape Painting: Letter IV," *The Crayon* 1 (1855): 98.

50. Emerson, *Nature,* sec. 3, in *Selected Writings,* pp. 7, 6; "The American Scholar," sec. 1, in *Selected Writings,* p. 48, and sec. 3, p. 52.

51. Jean-Paul Sartre, *Nausea,* trans. Lloyd Alexander (New York: New Directions, 1964), pp. 171–172.

52. Henry David Thoreau, *The Maine Woods* (New York: Crowell, 1961), p. 93.

53. Ibid., pp. 90–91.

54. "Kendal and Windermere Railway: Two Letters," in *Wordsworth's Guide to the Lakes,* app. 2 (pp. 146–166).

55. Ibid., p. 70.

56. Catlin, *Letters and Notes,* vol. 1, p. 260.

57. George Edward Moore, *Principia Ethica* (Cambridge: Cambridge University Press, 1965), pp. 194–195.

58. Ibid., p. 115.

59. William James, "On a Certain Blindness in Human Beings," in *The Moral Philosophy of William James,* ed. John K. Roth (New York: Crowell, 1969), pp. 215–216.

60. Whitehead, *Science and the Modern World,* p. 196.

61. Ibid., p. 206.

CHAPTER FOUR
WILDLIFE PROTECTION ATTITUDES

In "Animal Liberation: A Triangular Affair," J. Baird Callicott distinguishes among *humane moralism,* the ethical position held by proponents of animal rights or liberation; *ethical humanism,* the traditional ethical position opposed to animal rights; and the *land ethic,* an ecologically oriented position based on the writings of Aldo Leopold. He then argues that ethical humanism and humane moralism are merely extensions of "familiar historical positions [that] have simply been retrenched, applied, and exercised" and that only the land ethic, since it is derived from ecological science, represents any significant breakthrough in ethical theory.[1] While I am sympathetic to Callicott's analysis and have learned from it, I do not believe that he has succeeded in showing that the animal rights position, right or wrong, is nothing more than an extension of traditional ethical theory. Both the humane moralists and the ethical humanists, however much they may disagree, do accept that the proposal to replace rationality with sentience as the primary criterion for identifying rights-bearing entities, if accepted, would be a very radical break with traditional theory. It is only as it is seen from the outside, from the standpoint of the land ethic, that the proposal seems too insignificant to be a bold step beyond.

Callicott's claim that ethical humanism and humane moralism have something fundamentally in common in opposition to the land ethic is, however, an important one that can be made fairly easily, I believe, if one turns from theoretical to historical considerations. Both John Passmore, an opponent of animal rights, and Peter Singer, a defender, present historical accounts of the evolution of our attitudes toward animals in support of their theoretical positions, and these accounts, for all practical purposes, are identical.[2] Both agree that in the nineteenth century, attitudes toward animals changed and that it became morally wrong to inflict unnecessary suffering on animals. They disagree only as to how the new moral practice associated with these attitudes should be interpreted theoretically: as a restriction of human rights over animals, as Passmore claims, or as an extension of moral rights to animals, as Singer claims. While these interpretations are, of course, radically different from one another theoretically, they are nonetheless attempts to analyze and justify the *same* moral change, the *same* moral behavior. This is something that not only links them closely but also distinguishes them from the land ethic. Since supporters of the land ethic are not concerned with the suffering of individual animals, they clearly are not trying to interpret the nineteenth-century change in moral practice and attitude on which Passmore and Singer have focused. According to Callicott, pain is neither good nor evil; it is "primarily information": "In animals, it informs the central nervous system of stress, irritation, or trauma in the outlying regions of the organism."[3]

This historical approach to Callicott's distinction among the three views, while effective, points toward a new and unanswered question: If the land ethic has nothing to do with the history of ideas that philosophers like Passmore and Singer are trying to analyze, just what is its historical foundation or background? Callicott is not very helpful here, for, of course, he is not trying to be historical in his approach. When Callicott speaks of history in his article, he is speaking of the history of traditional ethics, not the history of the land ethic. One might suppose that the history is a short one, since Callicott asserts frequently that the land ethic is derived from the science of ecology, which has had a name for only a little over a century and has been a distinct discipline for only a few decades at most. Such a supposition, however, seems to be false, for, as I show, the concern for wildlife protection, but without regard for the suffering of individual animals, predates ecology and even the theory of evolution by more than a half-century.

In making this claim, I am not concerned with undermining Callicott's position that ecology supports the land ethic theoretically. As can be seen in the conflicting interpretations of Passmore and Singer, a theory and the history of ideas associated with it can be independent. Thus even though it may well be that ecology supports the land ethic theoretically and the land ethic can somehow be derived from it, it is probable that our present wildlife protection attitudes would have developed even if ecology and evolution had not become part of biological science.

In this chapter, I show that a history of ideas supports of our modern attitudes toward wildlife, and I argue (1) that the history of ideas does not support the animal rights position or the rights positions occasionally advanced by biologists, naturalists, and environmentalists, (2) that the theory of evolution and the science of ecology did not contribute positively to the establishment of our modern attitudes, and (3) that our attitudes actually emerged from an aesthetic interest in wildlife and nature generally that involved anthropocentric intrinsic value and treated animals as if they were exemplifications of an unusual kind of art.

I do not claim that the account I give is complete. There is, for example, also a legal tradition toward wildlife that is in some ways related and in some ways not. I am concerned with the history of the primary intuitions on which our modern attitudes toward wildlife are based, not the legal history of efforts to protect wild animals. The legal history begins in Europe with the establishment of royal forests and in the United States with a legal dispute, *Martin* v. *Waddell* (1842), over the right to take oysters out of the Raritan River in New Jersey.[4] My account begins with the American West just after Lewis and Clark's journey across North America and focuses on the attitudes of naturalists studying wildlife on the Upper Missouri River and in the Rocky Mountains. The wildlife of this area was studied and trapped extensively for nearly half a century before significant settlement began, and during this long period of time, significant disagreement over the treatment of wildlife developed between naturalists and trappers.[5] This dispute was made known to the general public in the eastern United States and in Europe by the travel accounts of the naturalists themselves and, I argue, formed the basis for our modern wildlife protection attitudes.

The people discussed in the account that follows were simply expressing attitudes, feelings, or sentiments without any philosophical pretension. They were not trying to formulate or articulate new ethical principles. This presentation, therefore, is intended merely as the starting point for a rational reconstruction that bridges the gap between our nineteenth-century attitudes toward wildlife and our contemporary ones. That reconstruction is the subject of all subsequent sections of this chapter.

THE HISTORY OF IDEAS

Primitive tribes often had customs according to which they asked the forgiveness and understanding of wild animals that they killed for food. Such customs or traditions, however, did not survive in Western civilization, in which a tradition of sport killing of wildlife for pleasure, not food, developed instead. The hunter, according to this tradition, derives enjoyment from the killing of animals without any feeling of guilt. Although naturalists of the eighteenth and nineteenth centuries did not consider themselves sport hunters, they all seem to have shared with sport hunters a complete lack of remorse when killing animals, an activity that they undertook with even greater frequency than sport hunters, since killing was the standard way to get close enough to an animal to study its properties. This lack of moral concern about the killing of individual animals continued throughout the period in which wildlife protection attitudes developed and continues for the most part among naturalists even today, although killing to study animals is no longer the normal practice in the field.

Occasionally naturalists were moved to sympathy under special circumstances, but these remained exceptions to normal practice. William Bartram, for example, was afflicted by pangs of moral conscience in the eighteenth century while accompanying a hunter who had just killed a bear with a cub.[6] Bartram was not, in principle, opposed to the killing of the adult bear; it was only the cries of the infant that stirred his moral sentiments. Had there been no cub present, Bartram would in all probability have derived some pleasure from the killing of the bear and afterward would have congratulated the hunter on his good marksmanship, not charged him with murder.

The journey of Lewis and Clark in 1804 up the Missouri River and across to the west coast of North America marked a new beginning in the scientific study of wildlife. Virtually any new animal encountered on the trip was shot immediately if Lewis and Clark or their guides and assistants could get within range. Although some of the accounts of these killings, especially the killings of the first grizzly bears, are exciting, there is nothing anywhere in the journals to suggest that Lewis and Clark harbored even the most latent wildlife protection attitudes. Perhaps had they encountered a bear cub, they might have felt a few moral qualms, but they did not and therefore simply had a good time killing and studying animals.

While Lewis and Clark were still on their journey, circumstances on the Upper Missouri changed in a way that affected the attitudes of nearly all subsequent naturalists traveling in the West. Shortly after Lewis and Clark departed, Manwell Lisa of St. Louis established a fur-trapping company and started up the Missouri, leading the first group of American fur trappers west of the Mississippi. The Lewis and Clark expedition met them as it was returning, and one of the men on the expedition, John Colter, left the party and was hired by Lisa right on the spot.[7] From that time on until after the Civil War, fur trappers were scattered over the Rocky Mountains and up and down the Missouri River. Naturalists encountered them everywhere, and since they used these men as guides and for logistic support, they were almost never out of sight of four or five of them for more than a few minutes. These fur trappers were uneducated people who could neither read nor write and who seldom had any cultured sensitivities. As Osborne Russell, one of the few who could write, notes, "My comrades were men who never troubled themselves about vain and frivolous notions as they called them[;] with them every country was pretty when there was weather and as to beauty of nature or arts it was all 'humbug.'"[8] In general, the lack of scientific and aesthetic appreciation of nature in their guides did not bother the naturalists, except for one bad habit that they all possessed—that of shooting animals indiscriminately for target practice.

The first naturalist to visit the Upper Missouri after the Lewis and Clark expedition was John Bradbury of London, a corresponding member of the Liverpool Philosophical Society and an honorary member of the literary and philosophical societies of New York. Bradbury traveled in the western interior of North America with fur trappers from 1809 to 1811 and published a diary account of his journeys in 1817. Initially Bradbury's moral sentiments about animals seem to be much like those of Bartram. He too is stricken with moral trauma when killing a mother bear.[9] Soon, however, Bradbury starts protesting repeatedly the unnecessary shooting of wild animals in general, and his diary begins to express moral indignation independent of any concern for the suffering of the individual animals.

Bradbury's disapproval of the fur trappers' behavior first appears in the following passage:

> Soon after we set out, we saw a great number of buffaloe on both sides of the river, over which several herds were swimming. Notwithstanding all the efforts made by these poor animals, the rapidity of the current brought numbers of them within a few yards of our boats, and three were killed. We might have obtained a great many more, but for once we did not kill *because* it was in our power to do so; but several were killed from Lisa's boat.[10]

Although this is the first mention of the subject in the account, it is clear that Bradbury had been upset about indiscriminate shooting for some time, judging by the use of the words "for once." Other passages of criticism follow: "Mr. Brackenridge joined me in preventing a volley being fired, as it would have been useless, and therefore wanton." And again: "The morning of the next day was very fine: we saw some buffaloe swimming, at which the men fired, contrary to our wishes, as we did not intend to stop for them." By the end of the journey, Bradbury has become so irritated that he is passing judgment over every shot fired by his guides.[11] Bradbury is clearly opposed to the killing of any wild animals on his trip unless the body can be recovered and used. To him, killing animals under any other circumstances is useless or *wanton*—done simply "*because* it was in our power to do so."

One might intuitively expect after Bradbury's trip to find a series of other naturalists lamenting the wanton destruction of wildlife with a gradual but growing awareness that something ought to be done to protect wildlife; in fact, however, the very next scientific expedition into the West formally proposed such protection in its official government report. Dr.

Edwin James of the Long expedition to the Rocky Mountains (1819–1820) urged in his part of the report that the entire area not be opened to settlement and that it be protected instead as a wildlife preserve. In the introduction to the report James writes: "The traveller who shall at any time have traversed its desolate sands, will, we think, join us in the wish that this region may forever remain the unmolested haunt of the native hunter, the bison, and the jackall." Later, in the main body of the report, he makes the proposal more specifically, in terms that reflect the attitudes of Bradbury:

> It would be highly desirable that some law for preservation of game might be extended to, and rigidly enforced in the country where the bison is still met with; that the wanton destruction of these valuable animals by white hunters might be checked.[12]

James' concern about the "country where the bison is still met with" comes at a point in history when only a handful of fur trappers had as yet gone west and when buffalo hides were of little value in the fur market in the East. Thus his conclusions could not have been based on concern about the actual numbers of buffalo being killed—as would be possible a few years later—and had to be based instead on a general displeasure at seeing the "wanton" destruction of individual animals.

Within ten years, it was possible for naturalists to make calculations about the enormous waste of wildlife through wanton destruction by white and Indian fur trappers. George Catlin, an artist studying Indians on the Upper Missouri during the early 1830s who had some interest in wildlife study (and protection), was one of the first to do so. Catlin is known today as the first American to call for a "*Nation's Park,* containing man and beast, in all the wild and freshness of their nature's beauty." Like Bradbury and James, Catlin too is concerned about the wanton destruction of wildlife, and his call for a national park—actually echoing James' earlier call—arises out of his desire to protect wildlife from fur trappers:

> This profligate waste of the lives of these noble and useful animals, when, from all that I could learn, not a skin or pound of the meat (except the tongue), was brought in, fully supports me in the seemingly extravagant predictions that I have made as to their extinction, which I am certain is near at hand.[13]

As other naturalists ventured into the American West, they too spoke out against the abuse of wildlife. In 1835, Prince Maximilian of Neu-Wied cited statistics similar to Catlin's and accused both the Indians and the fur trappers of endangering the buffalo. In 1839, John K. Townsend, traveling to Oregon, echoed the remarks of all the others, declaring the killing of wildlife by the fur trappers to be "a useless and unwarranted waste of the goods of Providence." As late as 1860, Captain Raynolds of the Raynolds expedition, the last to be guided by fur trappers, reported to Congress "that the wholesale destruction of the buffalo is a matter that should receive the attention of proper authorities" and predicted that "it is more than probable that another generation will witness almost the entire extinction of this noble animal."[14]

The lack of concern for the suffering of individual animals was conveyed in part by the silence of most naturalists about it. In some cases, however, naturalists blaringly omitted mention of it. George Catlin, for example, on one occasion wounded a buffalo and studied its suffering. In a long passage recounting the event, Catlin describes the immense aesthetic pleasure he experienced while admiring the death of the buffalo.[15] Without any feeling of guilt or twinge of conscience, he baits the bull so as to increase the sublimity of its expressions. He finally puts the animal out of its misery, not out of concern for its unnecessary suffering but simply because it is time to go. To Catlin, the death agony was not wanton, since it provided him with an opportunity for making valuable sketches.

Even when naturalists were moved emotionally by the killing of wildlife, the concern usually had nothing to do with the suffering of the individual animal. For example, when Townsend, overcome by his "evil genius and love of sport," committed an act of wanton destruction of his own, putting a ball through the side of a curious antelope following his party, he declared it an "unfeeling, heartless murder" for reasons completely different from those given by Bartram in the case of the bear with cubs.[16] As Townsend stresses, the killing of the antelope would have involved no cruelty if the animal had been needed for food. It was murder only because the act was wanton—that is, because it served no useful purpose. Presumably, had the travelers been in need of food, the antelope would have had no grounds for upbraiding Townsend and could have died satisfied that its death had not been in vain.

In 1872, at a time when the slaughter of the buffalo was at last at its height and the continued existence of the species was finally seriously endangered, Congress passed a bill to establish Yellowstone National Park. Although the purpose of the park was not to protect wildlife, the bill contained a passage directing the Secretary of the Interior to "provide against the wanton destruction of the fish and game for the purpose of merchandise and profit." As the discussion in the *Congressional Globe* indicates, there was strong sentiment in the Senate that the wording was not strong enough, and one Senator offered an amendment that the words "for merchandise or profit" be deleted, thereby prohibiting any killing of wildlife in the park for any purpose. The amendment was withdrawn, but only after the Senator proposing the amendment was reassured that the park was not intended as a "preserve for sporting" and that the powers given to the secretary of the interior would allow him to protect against this possibility as well as Congress could. Killing of animals was to be permitted only for the subsistence of parties traveling through the park.[17]

The inclusion of this passage in the Yellowstone park bill is not considered a legal milestone in the protection of wildlife because it provided no penalties for wanton destruction other than being escorted out of the park.[18] Whatever its legal failings, however, it signifies the existence of widespread public attitudes in favor of the preservation of wildlife in a fairly modern sense. Moreover, the phrase "wanton destruction" leaves no doubt that the introduction of the passage was intended as a partial response to the concerns about wildlife expressed by naturalists over the previous half-century. The naturalists cited in this section were appalled at what they considered the wanton slaughter of wildlife, particularly the buffalo. When they returned to civilization, all of them published reports of their adventures, just as naturalists do today, and these accounts spoke out against the useless slaughter of wildlife. Through these books, the complaints of the naturalists became the basis for a change in public attitude.

RECONSTRUCTING THE NINETEENTH-CENTURY VIEW

While it is clear that a favorable public attitude toward the preservation of wildlife had formed early in the second half of the nineteenth century and that this attitude is traceable directly to the expressed attitudes of naturalists earlier in the century, the justification of this new public attitude was not at all clear, for in the writings of these naturalists and in the legislation, no justification was given. The situation is comparable to the one faced by philosophers like Passmore and Singer with the other animal protection tradition: A change in attitude took place, but its significance remains a matter of interpretation. Possible foundations for the new attitude include the rights theories of the humane moralists, the ethical humanists, and even the land ethicists; the theory of evolution; and the science of ecology. In this section I show that none of these can account for the early nineteenth-century attitude toward wildlife, and I discuss three other possibilities: a scientific-aesthetic tradition in natural history, the theory of geological uniformitarianism, and the new system of biological and botanical classification developed by Linnaeus in the eighteenth century.

That the naturalist tradition is independent of the rights traditions cited by Passmore and Singer is obvious from the fact that the naturalists are never consistently concerned about the pain and suffering of animals, only about unnecessary (or wanton) killing of animals. If there was a good reason for a particular animal to be killed, the naturalists were indifferent, if not insensitive, to its suffering.

Even in contemporary form, the situation remains the same. For instance, Leopold's reservations about hunting emerged not from a belief that it was wrong to inflict unnecessary suffering on wildlife or that hunting in itself was in any way wrong but rather from a belief that predators killed prey animals more efficiently and kept them under better control ecologically than hunters did.[19] According to contemporary naturalists, people who worry about the pain and suffering of wildlife are victims of what has sometimes been called the "Bambi syndrome." Concern about pain and suffering, in fact, seems to become an issue among naturalists only when they wish to defend predators that kill their victims inefficiently.[20] In many cases, contemporary naturalists and the general public today take immense pleasure in the deaths of prey by predators—finding, for example, the film depiction of these kills a fascinating and aesthetically pleasing presentation appropriate for family viewing any evening on the television sets in their homes.

The naturalist tradition also does not support the claims of some contemporary biologists, such as Norman Myers, David Ehrenfeld, and Paul and Anne Ehrlich (or even Leopold), that animals have a right to exist.[21] As has been noted by a number of ethicists, rights theory focuses on individuals and their interests.[22] In contrast, nineteenth-century and contemporary concern for wildlife among naturalists is centered on the preservation of species and ecosystems, not the interests of the individual animals that make up those species and ecosystems.

In Chapter 3 I argued that nineteenth-century natural history scientists acquired preservationist attitudes toward nature on aesthetic grounds because of their close association with landscape artists and poets. Briefly, my argument was as follows: In landscape painting and poetry, the general desire that things of beauty be preserved was extended to include objects of beauty in nature, either actually represented in paintings and poetry or capable of being so represented. Natural history scientists—who were in fact studying the properties of nature of special interest to the painters, poets, and landscape gardeners of the time; secondary properties of rationalistic philosophy—developed a common aesthetic attitude toward nature with painters and poets as a result of the artistic training they routinely undertook in order to be able to illustrate their fieldwork. Among scientists with such artistic training, the desire to preserve objects of beauty in nature was extended to include objects of scientific interest.

Although this position is correct as the general framework within which modern preservationist attitudes arose in the nineteenth century, it cannot explain an important feature of the naturalists' attitude toward wildlife—the concern for preservation of the species without equal concern for the preservation of the lives of the individual animals making up those species. In actuality, my account helps to explain a growing concern for the preservation of material objects of unusual beauty or scientific interest, such as Yosemite and Yellowstone, but does not do justice to the more complex (and peculiar) concern for animals and plants.

It is important to note that concern for the preservation of wildlife did not arise among all natural history scientists, only among those specifically studying living organisms. Although nineteenth-century geologists certainly did develop strong preservationist attitudes, they did not necessarily follow the naturalists in their aversion to the wanton destruction of wildlife. William H. Holmes, for example, both a geologist and an artist who was deeply involved in the exploration and preservation of Yellowstone and the Grand Canyon, despite showing great sensitivity to the wonders of Yellowstone in his field notebooks, is completely casual in his attitude toward the animals living there. As his notes make clear, Holmes automatically attempted to kill any animal that came within range of his rifle. In one passage, written while working in Yellowstone, Holmes writes:

> Aiming at him near as possible at his heart I fired, but the animal turned and disappeared. Following up in the same direction with caution, hoping for still another shot I heard a thumping in the pine bushes and hurrying on was delighted to find the magnificent creature in his death throes.

Preservationist-oriented though he was, Holmes' tendencies toward wanton destruction of wildlife far exceeded those of the fur trappers, whom the naturalists had come to despise. Holmes took positive delight in the deaths of animals, especially bears and, judging by his personal papers, did not improve his attitudes until the 1920s, fifty years later.[23]

One way to account for the enormous difference between geologists and naturalists with regard to animal protection is to conclude that natural history scientists were primarily concerned with preserving the objects of their particular studies—rocks or animals, respectively—but did not generalize this concern beyond their own narrow professional interests. Geologists, not being professionally interested in animals except as decoration along with vegetation on their beloved rocks, failed to become sensitive to the wanton destruction that naturalists saw all around them and sometimes remained insensitive enough to continue as active contributors to that destruction when opportunities arose.

While this explanation has much to commend it, it is possible that theoretical differences in scientific outlook may have had some influence as well. The scientific world view of the natural history scientist in the early nineteenth century, however, does not appear on the surface at least to offer any basis for preservationist attitudes, since the theory of evolution and the science of ecology, both of which are considered central to modern preservationist thought, had not yet appeared on the scene. The places where naturalists studied animals were not ecological units. They were merely, as James put it, "the country where the bison is still met with" or "the unmolested haunt of the native hunter, the bison, and the jackall." The animals that the naturalists studied were simply natural objects that happened contingently to be where they were (probably because that is where God wanted them) and were not elements in a greater natural whole. The animals themselves, moreover, were representatives of species that were fixed and immutable. Thus, with ecology and evolution still largely unthought and unaccepted, there were really only two innovations in natural history science that could possibly have any relevance to preservationist attitudes: uniformitarianism in geology and the standardization of biological classification, following Linnaeus, among naturalists. Unlikely as these may seem as bases for preservationist arguments, the first is, I contend, the initial scientific foundation for all preservationist thinking, and the second accounts for the special features of early wildlife protection attitudes, distinguishing them from the mainstream trends.

Uniformitarianism was a geological theory, first advanced by Hutton at the end of the eighteenth century, that geological changes in the Earth's surface take place slowly: The present is like the past. It is in opposition to an earlier theory, which it eventually replaced, called catastrophism, according to which geological changes take place suddenly and cataclysmically: The present is radically different from the past. Early modern work in geology in the seventeenth century, to the extent that it was not focused on locating mineral deposits, was a quest to find geological evidence to substantiate the biblical account of the creation of the Earth. This research naturally came to be centered on attempts to verify the flood of Noah, a major catastrophic event. Evidence, however, soon suggested not just one catastrophic event but many. Recognition of the fossil remains of extinct species in rock layers, moreover, provided a role for these events—bringing past ages to an end through divine intervention. It was concluded, therefore, that God exterminated all life periodically and unexpectedly and then replaced it with improved versions of the previous animal forms—for how else could the great changes in animal life be explained?

Stephen Jay Gould has pointed out that uniformitarianism transformed geology from a branch of theology into a branch of science.[24] The transformation, however, was not without controversy and debate. As Charles Coulston Gillispie has shown, opposition to uniformitarianism—in support of catastrophism and foreshadowing future controversies over evolution—was focused on the relationship of God, man, and nature:

> In the nineteenth century, unlike the eighteenth century, orthodox natural theology was more interested in control than design. It was chiefly on this account that Huttonian and uniformitarian theories were suspect. And on the popularizing level, Combe and Chambers were attacked, not because they impugned the divine character of the physical universe, which, in fact, they were attempting to illustrate, but because they held that God's Providence, in the social and moral as well as in the organic and inorganic spheres, was a system of unvarying law, and that God never interfered in its workings.[25]

What uniformitarianism did religiously or theologically was to undermine the idea that God personally and consciously supervised and carried out the catastrophes that geologists had been studying. The history of early modern philosophy both illustrates and supports this role of God. Beginning with Descartes, we find an account of physical and mental existence that claims that God supervises the interaction of incompatible kinds of matter, making our hands (physical substance) obey our mental commands (mental substance). Indeed, Descartes even declares that God sustains everything from one individual moment to the next. Seemingly, if He became distracted for any one of those moments, we and everything else would completely, if only momentarily, disappear. This kind of intimacy with God is retained in catastrophism but rejected in uniformitarianism, in which mindless physical processes are blindly transforming the Earth.

Because an all-powerful and benevolent divine being is the primary geological agent in theological catastrophism, preservationist attitudes could not develop in connection with a scientific world view associated with it. Given the immense amount of scientific evidence that God periodically destroyed the Earth without advance notice, to have tried to save parts of the Earth for all time would have been presumptuous to say the least, since God might have decided at any moment to destroy everything, including all human life. Thus preserving the Earth was God's responsibility alone, carried out in accordance with His own plan. Human efforts to intervene were not only inappropriate but pointless.[26]

In terms of uniformitarian geology, however, the situation is very different. God is not involved at all. The Earth has slowly taken its current shape as a result of the slow working of uniform physical and chemical processes over incredible spans of time, which were then only barely beginning to be grasped. In this case, humans could change the world dramatically for the worse, and the Earth could not be expected to recover naturally in less time than it took for the damaged or destroyed objects to form to begin with, if at all. Thus, although theoretically those physical and chemical processes could reproduce what humans had destroyed, the time was so great that for all practical purposes the natural objects destroyed or damaged were irreplaceable. In this context, nature preservation now makes sense, since human action is significant, and responsible human action can prolong the existence of objects that are aesthetically or scientifically interesting or are needed to maintain human life on the Earth.

Although these connections were made by the middle of the nineteenth century, I do not believe that they had any direct effect on the preservation of wildlife at that time. From our standpoint in the twentieth century, arguments for the preservation of species could be made that are derived from the uniformitarian world view, but they would be in terms of the theory of evolution, which is the biological element of uniformitarianism. In terms of the theory of evolution, one could point out the length of time that was required to create this or that species and the extreme unlikelihood that this or that species could ever come into being again should we humans destroy it. Naturalists from the early nineteenth century, however, could not draw these conclusions for several reasons. First, they had probably never heard of evolution. Second, if they had heard of it, they had probably heard of it as a ridiculous consequence of uniformitarianism, which was supposed to reduce that geological theory to absurdity. Third, they undoubtedly all believed that the species were fixed and immutable.

Thus for lack of any substantive alternative, we are left with only one possibility: Naturalists were actually concerned with preserving the fixed and immutable species of preevolutionary biology. Though this may sound strange at first, it is not, for the species were fixed and immutable only in the sense that members of species could not acquire new properties. The immutability of the species, however, did not in any way guarantee that individual exemplifications of these species would continue to exist on Earth. In the late eighteenth and early nineteenth centuries, there was a growing awareness of the fact that species extinction could and did occur. American naturalists by that time had found dinosaur and mammoth fossil remains that confirmed that some very strange and large animals, which had once roamed the face of North America, had become extinct.[27] They also knew that large numbers of extinctions had occurred in Europe in recent historical times. It is in this context that the naturalists discussed earlier were voicing their objections to the wanton destruction of the buffalo: They do not want species to become extinct.

Today it is possible to express our concern for species protection in a way that is analogous to the concern for large natural objects. Just as natural objects like the Yosemite valley are gradually changing in accordance with the principles of uniformitarian geology, species are gradually changing in accordance with the principles of evolution. As a result, strictly speaking, we are not trying to preserve natural *things* so much as natural *processes.* In terms of fixed and immutable species, however, perhaps the best analogy is the periodic chart of chemistry. In the late nineteenth century, chemists found that chemical elements could be organized into a chart and that the chart could be so arranged that elements with similar properties were repeated throughout the chart in a regular or "periodic" manner. The naturalists were constructing a chart for species along similar lines. This chart was essentially the great chain of being, already obvious in the biological conceptions of Aristotle and used as the background structure for the worldwide species classification project that had been under way since Linnaeus standardized species classification methods in the early eighteenth century. In terms of the belief that species were fixed and immutable, the great chain of being was the periodic chart of elements for plants and animals. Most naturalists in the eighteenth century believed that God had created all possible creatures and that if they looked long and carefully enough, they would eventually find all of these animals and plants somewhere on the Earth's surface. Like the chemist, the naturalist could look forward to the day when all elements in his chart would be identified and studied. The realization that extinctions had occurred and would likely continue to occur, however, changed everything. The great chain of being was no longer a perfect listing of God's creation, for it was full of holes left by species that had ceased to exist on Earth. Moreover, the number of holes was likely to increase, perhaps even before the endangered species could be identified and adequately studied. It was the equivalent in chemistry of a discovery that, as some ancient Greek philosophers had suspected, matter did pop into and out of existence. In this context, the naturalists discovered that they were studying an idea, concept, or classificatory scheme exemplified in the natural world by individual entities that themselves were not very durable. If these individual entities all died, the object of their scientific research became nothing more than the object of memory and imagination. Species classifications became the equivalent of Platonic forms that were no longer formal causes and in which nothing in this world participated.

Seen in this way, the response of the early naturalists calling for wildlife protection was reasonable, even conservative. They understood that the creatures exemplifying the species they were studying also had instrumental value, sometimes even economic value. They therefore did not try to prevent all use of the individual animals, but rather tried to reduce wanton or useless destruction of them. Only in cases where *any* use of these creatures would clearly threaten the species with extinction did they try to prohibit all use. Consider the sequoias, for example. When word of their discovery first arrived and reports of wanton destruction soon followed, preservationist outcries began. When more trees at other locations were found, suggesting that the trees might not be rare at all, preservationist efforts stalled. When final appraisal confirmed that the trees were indeed reasonably rare, preservationist efforts were renewed, culminating in the inclusion of the Mariposa Grove in Yosemite.[28] In the case of the buffalo, rarity was not a factor, but the wanton destruction of the animals was so great that the naturalists became concerned anyway.

Curiously, unlike its geological counterpart, catastrophism, which provides no foundation for nature preservation, the biological concept of the great chain of being composed of fixed and immutable species—dependent, nevertheless, on the maintenance of exemplifications of each species on Earth—actually provides a better, stronger foundation for species preservation than our current concepts of evolution and ecology. In terms of the preevolutionary conception of species, extinction means a permanent gap in the great chain of being. Short of direct intervention by God, there is no way to reinstate individual exemplifications on the planet. In addition, extinction is the destruction by humans of God's work, going all the way back to the beginning of all creation. Thus extinction could be construed as a moral wrong against God. In terms of our evolutionary conception of species, however, there is no chain of being as such, only groups of individual entities, loosely classifiable under species designations, coming and going through time. Species are no longer Platonic, since the properties of a species are changing, evolving. Species may, for example, become extinct not only through evolutionary failure but also through evolutionary success as individual species evolve into new forms. In this conception of species, extinction is normal and natural. Since they are not the direct creations of God, we have not wronged Him if we extinguish all individuals of a species now and then. Moreover, in accordance with the evolutionary conception of species, unlike the preevolutionary one, there is the remote possibility that evolutionary processes could at some distant date reproduce a lost species or at least an adequate substitute.

With the introduction of ecology into the argument, the situation is no better. The loss of a species in an ecosystem is also natural and normal. When a species becomes extinct, the system simply adjusts. Some other creature comes forward and fills the ecological niche left vacant. Thus like evolutionary theory, ecological theory weakens the preservationist case. Since extinctions are natural, they are in principle morally neutral events. Claims that current rates of extinction are unnatural and therefore immoral are also unconvincing, since massive extinctions over short periods of geological time have occurred many times in the past.

In actual practice, however, the move from a fixed to an ecological and evolutionary conception of species has had no such weakening influence on our wildlife protection attitudes. There are apparently two reasons for this: First, a Platonic conception of the species/individual relation continues to dominate our aesthetic appreciation of wildlife. Second, the new theories did not require any reassessment of value in wildlife preservation.

THE AESTHETICS OF WILDLIFE PRESERVATION

Nature aesthetics evolved directly out of art aesthetics. As noted in Chapter 3, two main lines of development were landscape painting and landscape gardening. The parallel developments in these areas may be characterized as follows: In painting, there was a movement from the appreciation of composed paintings representing imaginary places to an appreciation of paintings accurately representing real places and finally to an appreciation of natural landscapes resembling picturesque paintings.[29] In gardening, there was a movement from improved, composed gardens to ones closely resembling natural landscapes and from plants viewed as building material to entities worthy of study and appreciation in a natural, unimproved state. In both cases, the movement was from the ideal to the actual or real, from the general or universal to the particular or individual, and from the artificial to the natural in such a way that aesthetic appreciation became focused on natural objects and living organisms as objects of interest for their own sake.

To a degree, these aesthetic developments also involved wildlife, since wild animals and plants often found their way into landscape paintings, and wild foreign plants routinely found their way into informal and botanical gardens. As noted earlier, naturalists, as part of their professional training, took art lessons, which provided them with the same general aesthetic perceptions of the artists with whom they trained. Moreover, the properties that they used to classify and identify animals and plants were the same secondary properties that were of special interest to artists and poets: colors, textures, shapes, smells, and the like. Nevertheless, there was no comparable movement aesthetically from the ideal to the real and particular, for the species classification system was composed of ideals in a very straightforward Platonic sense—they were *life* forms, to be sure, but *forms* nonetheless.

To illustrate this point, we do not need to reconstruct the wildlife perceptions of the early naturalists, for the contemporary perceptions of a tourist visiting a natural area or even a zoo are quite sufficient. A person who sees a wild animal for the first time will try to discern the properties that are characteristic of the species the animal represents. Because of the great diversity of appearance among animals of each species, the first sighting of a new animal may be misleading. Only after having seen many specimens will the tourist have an adequately generalized conception of what a member of that particular species should look like. The tourist may decide, upon reflection, that the first animal sighted was a good example, an outstanding one, or a poor one. This is an aesthetic judgment made in terms of a generalized, even idealized listing of essential properties for the species in question.

Phenomenologically, this activity is in most respects identical to the account that Locke, for example, gives concerning the creation of abstract ideas. Indeed, that is exactly what the tourist is doing—finding the properties in individual animals which are essential and putting them together as an idea by which animals encountered in the future can be identified and aesthetically evaluated (a good representative, a poor one, and so on). Once the "abstraction" is complete, the tourist's conception of the species is functionally a Platonic form. Any aesthetic judgment concerning a particular animal involves three elements: the perceiver, the object perceived, and the perceiver's conception of the particular species, the form. The animal is treated aesthetically as if it is supposed to "participate" in the perceiver's conception of the species. Individual differences or irregularities are considered "imperfections": The animal in question may be too large, too small, not quite the right color; there may be something unusual about part of its body, for example, peculiarly shaped ears or horns.

This kind of appreciation is very different from all other nature appreciation, which places great value on diversity and uniqueness. A tourist looking at mountains does not expect all mountains to look alike or judge their beauty in terms of a Platonic ideal for all mountains. The observer wants each mountain to be different, to be an individual, to offer something which he or she has not seen before. To be sure, it is eventually possible for the tourist to adopt a similar view with regard to wild animals with which he or she has become familiar so as to savor the unique qualities of each specimen encountered. In terms of the theory of evolution, for example, the observer may come to see each individual as an attempt in the natural history of the species at innovation and change. In terms of ecology, he or she may see each individual as an attempt to adapt to particular natural conditions. However, I submit, the Platonic idea continues in the background as the framework within which this diversity is appreciated in a way that it does not for natural objects such as mountains.

VALUE IN WILDLIFE PRESERVATION

The focus on the species, rather than the individual, in both nature appreciation and nature preservation creates interesting problems concerning the value of wildlife. Two kinds of value must be considered. The first is instrumental value. An entity is instrumentally valuable if its existence or use benefits another entity, usually a human being. The second is intrinsic value. An entity has intrinsic value if it is (1) valuable for its own sake or (2) valuable without regard to its use. These kinds of value may, moreover, be either anthropocentric or nonanthropocentric. An anthropocentric value is basically a human value. It is often customary to assume that all anthropocentric values are also instrumental, that is, valuable because they benefit human beings. It is nevertheless possible for values to be anthropocentric and intrinsic. An art object, for example, is appreciated and preserved in terms of human aesthetic values but is not regarded as being valuable instrumentally. Most environmental ethicists, however, have been critical of anthropocentric values of any kind and have attempted to develop some kind of nonanthropocentric value theory that can be used to establish environmental or ecological value independent of human judgment. It is within this framework—instrumental versus intrinsic and anthropocentric versus nonanthropocentric—that the value of wildlife must be sought.

In terms of preuniformitarian geology, in which natural objects are the work of God, nature appreciation, to the degree it existed, could be justified on completely traditional grounds. God could be viewed as an artist and natural objects, even species, as art objects in accordance with divine design. Such objects could be construed as having intrinsic value, since they were beautiful independent of human use, and as being nonanthropocentric, since the standards of beauty were obviously established by God at the time of creation. In terms of uniformitarian geology, nature appreciation could still be regarded as intrinsically valuable, but since appreciation was obviously an acquired taste that was developing with growing scientific interest in nature, it was also anthropocentric, dependent on the way that humans in Western civilization had (very recently) come to value natural objects.

There seem to be two possible ways to ground nature appreciation and nature preservation in nonanthropocentric value. First, in terms of a historical critique of the impact of the primary and secondary distinction of Descartes and Galileo on value theory, one may wish to propose a radical revision of the way in which we perceive the world so that we come to think of values existing in the world as facts do, not just in our heads as a secondary reaction to factual perception. Second, one may wish to ground value in nonhuman entities in terms of their interests and perceptions. In this way, we could conceivably come to speak of the instrumental value of objects to a creature such as a squirrel as well as the intrinsic value of various objects in terms of the squirrel's aesthetic experience. Neither of these approaches, however, can be grounded in a history of ideas connected with wildlife, for in reality they are contemporary criticism, indeed, rejection of the attitudes that form the basis of our wildlife intuitions.[30]

There is, furthermore, a great deal of confusion caused by the two conflicting meanings of *anthropocentric* used in environmental ethics. As already noted, the word is often used to mean "instrumental" and just as often to mean "human" or "conceived in terms of human consciousness." Nonanthropocentrists, on the one hand, thus frequently call for the recognition, or discovery, of nonanthropocentric value so that natural things will no longer be treated in a purely instrumental manner. Anthropocentrists, on the other hand, who do not wish to treat all natural things instrumentally and define the term in the second sense, respond that even if we attribute nonanthropocentric value to nonhuman animals and natural objects, the values will still be anthropocentric or "human," since they are still values created by human valuers.[31]

Bryan Norton has developed what he calls a weak anthropocentric position, which avoids the metaphysical issues involved in nonanthropocentrism, the search for value independent of the human mind, while also avoiding the perils of strong anthropocentrism, according to which all anthropocentric value is instrumental. In particular, Norton's discussion of societal ideals as the basis for environmental decision making leaves plenty of room for anthropocentric intrinsic value—human values cherished without regard to their instrumental value or use in terms of human interests.[32] This conception of intrinsic value provides the easiest and most straightforward foundation for nineteenth- and twentieth-century aesthetic interest in wildlife. Although it may eventually be possible to develop a nonanthropocentric conception of intrinsic value that conforms better to current twentieth-century intuitions, such a conception would probably still be in conflict with nineteenth-century intuitions, since aesthetic values at that time were generally thought of as matters of taste.

Viewed as a matter of taste, our aesthetic appreciation of art objects requires anthropocentric intrinsic value of some kind. There are three possibilities: (1) that the anthropocentric intrinsic value is in the object itself, (2) that it is in the aesthetic experience of the object, or (3) that it is in both the experience and the object itself. The third possibility seems to be the one that best fits our basic aesthetic intuitions and practice. Anthropocentrically, it seems to be correct to say that the value is in the object as long as we do not make a metaphysical claim that the value exists as a property of the object itself. Such an attribution of value to an object does not rule out the possibility that it may also possess intrinsic value nonanthropocentrically. It only means that humans aesthetically consider the object to be valuable without regard to its use or instrumental value. Whereas an object might be instrumentally valuable as a paperweight, an object intrinsically valued is valuable without regard to such use—that is, its intrinsic value is considered more important than and overrides its instrumental value. (For example, a tool of unusual beauty might be considered too beautiful or "good" to use.) It is also possible for humans to consider the aesthetic contemplation of an art object to be intrinsically valuable. There is nothing wrong with this position either unless it requires that we reject the first position—for example, that we conclude that the art object is merely instrumentally valuable as a trigger for the aesthetic experience. To attribute intrinsic value exclusively to the experience demeans the object of the experience by converting it into something that is merely instrumentally valuable. Likewise, it leads to the equally counterintuitive conclusion that the mind itself is merely instrumental to the creation of the intrinsically valuable experience.

The writings of most nature preservationists in the nineteenth century strongly imply that nature is intrinsically valuable aesthetically in this double sense. In the later part of the century, however, another kind of environmentalism, resource conservation, also developed, which tended to treat nature instrumentally. A forest, for example, in accordance with this view of nature, was primarily valuable as a source of wood for various human purposes, not simply as a place for wild animals to roam or for nature lovers to wander. By the turn of the century, many preservationists, following the conservationists, had come to see the aesthetic value of natural objects as an instrumental trigger for the aesthetic experiences of humans. Yosemite, in this value scheme, is not intrinsically valuable as such but rather is instrumentally valuable insofar as it aids in the creation of aesthetic experiences, position two above.

This conversion of natural objects into aesthetic instruments for the production of aesthetic experiences has created a dilemma for policymakers that would not have occurred had the intrinsic/instrumental distinction been retained for both objects and experiences of them. If the object, viewed instrumentally, is damaged by tourists trying to create aesthetic experiences in their minds by exposing themselves to the object, the object becomes expendable and is consumed by the efforts to create these mental states or feelings. For example, cave formations and prehistoric cave paintings can be damaged and destroyed by fungus that grows using the light required for tourist viewing. When such objects are protected by turning out the lights and discontinuing the tours, they are considered to be of intrinsic value. If the tours are continued until the objects are destroyed and the tours are no longer profitable, the value of the objects is instrumental only, as a trigger for intrinsically valuable aesthetic experiences in humans.

The misguided efforts to establish rights for natural objects in this century is a reaction against this conversion of intrinsic value into instrumental value. The best way to resolve the problem, however, is simply to reinstate the intrinsic/instrumental distinction. Such confusion does not occur with art, since art objects are routinely removed from public viewing whenever such viewing starts to damage them. They are not, as our practice demonstrates, simply instrumental triggers to aesthetic experience. If natural objects are once again treated like art objects, as intrinsically valuable entities, the dilemma of whether or not to consume natural beauty disappears. If the direct generation of intrinsically valuable aesthetic experiences threatens to destroy, damage, or consume the natural object, we take whatever steps are necessary to preserve the object, including limiting or terminating visitation. Usually these experiences can be generated indirectly through the contemplation of artistic or photographic reproductions or through the exercise of the imagination without external aid.

If the value is perceived (anthropocentrically or nonanthropocentrically) as being in the object, as in the case of mountains, one preserves the value by preserving the object. While it is true that natural objects are gradually changing in accordance with the principles of uniformitarianism, there is enough permanence or durability in the objects for long-term preservationist efforts (in human time scales) to make sense. This element of impermanence, moreover, is not unique to objects of natural beauty, for art objects are also subject to deterioration over time. If, however, the value of the nature object is in its *use*, as in the case of trees to be used for lumber and paper pulp, the idea of preserving the trees as individuals is inappropriate. Since in such cases the instrumental value takes precedence over whatever intrinsic value the object may have, the practice is to consume the object and, if possible, take steps to ensure that there will be more objects of the same kind to consume in the future on a regular basis.

When one tries to assess the value of wildlife within the context of nature preservation and conservation, difficulties immediately appear, for the protection of species seems to be a problem of nature preservation, while the protection of the animals making up those species is a conservation problem. Just as the mountains are gradually changing in accordance with the principles of uniformitarian geology, the various forms of life are evolving in accordance with the principles of evolution. In this context, long-term preservation efforts make sense, since specific actions can be taken with a high expectation of success. Provided that human beings cooperate, natural catastrophe is the only major threat. Individual wild animals, by contrast, do not endure long enough in terms of preservationist time scales for any efforts at this level to be of much consequence. Their lives are extremely hazardous: Under natural conditions, they may be killed or eaten at almost any time. The only way to be reasonably sure that any particular animals will have an opportunity to live out a full life span is to remove them from their natural habitat and place them in an artificial environment—such as a zoo or a park—where they are safe from predation and other hazards. Medical care, comparable to that provided for human beings, is also a must.

In terms of the intrinsic/instrumental distinction, there are also serious problems. Species, like mountains, seem to be valuable for their own sake, without regard (primarily) to their use. Unlike mountains, however, which do have some instrumental value, species have none at all. As a concept, a species does not really do anything for its member exemplifications, the environment, or human beings. Indeed, as a concept, it certainly does nothing to cause its exemplifications to be or to continue in existence in any Platonic sense. Yet when we look at individual animals from almost any standpoint, they have both intrinsic and instrumental value, and the instrumental value predominates over the intrinsic. This is the case not only from the standpoint of the hunter and the commercial trapper but also from the standpoint of the naturalist, the environmentalist, the ecologist, and the ordinary person seeking aesthetic experience in nature. In each case, there is something of value beyond the individual that it contributes to instrumentally—income, the ecosystem, the species. To think in terms of the intrinsic value of the animal, one must take the position of an animal liberationist of some kind and start worrying about the welfare, interests, and rights of the individual organism, which is contrary to our basic practice as it has evolved over the past several centuries. By common consent among most of those concerned about wildlife, this last position, the only one based on the intrinsic worth of the individual, is the abandonment of proper attitudes toward wildlife in favor of improper sentimentalism. Thus, although the preservation of the species as a life form conforms with the intrinsic value perspective of nature preservation, the preservation of the member animals of the species conforms best with the instrumentalist perspective of nature conservation.

Because the individual animal is valued primarily as a representation of something beyond and distinct from it, the species, we value it in much the same way that we value a reproduction of a painting. However, since we are still much more protective of prints than individual wild animals, perhaps the best analogy is a mass-produced toy, such as a *Star Wars* action figure. The child's interest in the figure is primarily as an exemplification of the design, just as our natural (or cultural) interest in the individual animal is as an exemplification of the species. The child is not interested in preserving the figure for all times, only in using it in various ways in acting out imaginary stories. This use is not necessarily in the best "interest" of the figure, for the child may do things with the figure that eventually cause its head or arm to fall off or completely destroy it—for example, dropping it from a great height, crushing it with a brick, or throwing it in a fire. Likewise, we are interested in using wildlife in ways that are not necessarily in the best interests of the individual animals—hunting them, letting them be eaten by other animals, or letting them starve to death so as to preserve the natural character of the landscape. If the factory stops making *Star Wars* figures or it becomes difficult to obtain them, the child may tend to be more careful during play. If animals belonging to a particular species become rare, more difficult to find or obtain, we may also tend to be more careful in the way we use these particular animals. The analogy seems to break down only in one respect: The animals produce their own replacements in most cases, whereas the figures are produced in a factory. Even this distinction, however, is not absolute, since various species of birds and fish are factory-farm raised and released into the wild to be caught or shot for sport.

ECOLOGY AND EVOLUTION RECONSIDERED

I noted at the beginning of this chapter that the history of ideas out of which an attitude develops may not necessarily have much to do with the justifications that eventually arise to explain it. This is certainly the case with wildlife protection attitudes, which are routinely justified in terms of ecology and evolution even though (1) they developed in terms of a pre-evolutionary and ecological conception of species as fixed and immutable and (2) were little affected by the new ecological and evolutionary perspectives that replaced that conception. Even today, in fact, the practical influence of the theory of evolution and the science of ecology on our behavior appears to be marginal at best. For example, if we look closely at our own intuitions, we will find, I believe, that we do care more strongly than evolution and ecology really allow. If a species faces extinction, even naturally, it is likely that there will be attempts to preserve the species in some way—for example, in zoos. Even if it is impractical to preserve a large enough population to maintain a healthy gene pool, there will be interest in preserving groups of individuals with an inadequate gene pool. Even if preservation efforts eliminate the natural behavior of the animals, considered by many to be properties of the species, the preservation of individuals lacking natural behavior will still be considered valuable by many people.

The conflict between these intuitions and the demands of the science of ecology or the theory of evolution is brought out rather dramatically in a paper by Callicott on the value of extraterrestrial life.

> Extraterrestrial life forms, assuming that they were not of Earthly origin and inoculated somehow on some foreign body, or *vice versa,* would not be our kin—that is, descendants of a common paleontological parent stock—nor would they be participants in Earth's economy of nature or biotic community. Hence, they would lie outside the scope of Leopold's land ethic.

While admitting that in terms of such reflections "the land ethic seems almost parochial in extent and even tribal in nature," Callicott is not especially disturbed, for this parochialism, "Earth chauvinism," "reveals at once its strength for Earth-oriented environmental ethics—which is of course the only variety of environmental ethics with any genuine practical interest or application." But, Callicott asks with some reluctance, what if we do want to attribute some moral significance or status to life forms beyond the ecosystems and evolutionary splendor of the Earth? To muddle through, Callicott recommends a life-principle or reverence-for-life ethics, following Goodpaster or Schweitzer and in terms of the weak anthropocentrism of Norton: "In other words, the life-principle/reverence-for-life ethics are serviceable as extraterrestrial environmental ethics, but, ironically, fail miserably as terrestrial environmental ethics."[33]

To find out just how we behave toward extraterrestrial life, if it exists, we will probably have to wait until we locate some. But certain human reactions seem likely, even predictable. The discovery of creatures not part of our evolutionary history or our ecosystems would be sensationally exciting, provided, of course, that the organism or organisms had some adequate level of internal complexity, some properties worthy of scientific and aesthetic interest. Assuming a rarity similar to that of sequoias or tube worms in volcanic vents on the floor of the ocean, endangerment of these creatures would certainly bring forth strong preservationist outcries. Contrary to Callicott's intuitions, I suspect that the organisms would be considered more valuable because they were not part of our system or our history than if they were. In this regard, the land ethic, if it could not embrace such creatures, would simply become irrelevant, truly parochial. If evolution and ecology could not support our desire to preserve such creatures, we would revert not to a life-principle or reverence-for-life ethic, but a reverence-for-life-*forms* ethic, the ethic of the naturalists of the early nineteenth century, who sought to preserve the species classification, not promote the interests, welfare, or continued existence of individual exemplifications. Eventually, of course, if we looked hard enough and attended properly to subtle observations, we would undoubtedly uncover evolutionary and ecological data on these creatures that would permit the creation of an extraterrestrial land ethic. Should such an ethic come to be formulated, however, it would be very unlikely to displace the older life form ethic, which remains the foundation of concern for species even today, despite the demise of the fixed species theory.

This thought experiment does not mean, of course, that Callicott's position is completely wrong. It is possible, as already noted in the case of animal liberation, for the theoretical justification of culturally evolved intuitions, beliefs, and behavior to be distinct from the history of ideas that produced those intuitions, beliefs, and practices. It is even possible for them to persist without any justification at all. Moreover, it is not necessary that there be just one reason, one justification, to ground these intuitions, beliefs, and practices. There could be several, none of which is sufficient on its own. Each justification could be useful only in limited or special contexts. It is even possible for this set of justifications to change dramatically over time. Thus it is remotely possible that we could someday ground our concern for species in terms of some sort of animal liberationist position, assuming that our intuitions, beliefs, and practices change appropriately, perhaps through the persuasion of the animal liberation movement. It is much more likely, however, that we may come to ground them in an ecological perspective exclusively. Nevertheless, even this possibility is reasonably remote, for concern for wildlife in terms of its value to ecosystems fails to account for all aspects of our basic contemporary behavior. Thus, as I see it, to adopt an exclusively ecological perspective would require almost as intense a campaign as the animal liberationists would have to undertake for their position. The limitations of a purely ecological justification are evident not only in speculations about our treatment of extraterrestrial life but also, as already noted, in our behavior toward wildlife that has lost its habitat—that is, its ecosystem. If wild animals were valuable only as parts of ecosystems, we would not spend so much time and money preserving them in zoological gardens and parks under artificial and seminatural conditions.

Curiously, the history of ideas that shaped our basic intuitions about wildlife protection has been a movement not through a series of incompatible foundations but rather through a series that has sustained a basic set of intuitions. Although the fixed species theory is incompatible with the evolutionary view of species and perhaps with their role in ecological systems, all three of these supported a common view of wildlife as instrumentally valuable entities serving as a means to some greater intrinsically valuable end—maintaining the great chain of being, continuing the natural evolution of species, or preserving the health and natural functioning of various ecosystems. Moving from the fixed species perspective to the evolutionary to the ecological, wildlife has been consistently regarded as something instrumentally valuable in a sense that is independent of the specific value of the individual animals living at any given moment. This instrumentalist approach to wildlife, moreover, has been remarkably compatible with non-environmental uses of wildlife. Since wild animals are entities that have instrumental status from the standpoints of both environmentalists and their opponents, wildlife preservation and conservation have been able to coexist with sport and subsistence hunting, even with trapping to a large degree. As long as there are enough of each kind to support the needs of the given ecosystems and the needs of trappers and hunters, on the one hand, and to preserve the life form classifications in such a way that many exemplifications are able to exhibit natural behavior and lead natural lives, on the other, serious problems do not arise. What we end up with is a layering of perspectives that all have a role in producing and justifying our basic ethical beliefs and behavior toward wild animals.

What ties all these perspectives together and reduces the conflict between them is the aesthetic element in both the concern for and the appreciation of wild animals. Aside from subsistence hunting and commercial trapping, human interest in wildlife is fundamentally aesthetic. Although, as I argue, wild animals are not straightforwardly regarded as aesthetic objects analogous to art objects, they are a key ingredient in various kinds of human experiences that are aesthetic in a broad sense. As I have already noted, aesthetic and scientific interests in nature overlap significantly. Scientists and nature lovers frequently have aesthetic experiences through the study of nature—and wildlife is a fundamental element in such study. Sport hunting, like other forms of outdoor recreation, likewise has its aesthetic component. These various perspectives provide additional dimensions, almost a kind of depth. From the standpoint of these perspectives, it is possible to admire wildlife in terms of their evolutionary history, as exemplifications of unique life forms, as worthy opponents and/or trophies, and as fundamental elements in healthy ecosystems—without having to choose between these viewpoints. Given that none of these perspectives allows for the intrinsic value of individual animals to outweigh their instrumental value to something else, thereby nearly closing the door on the animal liberationist, grounding our wildlife intuitions, beliefs, and practices in such (anthropocentric) aesthetic experience seems to be the best approach—one that takes into account not only those intuitions, beliefs, and practices as they are now understood by most people but also the history of ideas that produced them.

NOTES

1. J. Baird Callicott, "Animal Liberation: A Triangular Affair," *Environmental Ethics* 2 (1980): 319–321.

2. John Passmore, "The Treatment of Animals," *Journal of the History of Ideas* 36 (1975): 195–218; Peter Singer, *Animal Liberation: A New Ethics for Our Treatment of Animals* (New York: Avon Books, 1977), ch. 5.

3. Callicott, "Animal Liberation." p. 332.

4. Michael J. Bean, *The Evolution of National Wildlife Law* (Washington, D.C.: U.S. Government Printing Office, 1977), pp. 8–10.

5. For detailed accounts of the scientific exploration of the American West and its settlement, see William H. Goetzmann, *Exploration and Empire: The Explorer and the Scientist in the Winning of the American West* (New York: Knopf, 1966), and Richard A. Bartlett, *The New Country: A Social History of the American Frontier, 1776–1890* (London: Oxford University Press, 1974).

6. William Bartram, *Travels of William Bartram,* ed. Mark Van Doren (New York: Dover Publications, 1955), p. 22.

7. Goetzmann, *Exploration and Empire,* pp. 17–19.

8. Osborne Russell, *Journal of a Trapper,* ed. Aubrey L. Haines (Lincoln: University of Nebraska Press), p. 63.

9. John Bradbury, *Travels in the Interior of America* (Ann Arbor: University of Michigan Microfilms, 1966), p. 35.

10. Ibid., p. 108.

11. Ibid., pp. 182, 183, 198.

12. Edwin James, "James' Account of S. H. Long's Expedition, 1819–20," in *Early Western Travels, 1748–1864,* ed., Reuben G. Thwaites (Cleveland: Arthur H. Clark Co., 1904–1906), vol. 14, p. 20; vol. 15, pp. 256–257.

13. George Catlin, *Letters and Notes on the Manners, Customs, and Conditions of the North American Indians* (New York: Dover Publications), vol. 1, pp. 262, 256–257.

14. Prince Maximilian of Neu-Wied, *Travels in the Interior of North America,* in *Early Western Travels,* vol. 22, p. 379; John K. Townsend, "Narrative of a Journey across the Rocky Mountains to the Columbia River," in *Early Western Travels,* vol. 21, p. 170; William F. Raynolds, "Report on the Exploration of the Yellowstone and the Country Drained by That River," U.S. Congress, Senate, 40th Cong., 2nd Sess., *Senate Executive Document,* No. 77 (1868), p. 11.

15. Catlin, *Letters and Notes,* pp. 26–27.

16. Townsend, "Narrative," in *Early Western Travels,* vol. 21, p. 178.

17. U.S., *Statutes at Large,* vol. 17 (1871–1872), ch. 24, pp. 32–33; U.S. Congress, Senate, *Congressional Globe,* 42d Cong., 2d Sess., 1 (January 30, 1872), p. 697.

18. Penalties for hunting and poaching were not provided until 1894. See U.S., *Statutes at Large,* vol. 28 (1893–1894), ch. 72, p. 73. Congress did not act until a poaching incident in the park was publicized in an issue of *Forest and Stream* magazine. See Hiram Martin Chittenden, *The Yellowstone National Park,* ed. Richard A. Bartlett (Norman: University of Oklahoma Press, 1964), pp. 121–125; Aubrey L. Haines, *The Yellowstone Story* (Yellowstone, Wyo.: Yellowstone Library and Museum Association and Colorado Associated University Press, 1977), vol. 2, pp. 54–64.

19. This is the main point of Susan L. Flader's book, *Thinking like a Mountain: Aldo Leopold and the Evolution of an Ecological Attitude toward Deer, Wolves, and Forests* (Columbia: University of Missouri Press, 1974).

20. For example, in Africa, hyenas, wild dogs, and jackals eat their prey alive using a method called "rapid disembowelment" rather than the method of suffocation used by larger predators. Since the victim displays a great deal more pain behavior in the former than in the latter, these smaller predators frequently develop bad reputations. In their defense, Jane Goodall writes:

> We still hate to watch it and yet, though it seems longer at the time, the victim is usually dead within a couple of minutes and undoubtedly in such a severe state of shock that it cannot feel much pain. Indeed, lions, leopards and cheetahs, which have the reputation of being "clean killers," often take ten minutes or more to suffocate their

> victims, and who are we to judge which is the more painful way to die? And so we do not join the ranks of those who condemn hyenas and wild dogs as vicious brutes that should be ruthlessly exterminated, for they kill in order to eat and to live in the only way for which evolution has fitted them.

Hugo and Jane van Lawick–Goodall, *Innocent Killers* (New York: Ballantine Books, 1970), pp. 17–18.

21. Norman Myers, *The Sinking Ark* (Oxford: Pergamon Press, 1979), p. 46; David Ehrenfeld, *The Arrogance of Humanism* (New York: Oxford University Press, 1978), pp. 207–209; Paul and Anne Ehrlich, *Extinction* (New York: Random House, 1981), p. 48; Aldo Leopold, "The Land Ethic," in *A Sand County Almanac, and Sketches Here and There* (New York: Oxford University Press, 1949), p. 204. In *A Wealth of Wild Species: Storehouse for Human Welfare* (Boulder, Colo.: Westview Press, 1983), Myers, seeing the practical weaknesses of his rights position, retracted it, replacing it with radical instrumentalist argumentation stressing the value of wildlife to the production of toothpaste and other commercial household products.

22. See Richard A. Watson, "Self-consciousness and the Rights of Nonhuman Animals and Nature," *Environmental Ethics* 1 (1979): 99–129; Bryan G. Norton, "Environmental Ethics and Nonhuman Rights," *Environmental Ethics* 4 (1982): 17–36.

23. William H. Holmes, Random Records, Smithsonian Institution, vol. 3, "Survey of the Yellowstone, Part 2, 1878," random note 101, p. 19; "Survey of the Yellowstone Park in Two Parts, Part I, 1872," r.n. 28, p. 17, and r.n. 27, p. 16; vol. 2, sec. 3, "Episodes and Adventures: 1872–1930": "The Bear Story," r.n. 16–17, and "Bear Adventure in Yellowstone Park—1872," r.n. 34.

24. Stephen Jay Gould, "Is Uniformitarianism Necessary?" *American Journal of Science* 263 (1965): 223–228.

25. Charles Coulston Gillispie, *Genesis and Geology* (New York: Harper & Row, 1959), p. 226.

26. I came to realize the importance of catatastrophism as an inhibition to preservationist concern while studying the attitudes of Clarence King, the first head of the U.S. Geological Survey. Although King had an appropriate aesthetic and scientific interest in nature and was influential in promoting landscape painting and photography, his concern for the preservation of nature was lackluster. In the chapter on Yosemite in his book, *Mountaineering in the Sierra Nevada* (Lincoln: University of Nebraska Press, 1970), King has very little to say in praise of the decision to preserve the Yosemite valley: "By Act of Congress the Yosemite Valley had been segregated from the public domain, and given—'donated,' as they call it—to the State of California, to be held inalienable for all time as a public pleasure-ground" (p. 134). The reason for his lack of enthusiasm, it turns out, was his belief in catastrophism. King simply could not accept the idea that land could be held "inalienable for all time" by "Act of Congress." While working for the California Geological Survey, King wrote:

> I have read in revelations of the passing away of the earth and all the beauty and grandeur of it. I read too of a new Heaven and a new earth beautiful in type. Well, then, if this is transitory why study so hard into all the intricate mazes of facts, which will be swept away and known no more. I have looked for lessons. I have believed that God created all with design[,] that all was a lesson [and] that lessons were taught in nature which were not elsewhere.

(Clarence King Papers, Huntington Library, D23, "Journal of Trip in Northern Sierras, Grass Valley, Northern Survey," p. 26). Since King does not believe that scientific principles will continue to hold true beyond the next catastrophe, there is even less chance from his point of view of Yosemite's enduring inalienably "for all time" by act of Congress. Thus his comment in *Mountaineering* is properly read with sarcasm, not just with regard to the idea that the United States could "donate" the valley but that the nation could preserve it for all time.

27. See Loren Eisely, *Darwin's Century* (Garden City, N.Y.: Anchor Books/ Doubleday, 1961), pp. 5–10.

28. In August 1958, the American Association for the Advancement of Science met in Albany, New York, and took an official stand on the preservation of the "famous fir-trees of California, the *Abils donglassei.*" According to Chester Dewey, who spoke on behalf of the trees, "The attention of the Association is called to the fact that these trees are being exterminated as the settlement of the country advances. But twenty-five of them, we are informed, are now left standing in the States, and they are not to be found but in one place." The AAAS resolved that "this matter be referred to Professor Henry, of the Smithsonian Institution, with the request that he correspond, in behalf of this Association, with the authorities of California or at Washington, in relation to the preservation of these trees; or take such other course as may seem more effective." See *Proceedings of the American Association for the Advancement of Science,* Tenth Meeting (New York: Putnam, 1857), pt. 2, p. 239. Although there appears to be no record of the action Henry took, the resolution was well known in California only a few months later. J. E. Clayton, a mining engineer for John Frémont, immediately thereafter made known his discovery of three other groves of trees, promising to count the trees the next time he visited them. See *California Farmer,* 7 (November 1856): 1. The original letter, dated October 30, 1856, is preserved in the Huntington Library.

29. The connection with painted landscapes still remains. A scenic view, for example, is a point from which a tourist may view a collection of natural objects in a way that would most closely approximate the composition of a painting. The tourist at the scenic view will often pace back and forth so as to "get a better view"—that is, to compose the objects better.

30. As Birch and Cobb have noted, nonanthropocentric value in nonhumans actually calls for a position very similar to the one according to which animals have rights: "The intrinsic value of experience confers rights." See Charles Birch and John Cobb, Jr., *The Liberation of Life* (Cambridge: Cambridge University Press, 1981), p. 205. Matters are not much improved if we reject the view that the animals have rights but nevertheless conclude that they have interests that we *ought* to respect, for we still treat animals in a manner that is counterintuitive to our current practice. For example, see Robin Attfield, *The Ethics of Environmental Concern* (New York: Columbia University Press, 1983), pp. 150–151, 156–160, where he argues that "the class of things with moral standing does not extend beyond that of individuals with a good of their own. Thus when species count it is because of their individual members" (p. 156).

31. See J. Baird Callicott, "Non-anthropocentric Value Theory and Environmental Ethics," *American Philosophical Quarterly* 21 (1984): 299–309. Callicott writes (p. 299):

> An anthropocentric value theory (or axiology), by common consensus, confers intrinsic value on human beings and regards all other things, including other forms of life, as being only instrumentally valuable, i.e., valuable only to the extent that they are means or instruments which may serve human beings. A non-anthropocentric value theory (or axiology), on the other hand, would confer intrinsic value on some non-human beings.

32. Bryan G. Norton, "Environmental Ethics and Weak Anthropocentrism," *Environmental Ethics* 6 (1984): 131–148. Norton himself creates some confusion by

insisting that his weak anthropocentrism allows one to forego the search for intrinsic value altogether. This is potentially confusing, since, of course, Norton cannot reject anthropocentric (noninstrumental) intrinsic value, as conceived by a human valuer, without collapsing into the strong position, according to which all anthropocentric value is instrumental. For a similar approach involving standards of moral character, see Thomas E. Hill, Jr., "Ideals of Human Excellence and Preserving Natural Environments," *Environmental Ethics* 5 (1983): 211–224.

33. J. Baird Callicott, "Moral Considerability and Extraterrestrial Life," in *Beyond Spaceship Earth: Environmental Ethics and the Solar System,* ed. Eugene C. Hargrove (San Francisco: Sierra Club Books, 1986), pp. 246–253.

Part III
Philosophical and Ethical Implications

CHAPTER FIVE
THERAPEUTIC NIHILISM AND ENVIRONMENTAL MANAGEMENT

In 1965, Iain Douglas-Hamilton went to Lake Manyara in Tanzania to study the effect of elephants on *Acacia tortilis* woodland in a national park. The elephants were destroying the forest by stripping the bark off of the trees. These trees were important because they were used by lions to sleep in, and the lions were the most famous tourist attraction in the park. Douglas-Hamilton was supposed to determine a management solution to this problem. There were two main alternatives based on two contradictory interpretations of what was happening in the park. One group of managers argued that protection of Manyara's elephants had created an overpopulation problem, with the result that the elephants were destroying their environment. According to the other group, the destruction of the acacia thorn woodlands was not damage but rather habitat modification that occurred cyclically. As the trees were destroyed in one area, new woodlands developed elsewhere, allowing the cycle of destruction and new growth to continue indefinitely. If the first account of the elephant-tree relationship was correct, large numbers of elephants probably had to be culled (killed) to reduce the herd to save the ecological system and the trees for the lions. If the second was correct, the elephants' activities could be disregarded, and no action of any kind was required.[1]

Douglas-Hamilton found what he called a "unique" scientific solution: He recommended, first of all, that farmland be purchased to serve as a corridor to a nearby forest, so that the elephants could spread their damage among more trees over a larger area, thereby reducing the impact on the most endangered trees in the park. Second, since his research revealed that the lions really liked to climb only seventeen trees in the park, he advocated giving them special protection by wrapping their trunks with wire, thereby preventing the elephants from stripping the bark but still allowing lions easy access when they wanted to sleep in them. This solution was unique because it solved the problem in terms of both theories. If there was a population problem, it was taken care of by increasing the number of the trees available to the elephants. At the same time, by not interfering with the elephants, it still allowed the system to continue through its natural cycles. The only unnatural intrusion was the wire on the seventeen trees used by the lions.[2]

When Douglas-Hamilton proposed his solution, it was quickly accepted. As he put it:

> No one opposed this idea and indeed everybody at the seminar seemed relieved that there might be an alternative to decimating the Manyara elephants by shooting, and that the loss of the *Acacia tortilis* woodlands could be accepted with equanimity.[3]

The reason for the quick acceptance of this solution was partly because no one wanted to kill elephants and partly because it did not require a resolution of the conflict of the two opposing accounts of the situation, but primarily it was because everyone involved wanted a management approach in which the managers intervened in the ecology of the park as little as possible. This was an occupational preference more than a personal preference: Like most ecologists, environmentalists, and environmental managers, they preferred a management approach that advocated doing nothing whenever feasible.

This preference, and its implications for environmental management and environmental ethics, is the subject of this chapter. Although the preference was not popularly accepted at the time Douglas-Hamilton made his study in Manyara, a few years later it was elevated to the status of a law of ecology in Barry Commoner's book, *The Closing Circle.* According to Commoner, the third law of ecology is "Nature knows best." Stated baldly, this law means that "any major man-made change in a natural system is likely to be *detrimental* to that system." In terms of this law, doing nothing is better than doing something, because any action will most likely have bad consequences whether it succeeds in solving the initial problem or not.[4]

Since the promulgation of Commoner's law, this preference has gained broad public acceptance even among people who do not support environmental attitudes and ideology. Peter Singer, for example, who is very critical of environmentalists in his book *Animal Liberation,* nevertheless, accepts the approach as the best one for dealing with wildlife. As he puts it:

> Judging by our past record, any attempt to change ecological systems on a large scale is going to do far more harm than good. For this reason, if for no other, it is true to say that except in a very few and limited cases, we cannot and should not try to police nature.[5]

Although the general public's knowledge and approval of this managerial approach can probably be traced back to Commoner's book, the approach was already well known to environmental professionals and environmentalists not only at Lake Manyara but throughout North America and elsewhere around the world. It is, for example, implicit in many of Aldo Leopold's essays in *Sand County Almanac* and *Round River.* It is perhaps most explicit in the essay "Round River," where Leopold writes:

> The outstanding scientific discovery of the twentieth century is not television, or radio, but rather the complexity of the land organism. Only those who know the most about it can appreciate how little is known about it. The last word in ignorance is the man who says of an animal or plant: "What good is it?" If the land mechanism as a whole is good, then every part is good, whether we understand it or not. If the biota, in the course of aeons, has built something we like but do not understand, then who but a fool would discard seemingly useless parts? To keep every cog and wheel is the first precaution of intelligent tinkering.[6]

Picking up on the same theme in his more famous essay, "The Land Ethic," Leopold goes on to assert that although ordinary citizens believe that scientists know how nature works, "the scientist is equally sure that he does not. He knows that the biotic mechanism is so complex that its workings may never be fully understood."[7] Manipulations or alterations in ecological systems may, Leopold argues, often have unforeseen and devastating consequences. According to Leopold, the cutting of the cane fields of Kentucky might have adversely altered the course of the settlement of the United States, if the cane had been replaced not by bluegrass but by "some worthless sedge, shrub, or weed."[8]

In recent years, this let-it-be approach has come to be interpreted as the official policy of the National Park Service, in part because of the influence of a study of the park service's game management programs, conducted by a committee of ecologists, chaired by Starker Leopold, Aldo Leopold's son.[9] Although the Leopold report advocates active, rather than passive, management of national parks, the authors admit in the report itself that "in essence, we are calling for a set of ecological skills unknown in this country today."[10] In this context, the resource management policy evolved into "the application of ecological management techniques to neutralize the unnatural influences of man, thus permitting the natural environment to be maintained essentially by nature."[11] According to Alston Chase, the policy became official in 1978 when the following statement was added to the National Park Service's *Management Policies:* "The concept of perpetuation of a natural environment or ecosystem, as compared with the protection of individual features or species, is a distinguishing aspect."[12] In terms of this policy, for example, the elk herd in Yellowstone was to be kept under control not by culling as before but by allowing the herd to fall into ecological balance with the rest of the surrounding natural system.[13]

In part, the policy is a commonsense approach based on our limited scientific ability to understand and manipulate natural areas, but it is also something more. Most fundamentally, it represents a kind of scientific pessimism that is virtually the mirror image of the scientific and technological optimism that pervades the physical sciences and engineering. Whereas scientists and technologists generally assume that it is only a matter of time before this or that problem will be solved through additional research or technological innovation, many environmentalists and environmental managers have come to assume that scientific answers to most of their problems may never be found. The consequences of these two attitudes are strikingly different. In accordance with scientific and technological optimism, one forges ahead, confident that later discoveries and techniques will solve the problems created by current actions—later on, but before they become too bad. In accordance with environmental pessimism, however, one tries to do as little as possible, feeling that there will be large numbers of bad consequences from any active manipulation that either cannot be solved at all or will in practice be too costly to deal with adequately. Essentially, from this perspective, the cure is considered to be worse than the disease.

Alston Chase uses various terms and phrases to identify and describe this environmental management approach in his book, *Playing God in Yellowstone:* "natural regulation," "noninterference with wildlife," "ecosystems management," and "self-regulation." While these tags serve as adequate identification in scientific and management contexts, at least one other term is more appropriate in historical and philosophical contexts: *therapeutic nihilism,* a term frequently used by the Viennese medical community in the nineteenth century.

TRADITIONAL THERAPEUTIC NIHILISM

Nihilism was originally the name for an anarchical and revolutionary political movement in Russia in the early nineteenth century that held that existing social, political, and economic systems had to be destroyed before new institutions could be established. The term quickly spread throughout

Europe, but in doing so it lost its political meaning, finding a home instead in intellectual debates about atheism, moral skepticism, and the meaninglessness of life. In the twentieth century, it has also been connected with controversy about the limits and foundations of knowledge. *Webster's New World Dictionary* defines it as "the denial of the existence of any basis for knowledge or truth," "the general rejection of customary beliefs in morality, religion, etc.," and "the belief that there is no meaning or purpose in existence."[14]

Therapeutic nihilism is closely associated with the establishment of modern medical practice in the nineteenth century in Austria. William Johnston traces its origin back to a Dutch physician in the eighteenth century, Hermann Boerhave, who advocated the "slow accumulation of observations" aimed at discrediting "quack practices," and to Gerhard van Swieten, a student of Boerhave, who founded the Vienna Medical Faculty in 1745 and put Boerhave's teachings into practice as standard procedure. Followers of van Swieten, for example, "revived Hippocrates' doctrine of the healing power of nature in order to diminish the frequency of blood letting." One early name for this new approach was *passive therapy;* another was *expectant therapy*. Doctors who practiced this kind of therapy usually did little or nothing for their patients except wait for nature to cure them.[15]

This new approach was especially useful in helping doctors move beyond folk medicine into modern medical practice. In particular, it revealed the ineffectiveness of most traditional cures. In a wide range of cases, doctors were able to show that patients who were passively treated were as likely to recover as those subjected to most traditional remedies. This advance in medical knowledge, however, did have some unpleasant consequences. In its extreme form, as therapeutic nihilism, as Johnston notes, it "encouraged neglect of patients and indifference to human life."[16] Gradually the focus shifted from treatment to diagnosis, from prescribing remedies to analyzing illness, and with this shift came an increase in unnecessary human suffering. Since medicine given to patients to reduce their suffering also distorted symptoms that were important to the patients' diagnoses, doctors stopped prescribing medication to relieve pain. By 1850, cherry brandy was the only painkiller used in the General Hospital in Vienna.[17]

Lack of success in finding cures was generally taken as support for therapeutic nihilism: It encouraged doctors to believe that there really were no cures for most health problems and that it was useless to look for any. The most famous example of this self-fulfilling skepticism was the problem of childbed fever. In Vienna in the 1840s, it was very dangerous to have a baby delivered in the hospital, for the mortality rate was inversely proportional to the degree of professional care given. There were two divisions in the General Hospital, the First Maternity Division, administered by the doctors of the Medical Faculty, and the Second Maternity

Division, administered by midwives. In 1846, some 20 to 30 percent of the women admitted each month to the first division died of childbed fever, for a total of 451 women for the year. In contrast, the chance of dying from the disease was five times less for a woman if she received treatment from a midwife in the second division, and the lowest mortality rate was among women who had their babies on the street on the way to the hospital. The obvious conclusion reached by doctors and patients alike was that it was safest not to go to the hospital at all, a conclusion completely in keeping with the spirit of therapeutic nihilism.[18]

The influence of therapeutic nihilism on the treatment of childbed fever was so inhibitive that doctors paid no attention when Ignaz Semmelweis, the head of the first division, discovered that most of the deaths could be avoided if doctors disinfected their hands after dissecting cadavers and before examining their patients.[19] Incredibly, because he was considered to be devoting excessive attention to the problem, Semmelweis was actually demoted one year later and eventually forced to leave the hospital. His discovery, moreover, continued to be ignored by the medical community. Upon his departure, the death rates for childbed fever in the first division, which had been sharply reduced, returned to normal. Semmelweis' discovery was not universally recognized, and hospital practice appropriately altered, until fourteen years later, when his emotionally charged, but carefully documented book on the subject was published.[20]

Although Carl Hempel cites Semmelweis' research on childbed fever as a model for scientific inquiry,[21] his contemporaries, quite to the contrary, did not perceive his work as being scientific at all. In accordance with the dictates of therapeutic nihilism, a doctor was not supposed to treat a patient for an illness until the cause of the illness was properly identified. This Semmelweis was unable to do. The general medical wisdom at that time was that childbed fever was "an unknown epidemic influence of an atmospheric-cosmic-telluric nature," and Semmelweis' speculation that it was blood poisoning caused by "putrid animal matter" was not considered a theoretical improvement.[22] If Semmelweis could have identified hemolytic streptococcus as the cause of childbed fever, he probably would not have had much trouble convincing doctors to practice the hygienic procedures he recommended. He was not, however, in a position to do so, since the very existence of bacteria and viruses was in those days still unknown.

Although it is tempting to treat therapeutic nihilism as a misstep in the development of modern medicine, that would be a mistake, for therapeutic nihilism is in fact alive and well today both in medical research and medical practice. A computer search of medical journals, for example, would reveal frequent use of the term in research papers on almost every aspect of medicine (a preliminary search I made of *Excerpta Medica* turned up twenty-nine citations).[23] In theory, doctors today, if confronted with an unknown disease, would, in accordance with therapeutic nihilism, study the disease and as much as possible avoid medication that might distort symptoms.[24]

All in all, therapeutic nihilism deserves neither wholehearted praise nor denunciation. There are both pluses and minuses to be considered. It cannot be denied that the practice of therapeutic nihilism has been beneficial in the past and will continue to be so in the future. The benefits, however, are usually long-term—to future patients, not to current ones. The first victims of a newly identified disease are able to benefit only if doing nothing really does allow their recovery. When this is not the case, the patients serve simply as objects of scientific study, a step toward the theoretical understanding of a medical condition, not its cure. Moreover, they serve in a dehumanizing way when analysis takes precedence over treatment and to the degree that medication that might ease their suffering is withheld in order to avoid distorting symptoms and to aid in the collection of valuable medical information. To be sure, this approach is often the most efficient way in which to study a medical problem. It is not, however, always the most efficient way to find a cure or to treat terminally ill patients humanely, for, as Semmelweis clearly demonstrated with childbed fever, it is possible in some cases to find a cure without the theoretical understanding therapeutic nihilism calls for.

THERAPEUTIC NIHILISM AND MODERN SCIENCE

As the nineteenth century progressed, therapeutic nihilism began to have a significant intellectual impact outside medicine. Johnston notes its importance in the thought of Karl Kraus and Albert Ehrenstein in literature, Richard Wahle and Ludwig Wittgenstein in philosophy, Carl Menger and Ludwig von Mises in economics, and Otto Weininger in psychology. Even in politics, the stagnation caused by the long reign of Kaiser Franz Joseph I was eventually deemed preferable to any conceivable political change. Although Johnston argues that Freud's contribution to psychology was a rejection of therapeutic nihilism (favoring compassion for patients), his methods were similar enough that an English-language version of therapeutic nihilism, *therapeutic positivism,* was sometimes characterized as a kind of psychoanalysis. It is largely because therapeutic nihilism can be given a positivistic look, thereby transforming it into something that is compatible with early twentieth-century philosophy of science, that the position has some plausibility as a scientific approach to environmental management.[25]

Positivism is a philosophical position that originated in the early nineteenth century in the writings of Henri, Comte de Saint-Simon, and of Auguste Comte, according to which scientific knowledge is treated as the only legitimate kind of knowledge possible. This view was rigorously developed and defended as "logical positivism" in the early twentieth century by a group of philosophers of science in Vienna, collectively known as the Vienna Circle, and was spread to various English-speaking countries around the world in the 1930s when the members of the group left Austria just before World War II. Because the connotations of nihilism and positivism are so very different, the idea that therapeutic nihilism could surface in positivism may at first seem almost counterintuitive. However, the positivists differed dramatically from nihilists only in claiming that objective, scientifically verifiable knowledge was possible. When it came to subjects such as ethics and religion, the conclusions they reached were as negative and as skeptical as those of the nihilists, if not more so: Ethical, aesthetic, and religious statements were declared meaningless because they are not scientifically verifiable; ultimately they were treated as nothing more than nonsensical outpourings of emotion.[26]

Although the first logical positivists did not themselves officially embrace therapeutic nihilism, as Viennese they were undoubtedly familiar with the position, and their recommendations concerning the treatment of nonscientific issues—to ignore them—was a straightforward application of therapeutic nihilism in an academic and scientific, rather than a medical, context. They were, moreover, heavily influenced by the early writings of Ludwig Wittgenstein, another philosopher from Vienna, whose work, both early and late, shows the mark of therapeutic nihilism. Because Wittgenstein's work remained oriented toward therapeutic nihilism even after he rejected and broke free from logical positivism, his writings are one of the best applications of the general position in twentieth-century philosophy. While the later Wittgenstein and his students are most appropriately classified as ordinary language philosophers, they had the distinction of being labeled therapeutic positivists in a critical article in *Mind* in 1946.[27]

As the positivists interpreted Wittgenstein's writings, especially his early work, his basic position was an excellent model for their own scientific approach. According to this interpretation, the study of philosophy, ethics, aesthetics, and religion should be disregarded in favor of scientific research on the grounds that our inability to verify hypotheses scientifically in these nonscientific fields of inquiry makes such inquiry pointless activity that contributes nothing to our pursuit of knowledge and indeed frequently inhibits it by treating nonsense as if it is in some way meaningful.

On the surface, this interpretation is supported by most of Wittgenstein's writings throughout his philosophical career. The influence of therapeutic nihilism on Wittgenstein's philosophy is most obvious in his characterizations of philosophy and philosophical method in his book *Philosophical Investigations*. Here he openly declares that "the philosopher's treatment of a question is like the treatment of an illness."[28] The treatment as such is not really a cure but rather a demonstration that there is nothing to cure. One is supposed to study a philosophical problem until it becomes clear that the problem does not really exist: "The clarity that we are aiming at is indeed *complete* clarity. But this simply means that philosophical problems should *completely* disappear." The therapeutic result is an end to a kind of psychological torment brought on by the contemplation of philosophical puzzles: "The real discovery is one that makes me capable of stopping doing philosophy when I want to.—The one that gives philosophy peace, so that it is no longer tormented by questions which bring *itself* in question."[29]

For Wittgenstein, philosophical problems are intellectual confusions resulting from attempts to say what cannot be said in language, to thrust against and try to go beyond the limits of language. As he put it in his first book, *Tractatus Logico-Philosophicus,* what can be said is subject to scientific investigation and what cannot be said is mystical (nonscientific) and must be passed over in silence:

> We feel that even when *all possible* scientific questions have been answered, the problems of life remain completely untouched. Of course there are then no questions left, and this itself is the answer.
>
> The solution of the problem of life is seen in the vanishing of the problem.[30]

This approach to philosophy is nihilistic to the degree that it rejects the idea that it is possible to find solutions to philosophical problems; it is positivistic in that it accepts the view that scientific problems can be solved through rational and scientific inquiry.

The *Tractatus* was intended as a reductio ad absurdum proof that traditional philosophical inquiry is impossible. Knowing that not everyone would accept his proof, Wittgenstein offered an alternative method—"the correct method"—at the end of the *Tractatus* that would allow doubters to verify his conclusions independently. In accordance with this method, one is supposed to say

> nothing except what can be said—i.e. propositions of natural science—i.e. something that has nothing to do with philosophy—and then, whenever someone else wanted to say something metaphysical, to demonstrate to him that he had failed to give a meaning to certain signs in his propositions.[31]

This method is the one used by Wittgenstein in all of his later writings. Its purpose is to quiet the urge to go beyond the limits of language.

In the *Investigations,* Wittgenstein compares thrusting against the limits of language with banging one's head against a wall: "The results of philosophy are the uncovering of one or another piece of plain nonsense and of bumps that the understanding has got by running its head against the limits of language."[32] There are at least two sources for this remark. First, it is a paraphrase of an aphorism by Karl Kraus that recommends the inactivity of traditional therapeutic nihilism: "If I cannot get further, this is because I have banged my head against the wall of language. Then with my head bleeding, I withdraw."[33] Second, it is supported by Wittgenstein's own experiences as documented in a series of notebooks that he kept in preparation for the writing of the *Tractatus*. Here we find him actually thrusting against the limits of language trying to define ethical terms and eventually concluding that such definitions are impossible because they exceed the limits of language.[34] Because of such documentation in Wittgenstein's writings and lectures, it is easy to characterize him as a very straightforward traditional therapeutic nihilist. As it turns out, however, his actual position is much more complicated and includes elements that essentially turn therapeutic nihilism on its head.

One early indication that Wittgenstein's interpretation of his own writings is incompatible with the positivists' understanding of them is a letter written to Ludwig von Ficker about the *Tractatus* in which he states that the things that we cannot speak about are more important than the things that we can:

> My work consists of two parts: the one presented here plus all that I have *not* written. And it is precisely this second part that is the important one. My book draws limits to the sphere of the ethical from the inside as it were. . . . In short, . . . I have managed in my book to put everything firmly into place by being silent about it.[35]

Commenting on this passage, Paul Engelmann, a Viennese friend of Wittgenstein, distinguishes the positivistic interpretation of Wittgenstein's writings from his own views as follows:

> A whole generation of disciples was able to take Wittgenstein for a positivist because he has something of enormous importance in common with the positivists: he draws the line between what we can speak about and what we must be silent about just as they do. The difference is only that they have nothing to be silent about. Positivism holds—and this is its essence—that what we can speak about is all that matters in life. *Whereas Wittgenstein passionately believes that all that really matters in human life is precisely what, in his view, we must be silent about.* When he nevertheless takes immense pains to delimit the unimportant, it is not the coastline of that island which he is bent on surveying with such meticulous accuracy, but the boundary of the ocean.[36]

Seen in this way, the difference between Wittgenstein and his positivistic followers becomes a matter of value. While they hold that only scientifically verifiable statements are worthy of attention, Wittgenstein holds that they are less important than the unverifiable ones, which are frequently worth investigating whether or not any positive epistemic result is achieved.

Although Wittgenstein's initial experiences thrusting against the limits of language were in accordance with the traditional model for therapeutic nihilism—that is, he himself stopped trying to go beyond the limits of language—by the early 1930s at the latest, and probably much earlier, he concluded that there is a natural tendency in human beings to try to solve philosophical problems and that such activity is beneficial whether it is successful or not. He stresses this point, for example, at the end of his "Lecture on Ethics":

> This running against the walls of our cage is perfectly, absolutely hopeless. Ethics so far as it springs from the desire to say something about the ultimate meaning of life, the absolute good, the absolute valuable, can be no science. But it is a document of a tendency in the human mind which I personally cannot help respecting deeply and I would not for my life ridicule it.[37]

As this passage makes clear, the major change in Wittgenstein's attitude toward therapeutic nihilism between the early and late periods was his gradual realization that his method of dissolving philosophical problems had therapeutic value. In the *Tractatus,* as mentioned, after describing his alternative method, Wittgenstein goes on to suggest that the people who want philosophical answers will not find the method "satisfying." By the time he had returned to England to begin his second period of philosophical work, however, he had changed his mind completely. G. E. Moore, who attended Wittgenstein's lectures in the 1930s, records this change in his notes on those classes, specifically with regard to the alternative method of the *Tractatus,* which was then being put into action:

> He did not expressly try to tell us what the "new method" which had been found was. But he gave some hints as to its nature. He said . . . that we had to follow a certain instinct which leads us to ask certain questions, though we don't even know what these questions mean; that our asking them results from "a vague uneasiness," like that which leads children to ask "Why?"; and that this uneasiness can only be cured "either by showing that a particular question is not permitted, or by answering it."[38]

Wittgenstein's reevaluation and approval of the thrusts against the limits of language dramatically transformed his therapeutic positivism into something very different from the therapeutic nihilism upon which it was initially based. For medical therapeutic nihilists, it was a complete waste of a doctor's time to thrust against the limits of medical knowledge—to attempt to cure patients when the theoretical knowledge of a disease was still unknown. The therapy was supposed to come from doing nothing, letting nature take its course. In philosophy, likewise, it could be said that the logical positivists followed their Viennese medical counterparts in rejecting investigations that were not aimed at uncovering scientific knowledge in accordance with standard scientific methods. Wittgenstein, however, was not so much interested in uncovering scientific knowledge as in clearly defining the limits to scientific knowledge, and for him what lay outside those limits was more interesting than what was within. The therapy, moreover, came from trying to thrust against the limits of philosophical, religious, and ethical knowledge, whether one succeeded or failed, and despite the likely prospect that failure would be the final result.

This shift of emphasis from concern about the value of the product of the therapeutic activity to the value of the activity itself, regardless of its consequences, reveals an unexpected valuational flexibility in therapeutic nihilism that will haunt its application in environmental affairs.[39] Although a direct application of therapeutic nihilism, following the positivistic model, would discourage environmental manipulation on the grounds that the results are nearly always damaging, it is nevertheless possible, taking an approach analogous to Wittgenstein's approach in philosophy, to conclude that environmental manipulation is good for its own sake or in terms of various nonenvironmental consequences—for example, the expansion of the economy or the humanizing or civilizing of the world[40]—and argue that these goods override concern about environmental damage.

THE ORIGINS OF ENVIRONMENTAL THERAPEUTIC NIHILISM

Unlike Wittgenstein's therapeutic positivism, which arose directly out of medical therapeutic nihilism, environmental therapeutic nihilism seems to be historically independent of it. In particular, there is no evidence that those who have supported the position drew any inspiration from therapeutic nihilism of any kind or even knew what it was. Thus the first step in examining the environmental variant is to take a look at the reasons that environmentalists give for holding their version of the general position.

Since Barry Commoner's third law of ecology, "Nature knows best," is the official and most popular formulation of environmental therapeutic nihilism, one might suppose that it would be the starting point for any analysis of the position. In fact, however, Commoner provides very little support for the law: He tries to explain it, but he does not make any attempt to justify it; he does not even provide an anecdotal account of how he came to hold the view. Although he provides examples, they are not ecological examples.

The purpose of Commoner's explanation is to provide "a properly defined context" for his claim that "any major man-made change in a natural system is likely to be *detrimental* to that system." He proceeds by analogy with an example about a watch. He argues that random thrusts into the works of the watch are more likely to damage the watch than to make it work better because the watch is a finely tuned mechanism with a great deal of research and development behind it. From here he moves on to random changes in an organism induced by X-radiation. The living organism, he maintains, is also more likely to be damaged than benefited because of the biological research and development that it has acquired through evolution. Based on these two examples, Commoner goes on to suggest by analogy that random interference in the organization of natural systems will result in damage in the same way.[41]

There are a number of problems with Commoner's exposition. First, there are the analogies themselves. Since the rationalist world view of nature as a machine is often cited as one of the most fundamental causes of the environmental crisis in this century, it is odd that Commoner immediately turns to a mechanistic example to defend his ecological principle. Even his shift from a machine to an organism falls short, since ecosystems are usually treated as communities of organisms, not as superorganisms. These analogies, moreover, work only if the organization of an ecosystem really is as rigidly structured as that of a watch or an organism, and it is very doubtful that this is the case. Random changes in the watch and the organism are usually damaging because these entities are able to function well only within very limited mechanical or biological parameters. The organization of an ecosystem, by contrast, is obviously more loosely structured than a watch or an organism and does not have comparable functions and purposes built into it. Losing a species to extinction in an ecosystem, for example, is usually not anything like losing the mainspring in a watch or a vital organ in an animal. The ecosystem does not break down or die; it simply changes, taking on different "functions" and "purposes." Described in this way, it is hard to assess whether particular changes constitute damage. Usually, depending on various contexts and perspectives, such changes are damaging to some parts of the system but not to the whole.

In short, Commoner's examples fail to take into account the resilience of the ecological system, which, unlike a watch or an organism, can avoid destruction by changing its structure. In this respect, an ecosystem is more analogous to an economic system, for example, a market system, than to a machine. Virtually any change in such a system has innumerable good and bad consequences. A drop in the price of oil, for example, may devastate some parts of the system, such as oil-producing companies that have trouble continuing to provide oil at the reduced price, while dramatically improving other parts of the system, such as oil-using companies that do a booming business selling cheaper products. Even the near or complete destruction of a commercial or industrial activity does not necessarily have any long-term impact on the market system, since other related activities may produce a new surge of growth, in some cases bolstering the same activities that they very nearly destroyed. The appearance of new products such as television and videocassette players that initially hurt the motion picture industry has over the long term provided it with new commercial opportunities. Similarly, the loss of particular species in an ecosystem may have negligible impact if other species are waiting in the wings—as, for example, when coyotes replace wolves—and may even benefit some species that might otherwise have been lost—for example, from wolf predation, but not from coyote predation. In this context, the claim that any change is likely to be detrimental is, on the one hand, a trivial truth, since in principle all change is likely to produce damage of some kind, and, on the other hand, a serious falsehood, if it fails to note that the same change is also just as likely to produce benefits.

Finally, there is the problem of Commoner's emphasis on randomness. While it is reasonable to assume that random pokes at a mechanism will damage the watch, it does not follow that skilled pokes by a watch repairman will have a similar effect. Likewise, although random doses of radiation are bad for an organism, carefully administered doses by a doctor for medical purposes often benefit the organism. Thus Commoner's analogies suggest only that any *random* man-made change in a natural system is likely to be detrimental, not that *any* man-made change most likely will be. To justify his law, or even to explain it adequately, Commoner needs to demonstrate that ecological adjustments to ecosystems, comparable to competent watch repair service or to good medical treatment, are impossible.

Traditional therapeutic nihilism is supported by a belief that there are definite limits to medical knowledge. Therapeutic positivism is supported likewise by a belief that traditional philosophical problems are puzzles that can never be solved. In neither case, however, is this belief based on a proof that the limits can never be overcome. Rather, a kind of pessimism is generated by the experience of many people who fail to go beyond those limits. As Johnston has noted, poor results in surgery and other fields of medicine in Vienna gave strong support to a general feeling that further research was futile.[42] In therapeutic positivism, Wittgenstein's failure in his attempts to define certain ethical terms, together with his studies of Kierkegaard and other philosophers, had a similar effect on him. Although Commoner provides us with no comparable accounts in ecology, personal or otherwise, it seems safe to assume that his ecological principle must be based on experiences of this kind, which, while not constituting a final proof, provide psychologically convincing evidence. Furthermore, given the widespread acceptance of environmental therapeutic nihilism, it is reasonable to assume that many other people have had such experiences as well.

Susan Flader skillfully documents one such case in her intellectual biography of Aldo Leopold, *Thinking like a Mountain.*[43] Much of Leopold's life was devoted to uncovering ecological management principles that would allow the manipulation of ecosystems for the benefit of human beings, most specifically for the benefit of those who wished to hunt deer. His early work in the U.S. Forest Service was directed toward finding ways to increase the uses of national forests by maximizing the size of deer herds in those forests for recreational hunting. Leopold's studies culminated in his book *Game Management,* in which he provided what he thought were the principles necessary to "substitute a new and objective equilibrium for any natural one which civilization might have destroyed."[44] Leopold argued that he had identified a series of factors that could be manipulated independently of one another to maintain ecosystem stability and to provide products like deer for recreational consumption. These factors are hunting, predation, starvation, disease parasites, accidents, food supply, water supply, coverts, and special factors.[45] Leopold believed at that time that these factors could be manipulated with great subtlety. For example, on one occasion, in order to avoid a doe season on the Gila, he suggested to Frank Pooler that "concentrating the predatory animal work on coyotes and letting the lions alone for awhile might be a better remedy."[46] According to Leopold, such manipulation represented the domination of nature by civilization. As he put it in his book, "Civilization is, in its essence, the will to interpret and govern [the fundamental behavior of all aggregations of living things]."[47]

Leopold's book was published the same year that he made the transition from game manager to teacher, accepting a newly created chair of game management at the University of Wisconsin. Within three years, he denounced the management techniques that he had so carefully developed and embraced instead environmental therapeutic nihilism. This major change in his view of game management was the result not so much of any particular scientific experimentation as of his reflections on the consequences, out in the field, of the kind of manipulation he had encouraged.

As Flader presents it, Leopold was primarily influenced by deer irruptions on the Kaibab plateau, north of the Grand Canyon, and especially in a game refuge called Black Canyon that Leopold had been instrumental in establishing.[48] The Black Canyon refuge was supposed to be a breeding ground for deer where they would be free of both predators and hunters. In theory, the overflow from the refuge was supposed to supply greatly increased numbers of deer for recreational hunting around the perimeter of the refuge. In practice, the deer, free from hunting and predation, increased as expected but remained in the refuge, destroying the carrying capacity of the land. In the end, the result was less deer rather than more, and a severely damaged ecosystem as far as deer farming was concerned. During the same period, a similar disaster occurred on the Kaibab plateau for the same reasons: The deer population increased from four thousand in 1904 to one hundred thousand in 1924, followed by massive depletion in the herd through starvation in the next few years and a drop in the carrying capacity below the 1904 level.[49]

Although Leopold was very much aware of the problems with deer in Black Canyon and on the Kaibab plateau when he was writing *Game Management,* he did not at that time view them as problems that his general management approach could not overcome. Indeed, he cited them "as illustrations of the effectiveness of management."[50] It was not until Leopold was busy with another excess deer problem, this time in Wisconsin, that he finally began to rethink his factor manipulation management approach. According to Flader, what finally changed Leopold's mind was a trip to Dauerwald in Germany in 1935, where a policy to maximize forest growth and deer populations had been in force for centuries, followed by a trip to Chihuahua in Mexico the following year, where no management policies had been undertaken and the land was in a reasonably natural condition.[51] In Dauerwald, Leopold saw that efforts to maximize both deer and forest were mutually contradictory, since maximized forest growth created conditions in which there was no undergrowth for the deer to eat: Food had to be grown on farms and brought in. In Chihuahua, in contrast, he found stable natural conditions in which deer, wolves, and forest were coexisting, seemingly in harmony, and without the deer irruptions that were now occurring with some regularity north of the border. These observations, Flader argues, convinced Leopold that active manipulation of the environment, with the goal of maximizing particular elements, could lead only to the artificial conditions he had found in Germany. To avoid this outcome, Leopold began reformulating his management approach to retain and rely on the ecological harmony he had found in Mexico—that is, he turned to natural regulation.

Although theoretically Leopold could have embraced natural regulation without radically changing his mind about his factor management approach, and perhaps thereby avoiding environmental therapeutic nihilism, this was not the case. Leopold had, in fact, already clearly rejected factor manipulation months before his trip to Mexico in a lecture given at Beloit College in 1936 called "Means and Ends in Wildlife Management." At the outset, Leopold takes back his earlier claim that game management—now wildlife management—can "substitute a new and objective equilibrium for any natural one that civilization might have destroyed." He writes:

> Agriculture has assumed that by the indefinite pyramiding of new "controls" an artificial plant-animal community can be substituted for the natural one. There are many omens that this assumption may be false. Pests and troubles in need of control seem to be piling up even faster than new science and new dollars for control work.

Because of these problems, Leopold continues, "Wildlife management . . . has already admitted its inability to replace natural equilibria with artificial ones, and its unwillingness to do so even if it could." According to Leopold, wildlife management is not only unable to synthesize wildlife environment but is not even able to "isolate variables in research." In turn, this "inability of isolating variables leads the game manager to place dependence on observation in the wild." While these observations can suggest "items which are susceptible [to] experimental verification," "the unnatural simplicity of his controlled tests forces [the wildlife manager] to be suspicious of even the most carefully verified results." Few such conclusions, Leopold adds, "stay put for a long period."[52]

Leopold's loss of confidence in the reductionist method as a foundation for ecological manipulation, together with his realization in Chihuahua that ecosystems, if left alone, can be expected to remain reasonably stable, except for some cyclic change, seem to be the primary sources of the environmental therapeutic nihilism that surfaces in "Round River" and "The Land Ethic." Leopold's path is similar to the one Wittgenstein took when he encountered seemingly insurmountable difficulties trying to define ethical and metaphysical terms. The failure of all attempts to solve particular ecological problems—for example, deer irruptions—provided Leopold with psychologically convincing evidence that such problems probably cannot be solved, a conclusion straightforwardly in the tradition of medical therapeutic nihilism. Thwarted in his efforts to maintain ecosystem stability through active manipulation, Leopold opted for passive therapy, placing his faith in self-regulation as the best basis for what he came to call land or ecosystemic health. Like his medical counterparts in Vienna, he decided to rely on the healing powers of nature, concluding that doing nothing is better than doing something, since the former permits self-healing while the latter produces random and unpredictable damage to the system as a whole.

This version of therapeutic nihilism, although most prominently aligned with the traditional medical position, not only has some features in common with therapeutic positivism but also has some special features of its own. First, just as Wittgenstein did not try to discourage the utterly hopeless thrusts of others against the limits of language, Leopold does not try to discourage continuing research into factor manipulation. In a closing section of "Means and Ends," Leopold discusses cycles, which he characterizes as "a problem defying the experimental method." Although he makes it clear that he considers the problems in this area unsolvable, he nevertheless provides practical advice, suggesting that it may be possible to split the problems into smaller parts, which might be testable on domesticated animals, and notes, with a hint of optimism, that "a virgin field awaits the investigator who is able to do the splitting."[53] Even though Wittgenstein thought that no one really could go beyond the limits of language, he did feel that it was possible that someone trying to do so might achieve positive results. A successful effort, however, would not constitute a thrust beyond the limits but a clarification of the limits in an area where they had been too narrowly understood. Similarly, in Leopold's therapeutic nihilism, the solution of a difficult problem in ecology can alternately be taken as a clarification of the limits of ecological knowledge rather than as an indication that those limits can be or have been broken. In this context, ecological research is still worth doing, not for its own sake, as in Wittgenstein's therapeutic positivism, but because of the scattered positive results it might bring from time to time.

Second, a unique valuational feature separates Leopold's therapeutic nihilism from the two versions already discussed. Leopold spent most of his life trying to identify the principles that would allow us to dominate nature—to substitute an artificial equilibrium for a natural one. When problems with his factor approach convinced him that such artificial equilibria could not be maintained, the result was a transformation not simply in his method but also in his values. In "Means and Ends," when Leopold writes that wildlife management "has already admitted its inability to replace natural equilibria with artificial ones," he adds that it has also admitted "its unwillingness to do so even if it could." Throughout the lecture, wild things are treated as aesthetically valuable objects on the model of art objects:

> The value of wild things is in part a scarcity value, like that of gold. It is also in part an artistic value, like that of a painting. The final arbiter of both is that elusive entity known as "good taste." There is though the residual difference: a painting might conceivably be recreated, but an extinct species never.[54]

This change in value is a step beyond that of Wittgenstein's therapeutic positivism, in which the activity of thrusting against the limits of language is valued for its own sake and without regard to its success or failure. Leopold has gone on to admire the intractable object of his study—the natural ecosystem—a shift analogous in traditional therapeutic nihilism to doctors coming to admire the diseases they are trying to cure. It is a transvaluation of values that highlights the central problem of environmental therapeutic nihilism: its relationship to nature preservation.

ENVIRONMENTAL THERAPEUTIC NIHILISM AND NATURE PRESERVATION

In assessing the importance of therapeutic nihilism in nature preservation arguments, we need to look at two very different kinds of things: first, the relationship of therapeutic nihilism to environmental values, and second, the long-term viability of therapeutic nihilism as an ecosystem management approach.

In some important ways, therapeutic nihilism may not promote appropriate environmental values at all. First, it seems likely that environmental therapeutic nihilism has contributed to a peculiar kind of callousness toward wild animals. Just as the seeming inability to help patients in the nineteenth century hardened most doctors and encouraged neglect and indifference to human life and suffering, our seeming inability to manipulate ecosystems beneficially appears to have fostered a similar indifference to the suffering of animal life in natural settings. The perpetuation of such an attitude not only runs counter to our basic moral sentiments but may also be counterproductive in terms of environmental management. Letting a buffalo freeze to death in a river in winter certainly conflicts with our moral intuitions, and it is hard to believe that an occasional rescue will have any serious environmental, ecological, or evolutionary consequences. Even when large numbers of animals are involved, assisting them may in many cases produce less damage than leaving them to their fate. For example, it probably would have been better to have treated the sheep in Yellowstone for pinkeye than to have watched most of the animals die from accidents caused by blindness. Similarly, Jane Goodall's decision to inoculate the chimpanzees she was studying against polio was probably less damaging than her decision to set up a banana feeding station.[55]

Second, therapeutic nihilism may sometimes allow environmental managers to avoid confronting their environmental values altogether. There is, of course, a strong tendency among scientists to defend their positions exclusively in terms of scientific research whenever possible: to argue in terms of facts rather than values. Douglas-Hamilton, for example, brings this point up specifically in connection with the problem of the elephants and the trees. He had not been at work very long, he writes, before he concluded that "scientifically there was no objective reason either for or against shooting the elephants that were doing the damage" and that the fate of the elephants had to depend on nonscientific factors:

> Here was an issue that could only be decided in relation to aesthetic, economic or political considerations. In ecological terms the Seronera tree damage was insignificant. The very desire to preserve the animals was a subjective statement of faith in the animals' intrinsic worth. It was a feeling possessed by most of the scientists there, who regarded the wildebeest migration with the same awe that others feel for the Mona Lisa, but they would not admit this sentiment into their arguments because it could not be backed up by facts; the right and wrong of aesthetics being imponderables not open to scientific analysis.[56]

Of the three factors listed, Douglas-Hamilton was most concerned about the first. He wanted to place great emphasis on the aesthetic worth of elephants, their intrinsic worth, which he equated with the value of art objects. Nevertheless, he was reluctant to do so because "this sentiment . . . could not be backed up by facts" and is "not open to scientific analysis." As a result, the aesthetic factor, which he considered so important, did not enter into his study and his conclusions, since it was not scientific, and he instead opted for a "unique" scientific solution that among all the possible alternatives was most compatible with therapeutic nihilism, doing almost nothing.

Since these considerations suggest that there is often no positive, straightforward connection between therapeutic nihilism and environmental values, it is probably best to say that while a management approach based on therapeutic nihilism cannot in general be depended on to promote environmental values, it at least establishes a scientific context in which they can persist without direct challenge. By contrast, much less can be said for the factor manipulation approach to management, since anyone who practices it must consciously act so as to destroy or replace natural environmental values on a regular basis. Leopold's own flirtation with the factor manipulation approach illustrates this point fairly well: His early preference for natural environmental values was suppressed during the time he actively sought to manipulate natural systems and reappeared in full only when he lost confidence in the approach and turned to therapeutic nihilism. Although Leopold was throughout his life well aware of and very appreciative of the aesthetic value of nature, his Pinchotian training at the Yale Forestry School, which stressed the instrumental use of nature for human purposes, was not entirely consistent with this value perspective. To become enthusiastically involved in factor manipulation of the environment, Leopold needed to resolve the tension between these two perspectives, and he did so by concluding that natural systems in civilized countries had already been so disrupted that the original natural environmental values no longer existed. As Leopold puts it in the first chapter of *Game Management:*

> A state of undisturbed nature is, of course, no longer found in countries facing the necessity of game management; civilization has upset every factor of productivity for better or worse. Game management proposes to substitute a new and objective equilibrium for any natural one which civilization may have destroyed.[57]

The replacement of the natural but disturbed equilibrium with an artificial one meant at the same time the replacement of natural values with a set of humanly imposed artificial ones. Once this intellectual hurdle was overcome, Leopold was able to look on the management of natural systems as nothing more than a special kind of landscape gardening. In the chapter "Game Management and Aesthetics" in *Game Management,* for example, he argues that the conservation of game and nongame animals (such as songbirds) alike requires nothing more than the identification of the habitats required and their construction by artificial means: "Environments can, by judicious use of those tools employed in gardening or landscaping or farming, be built to order with the assurance of attracting the desired bird."[58] This reluctant acceptance of artificial systems and artificial values persisted until Leopold finally came to realize that the factor manipulation approach did not work after all and that permitting natural systems to regulate themselves was the best he and other environmental managers could do, given the state of ecological science.

Within this context, nevertheless, there may still be some ways in which therapeutic nihilism positively influences our environmental values, especially instrumental values. That environmental therapeutic nihilism enhances our awareness of the importance of the instrumental value of natural systems seems fairly obvious. Leopold makes this point quite clearly in the passage from "Round River" quoted earlier in which he concludes, "To keep every cog and wheel is the first precaution of intelligent tinkering." At the end of Commoner's discussion of therapeutic nihilism, he also seems to take the same position, suggesting that following his principle, "Nature knows best," is basically a matter of "prudence" or "caution," an admonition to be careful when we are not sure what our man-made changes will do to the environment.[59] Just what therapeutic nihilism has to do with intrinsic value, however, is far less obvious. There are several possibilities. First, it may be that the relationship of therapeutic nihilism to the preservation of natural systems for their own sake is merely a pragmatic one. They are connected because the support therapeutic nihilism happens to provide to arguments for maintaining natural systems instrumentally can be extended uncritically and informally to include intrinsic value positions, but not because intrinsic value arguments in any way follow in deductive sense from the basic principles of environmental therapeutic nihilism. Second, as suggested by Leopold's "Land Ethic," it is also possible that our ignorance about underlying causal interrelationships in nature may force us to rely intuitively on aesthetic properties of ecosystems as "second-best" indicators of ecosystemic health, in much the same way that rosy cheeks and a twinkle in the eye might suggest health in a human. Leopold's remark in "The Land Ethic," "A thing is right when it tends to preserve the integrity, stability, and beauty of the biotic community," suggests such an approach.[60] Although these values are unscientific, they remain useful, since the alternative to using them may be to use nothing at all. In this context, however, the value orientation ultimately remains instrumental in spirit and in deed.

Regardless of what Leopold narrowly and historically might have had in mind in writing "The Land Ethic," it is still possible to draw a positive connection between therapeutic nihilism and the preservation of natural values independent of their instrumental value to humans. Mark Sagoff, for example, has identified two medical analogies in which concern for the promotion of certain moral values frequently overrides the desire for the efficient and effective treatment of human patients. The first is an analogy between ecology and medicine. According to Sagoff, doctors can prescribe medication either to help maintain normal good health or, for example, in the case of an athlete, "to change the normal healthy functioning of a person's body to allow that person to do abnormal or extraordinary things."[61] In the context of ecosystemic health, nature preservationists want the former, conservationists and related commercial interests want the latter. In going from the first to the second, certain values are lost because, once the transition is made, the human or the ecosystem ceases to function naturally. If it is discovered that the athlete's victory was due to special drugs, it alters our admiration for his or her achievement. Likewise, when we discover that an ecosystem is being maintained artificially to maximize the production of certain animals or plants, our appreciation of and admiration for the system are frequently diminished in a similar way. Although we may on some occasions find values to admire in such an ecosystem, they will not be the values of a natural system but values introduced technologically by humans. Regardless of what has been conserved, what the nature preservationists want to preserve has been lost.

A similar loss of value also occurs in the second analogy, in which the factor manipulation and ecosystem management approaches are compared to behavioral and therapeutic pyschology.[62] As Sagoff points out, although the behavioral approach is usually very effective and the therapeutic approach rarely works at all, nearly everyone nonetheless prefers the therapeutic approach over the behavioral, since the therapeutic approach respects the autonomy of the individual and various associated values, for example, freedom and dignity, whereas the behavioral approach does not. For many people, there is a similar contrast between the factor manipulation and therapeutic approaches in environmental management. Once the manipulation begins, the system is transformed into a living machine controlled and dominated by humans for exclusively human purposes: It is enslaved; it is no longer wild and free; and the values that we respect and admire in nature are destroyed.

Although these analogies clearly demonstrate that therapeutic nihilism can promote appropriate noninstrumental values *in theory,* we still need to consider carefully whether we can depend on such associations to arise and flourish *in practice* and whether such value promotion counterbalances other negative aspects of the general therapeutic approach. A number of problems frequently arise when we turn to practical application. First, doing nothing may be as unnatural as doing something. If, as Chase argues, the American wilderness was consciously managed by the Indians, it probably cannot remain in the condition in which whites originally found it without continued management.[63] Second, it may not really be possible to do nothing. It is very difficult for a doctor to deny medication to a patient even when he or she knows that it probably will not help. Moreover, when humans can affect the outcome, it is often hard to say that choosing not to intercede is simply doing nothing. As Sartre once put it in another context, choosing to do nothing is still choosing to do something: to let the current state of affairs reach its final conclusion unhindered.[64] Third, it is easy to drift into factor manipulation while trying to follow an approach based on therapeutic nihilism, for example, when a manager decides to counter outside influences so as otherwise to allow the unfolding of natural history within the protected area. Once this kind of factor manipulation begins in the name of therapeutic nihilism, there is the very real possibility that the values being protected will be lost by trying to protect them. Since it can be difficult or even impossible to distinguish between natural and humanly induced change, managers may either unconsciously or consciously (through pressure from the general public) try to freeze the natural area in its current state or return it to an earlier state, as a museum piece, thereby bringing its natural history to an end and unwittingly destroying the very thing that the therapeutic approach was supposed to protect.

The problem of creeping factor manipulation in a therapeutic context, moreover, highlights what is probably the single most serious difficulty with therapeutic nihilism as a preservationist strategy, for the aim of the mainstream argument for this approach is not to preserve values but to avoid damage through the employment of ineffective or inept ecological technology. This is especially clear when one considers alternative interpretations of Commoner's "Nature knows best" principle. There are really two interpretations with very different consequences: (1) that we ought to be careful until we have developed appropriate techniques to manipulate the environment without random damage occurring and (2) that we ought to be careful permanently because it will never be possible to develop the appropriate techniques needed to manipulate the environment without random damage occurring. If it is true that we will never develop the ability to manipulate nature as Leopold originally intended in his factor approach, environmental therapeutic nihilism is a strong foundation for nature preservation arguments. There is, however, a great danger here, for it is a strong foundation only as long as there is good reason to believe that the second interpretation is true. If it ever turns out that ecological engineering on a substantial scale is feasible, nature preservation arguments and environmental ethics in general, to the degree that they depend on environmental therapeutic nihilism, will be based on false premises. For this reason, it is probably best pragmatically to guard against this possibility by separating intrinsic value arguments from therapeutic nihilism and interpreting Commoner's principle as a temporary precaution to be followed until such time, if ever, that ecological engineering becomes a practical reality.

Humans have most successfully manipulated nature by applying principles from the physical sciences, for example, in making steel, plastic, gasoline, and the like. No comparable degree of manipulative ability has as yet been developed in the environmental or natural history sciences. Although it is sometimes suggested that complete technological mastery of the environment might be possible if environmental science could somehow be reduced to physics and chemistry, it is important to recognize that these sciences are based on a reductionist method that may be only partially appropriate to environmental science, thereby making this possibility very unlikely. Everything depends on whether environmental factors can in fact, and not just in theory, be isolated and manipulated independently. David Kitts argues that geology, in particular, is fundamentally different as a science from physics and chemistry: that unlike the physical sciences, which focus on the discovery of universal laws that work in isolation, geology is historically oriented, that is, primarily concerned with the generation of singular historical statements that aid us in reconstructing the history of the Earth. As a result, Kitts contends, geology is more concerned with explanation than prediction, and the methods used to produce geological explanation have little use in formulating predictions about future events.[65] Can geology and other environmental sciences become adequately future-oriented? It is probably not possible for the therapeutic nihilist to prove in advance that the environmental sciences will not develop the ability to make the precise predictions needed for factor manipulation of the environment any more than it is possible for the technological optimist to prove that he will always be able to find solutions to the various problems that his new technologies generate. If factor manipulation can be done successfully, humans will almost certainly figure out how to do it. If it cannot, it will remain an intriguing possibility as long as Western science and technology continue to be practiced.

Even if successful, nondisruptive factor manipulation technology is never developed, there is still a serious problem with any association of therapeutic nihilism in the strong sense with nature preservation arguments. While there might not be much danger of these arguments being factually undermined in terms of a therapeutic nihilism that demands full theoretical understanding before factor manipulation begins, one of the lessons of Semmelweis' discovery is that rules of thumb can be found and applied whether theoretical underpinnings exist or not. Thus it is always possible, whether or not an ecological technology ever materializes, that procedures for maximizing particular elements of ecosystems without excessive damage might be found that work well even though we do not know why they do. If such procedures are discovered, the argument that in general we cannot manipulate ecosystems without random damage will be overridden by the fact that we can in such and such cases, and environmentalists will be forced to defend their positions on the basis of their value preferences alone without the aid of arguments about the limits of ecological knowledge.

As I noted earlier, scientists, environmentalists, and policymakers are naturally reluctant to defend their positions in terms of value considerations, and therapeutic nihilism, at this time, at least, provides everyone with an easy way to stick to the facts. Instead of arguing that we ought not to do this or that because it conflicts with the kinds of environmental values we want to promote individually or as a society, they can argue that we ought not to do it because we cannot, because it is not scientifically or technologically possible. What we end up with, then, is a counter to the technological *ought* (if we can, we ought to) by a technological *ought not* (if we cannot, we should not), an argument that is effective only as long as it is factually true.

In summary, for the time being, environmental therapeutic nihilism as precaution or prudence continues to be a pragmatically useful foundation for nature preservation. However, whether it will continue to be in the future depends on whether breakthroughs in ecology occur, and the prospects for such breakthroughs are better than most environmentalists might imagine. Environmental therapeutic nihilism is really an outgrowth of historical developments in ecology and environmental management, and although it is still widely held by most environmentalists and many applied ecologists working in environmental management, it no longer represents the attitudes prevalent among contemporary ecologists, most of whom now believe that it is possible to make accurate recommendations for action in many circumstances, including deer herds. While the improvements in the ability to make ecological predictions since Leopold's time are not a revolutionary leap forward, they are substantial and can be expected to translate into greatly improved expertise at the applied level in the near future. If these improvements continue, with or without a major breakthrough, therapeutic nihilism will almost certainly become indefensible as a mainstream preservationist position: As in medicine today, it will then become an approach that is relevant and useful only in cases in which an appropriate technical solution is not yet available.

The vulnerability of therapeutic nihilism to future developments in ecology puts environmentalists in an unusual and unpleasant position. They must either actively root against advances in ecology or look for better preservationist arguments. Because the science of ecology has played such an important role in the development of modern environmental attitudes, the first alternative would certainly be a sad and probably also a self-defeating course of action. Although the second alternative may seem equally unappealing, the prospects may be good, if environmentalists are willing to bring their values to the surface and turn them into ethical and aesthetic arguments in defense of nature. How they might go about doing so is the subject of the next chapter.

NOTES

1. Iain and Oria Douglas-Hamilton, *Among the Elephants* (New York: Viking Press, 1975), pp. 31–33, 74–75.
2. Ibid., pp. 259–263.
3. Ibid., p. 263.
4. Barry Commoner, *The Closing Circle: Nature, Man, and Technology* (New York: Knopf, 1971), p. 41.
5. Peter Singer, *Animal Liberation: A New Ethics for Our Treatment of Animals* (New York: Avon Books, 1975), pp. 238–239.
6. Aldo Leopold, "Round River," in *A Sand County Almanac: With Essays on Conservation from Round River* (New York: Ballantine Books, 1970), p. 190.
7. Leopold, "The Land Ethic," ibid., pp. 240–241.
8. Ibid.
9. See A. S. Leopold et al., "Wildlife Management in the National Parks," in

National Park Service, *Compilation of the Administrative Policies for the National Parks and National Monuments of Scientific Significance (Natural Area Category)*, rev. ed. (Washington, D.C.: U.S. Government Printing Office, 1970), pp. 99–112.

10. Ibid., p. 106.

11. A. S. Leopold et al., "Resource Management Policy," in *Compilation of Administrative Policies*, p. 17.

12. Alston Chase, *Playing God in Yellowstone: The Destruction of America's First National Park* (Boston: Atlantic Monthly Press, 1986), p. 42. Quotation from National Park Service, *Management Policies* (Washington, D.C.: U.S. Government Printing Office, 1978), p. iv-I.

13. See "A Solution to the Elk Problem," in Chase, *Playing God*, pp. 49–70.

14. For a short, concise discussion of nihilism, see Paul Edwards, ed., *The Encyclopedia of Philosophy*, vol. 5 (New York: Macmillan and Free Press, 1967), pp. 514–517.

15. William M. Johnston, *The Austrian Mind: An Intellectual and Social History, 1848–1938* (Berkeley: University of California Press, 1972), pp. 71, 223–224.

16. Ibid., p. 71.

17. Ibid., pp. 224–225.

18. Ibid., p. 226; for a fuller account of this problem, see Paul de Kruif, *Men against Death* (Orlando, Fla.: Harcourt Brace Jovanovich, 1932), pp. 35–58.

19. For a philosophical discussion of Semmelweis' discovery, see Carl G. Hempel, *Philosophy of Natural Science* (Englewood Cliffs, N.J.: Prentice-Hall, 1966), pp. 3–8.

20. Johnston, *Austrian Mind*, p. 226; de Kruif, *Men against Death*, pp. 49–50.

21. Hempel, *Philosophy of Natural Science*, p. 3.

22. De Kruif, *Men against Death*, pp. 39, 54.

23. Therapeutic nihilism is frequently discussed in connection with health care in the elderly, psychiatry, deafness, breast cancer, liver disease, the common cold, and other problems. In most cases, authors analyze a particular health issue and argue that there are now good reasons why therapeutic nihilism is no longer justified. See, for example, Carl Eisdorfer, "Therapeutic Nihilism and Other Rationalizations for Avoiding the Issues in Health Care," *Geriatrics* 31 (1976), no. 1: 35–42. In some cases, nearly all medical practice is depicted as therapeutic nihilism. See, for example, Paul Starr, "The Politics of Therapeutic Nihilism," *Hastings Center Report 6* (1976), no. 5: 24–30.

24. Because the victims of Legionnaires' disease returned home before showing symptoms, all of them were randomly given antibiotics as a general treatment for the symptoms of pneumonia, even though a bacterial agent had not been identified. However, the fact that most patients responded to antibiotics, and reasonably well to tetracycline and erythromycin, was not taken as an important clue in narrowing the search for the cause of the disease. Only after the bacterial agent was conclusively identified did doctors seek to determine which antibiotic was most appropriate. See Gary L. Lattimer and Richard A. Ormsbee, *Legionnaires' Disease* (New York: Marcel Dekker, 1981), pp. 19–22, 86–90. In the middle of the following summer, during an outbreak of the disease in Vermont, more patients were systematically given a variety of antibiotics, and erythromycin, one of the most commonly used antibiotics, was determined to be the correct medication. For a straightforward account of the discovery and cure of Legionnaires' disease from the perspective of the researchers themselves, see "The Hunt for the Legion Killer," *Nova* (Program No. 904, 1982). The organism was discovered by Joseph McDade in early August 1976, but he ignored it, since he was supposed to be looking for signs of rickettsias (p. 6). In late December, when he learned that the identity of the

organism was still unknown, he took another look at his slides, finding the rodlike organism once again (pp. 9–10).

25. Johnston, *Austrian Mind,* pp. 71, 223, 228–229; Norman Malcolm, *Ludwig Wittgenstein: A Memoir* (London: Oxford University Press, 1958), p. 56.

26. See Alfred Jules Ayer, "Critique of Ethics and Theology," in *Language, Truth, and Logic* (New York: Dover Publications, 1952), pp. 102–120.

27. See B. A. Farrell, "An Appraisal of Therapeutic Positivism," *Mind* 55 (1946): 25–48, 133–150.

28. Ludwig Wittgenstein, *Philosophical Investigations,* trans. G. E. M. Anscombe, 3d ed. (New York: Macmillan, 1958), par. 255.

29. Ibid., par. 133.

30. Ludwig Wittgenstein, *Tractatus Logico-Philosophicus,* trans. D. F. Pears and B. F. McGuinness (London: Routledge & Kegan Paul, 1961), par. 6.52–6.521.

31. Ibid., par. 6.53.

32. Wittgenstein, *Philosophical Investigations,* par. 119.

33. Quoted in Eric Heller, "Wittgenstein: Unphilosophical Notes," in *Ludwig Wittgenstein: The Man and His Philosophy,* ed. K. T. Fann (New York: Dell, 1967), p. 101, n. 28.

34. Ludwig Wittgenstein, *Notebooks, 1914–1916,* ed. G. H. von Wright and G. E. M. Anscombe (New York: Harper & Row, 1961), pp. 78–79e.

35. Quoted in Paul Engelmann, *Letters from Ludwig Wittgenstein, with Memoir,* trans. L. Furtmuller (Oxford: Basil Blackwell, 1967), pp. 143–144.

36. Ibid., p. 97; emphasis in original.

37. Ludwig Wittgenstein, "Wittgenstein's Lecture on Ethics," *Philosophical Review* 74 (1965): 11–12.

38. G. E. Moore, "Wittgenstein's Lectures in 1930–33," *Mind* 64 (1955): 26–27. Wittgenstein's discussion here seems to have been significantly influenced by William James' general characterization of a religious experience as an uneasiness and its solution. See William James, *The Varieties of Religious Experience* (New York: New American Library, 1958), p. 383.

39. This distinction between the value of an activity and its product is an old one. See, for example, the first paragraph of Aristotle's *Nicomachean Ethics.*

40. Both views are strongly held by John Passmore in *Man's Responsibility for Nature.*

41. Commoner, *Closing Circle,* pp. 41–45.

42. Johnston, *Austrian Mind,* p. 225.

43. Susan L. Flader, *Thinking like a Mountain: Aldo Leopold and the Evolution of an Ecological Attitude toward Deer, Wolves, and Forests* (Columbia: University of Missouri Press, 1974).

44. Aldo Leopold, *Game Management* (New York: Scribner, 1933), p. 26.

45. Ibid., p. 29.

46. Flader, *Thinking like a Mountain,* p. 93.

47. Leopold, *Game Management,* p. 45.

48. Flader, *Thinking like a Mountain,* pp. 76–121.

49. Ibid., pp. 84–85. Although Flader's account of the Kaibab remains a historically accurate account of the situation as Leopold perceived it, the idea that the irruptions there were caused by the removal of predators has been challenged by Graeme Caughley in his paper "Eruption of Ungulate Populations with Emphasis on Himalayan Thar in New Zealand," *Ecology* 51 (1970): 53–56.

50. Flader, *Thinking like a Mountain,* p. 120.

51. Ibid. pp. 139–150.

52. Aldo Leopold, "Means and Ends in Wild Life Management," holograph,

LP 6-16, Leopold Papers, University of Wisconsin Archives, Madison; lecture delivered at Beloit College on May 5, 1936.

53. Ibid.

54. Ibid.

55. Chase, *Playing God,* pp. 81–82; Jane van Lawick–Goodall, *In the Shadow of Man* (Boston: Houghton Mifflin, 1971), ch. 8, 17.

56. Douglas-Hamilton, *Among the Elephants,* pp. 75–76.

57. Leopold, *Game Management,* p. 26.

58. Ibid., p. 405.

59. Commoner, *Closing Circle,* p. 45.

60. Leopold, "Land Ethic," p. 262.

61. Mark Sagoff, "Fact and Value in Ecological Science," *Environmental Ethics* 7 (1985): 112–113.

62. Ibid., pp. 114–116.

63. Chase, *Playing God,* ch. 9.

64. Jean-Paul Sartre, *Existentialism and the Human Emotions* (New York: Philosophical Library, 1957), p. 41.

65. David B. Kitts, *The Structure of Geology* (Dallas: Southern Methodist University Press, 1977), ch. 1–2.

CHAPTER SIX
AN ONTOLOGICAL ARGUMENT FOR ENVIRONMENTAL ETHICS

Some years ago, I took a tour of Onondaga Cave, one of the two most beautiful show caves in the state of Missouri. At that time, there was a plan to build a dam on the Meramec River. If constructed and put into service, the dam would have destroyed most of the cave through flooding. The owners of the cave, who were opposed to the dam and wished to save the cave, included a discussion of this problem in the tour as part of their effort to rally public support. After completing about three-fourths of the tour, the guide stopped in a large room and pointed to a water marker, placed high above us on a distant wall to illustrate the water level in the cave that would result from the building of the dam. All of the cave that we had seen so far, he told us, would be underwater, destroyed forever. Although nearly everyone in the group seemed disturbed by this revelation, one woman was not. In fact, her eyes beamed with joy, and she exclaimed spontaneously with great excitement and seeming insensitivity, "That would be wonderful!" "What?" I stammered in astonishment. "Why do you think that?" Recovering somewhat, I and the others on the tour waited for some rationale about the financial benefits of the dam versus the lesser aesthetic value of the cave; her explanation, however, took a completely different and very unexpected direction. The experience of seeing the cave was, she said, extremely pleasurable. It was an experience that she would remember all of her life whether the cave was destroyed by the dam or not. Nevertheless, if the cave was destroyed, she would be among a finite group of living people who had had that experience, which no others could ever have again. Gradually as the members of this group grew older and died, the size of the group would become smaller and smaller until she was at last part of a very tiny and elite group of people who could still remember and imaginatively re-create the experience that she was then having in the cave. Eventually, if circumstances favored her, she might even become the last person on Earth who had had this particular experience. But in any event, as the size of the group decreased, the value of her experience would increase as it became increasingly rare, and she could therefore cherish it throughout her life, and more so as she grew older, as an experience that most other people did not possess and never could have.

I cite this woman's explanation not because it is a commonly held view—indeed, to the contrary, I think it is probably not held by very many people at all—but rather because it helps identify some key issues at the heart of any attempt to justify the preservation of parts of the environment in a natural state. To a very great extent, the preservationist wing of the environmental movement is strongly committed to the creation of the kinds of experience that the woman had in Onondaga Cave. It is, moreover, I believe, the general opinion of most environmentalists, the general public, and most public administrators that one of the chief purposes of national parks, as well as most other natural areas, is the generation of these kinds of experiences in the minds of park visitors. In addition, it is generally regarded as preferable to have these experiences than not to have them, and it is believed that people who have them are better off than those who do not. Does it follow, however, as the woman in Onondaga Cave claimed, that the best situation is one in which the object experienced is destroyed after it has been experienced? That is, what is the relationship of the pleasurable experience of a natural object to its continued existence?

This question has very broad significance and application. One can ask, for example, whether the fact that the dinosaurs do not exist in today's world constitutes a significant loss of value. Likewise, would the world be a better one if examples of the dodo or the passenger pigeon still existed outside of stuffed animal museums? Would a world without elephants and lions be a worse world than the world we live in now? Would a world in which a lake rather than a canyon existed at the current site of the Grand Canyon be a more valuable or a less valuable world? Note that in asking any of these questions, broad though they may be, we are nevertheless addressing a specific problem. We are not asking about the rights that any of these animals or natural objects may or may not have to exist; nor are we asking if they are valuable independent of human beings. We are asking a question about anthropocentric value, not nonanthropocentric value. Does the existence of any of these things have any importance in the value judgments of human beings?

This kind of anthropocentric question, of course, is not the only kind of question that is involved in our preservationist arguments. It is possible to base preservationist justifications on some nonanthropocentric conception of the rights, interests, or intrinsic value of particular organisms. This approach, however, is not a complete alternative to the anthropocentric approach considered in this chapter, since nonanthropocentric rights, interests, or intrinsic value justifications work less well, if they work at all, with nonliving natural objects than with living ones. While we can readily identify wants, needs, and interests of living things, such terms become metaphorical when applied to the nonliving. Onondaga Cave, for example, might have received some protection by appealing to the rights, interests, and nonanthropocentric intrinsic value of the creatures that live in it, especially if some of them are rare or endangered, but the cave itself, without regard to what lives in it, as a hole in a layer of sediment, does not seem to be the kind of object that can have wants, needs, or interests. It could even be argued that it is not an object at all, that as a volume of space it is, to paraphrase Wittgenstein in another context, not a something, but not a nothing either.[1] In the case of a cave, we must appeal to its beauty or its scientific interest as a foundation for our preservationist concern, and this appeal is anthropocentric, involving human or humanlike consciousness that is capable of perceiving and appreciating the noninstrumental aesthetic and scientific values of the cave. Unless we want nonliving natural objects like caves to be entirely dependent on the trickle-down effect of nonanthropocentric arguments for the protection of living organisms, we still need anthropocentric justifications in terms of anthropocentric or human values. While some critics may claim that such justifications compete with nonanthropocentric justifications, such a position is mistaken, for in addition to providing protection for nonliving things, anthropocentric justifications also provide the same protection for living things, and this protection can appropriately complement any nonanthropocentric justifications that may someday be developed.

My examination of the role of existence in preservationist arguments is also anthropocentric for two additional reasons. My aim is to provide the minimum justification for the type of concern that has developed out of the history of ideas detailed in Chapters 3 and 4—that is, the justification that most closely accounts for our current and historical intuitions and does so in terms of traditional concepts and ideas as much as possible. Such a justification seems desirable on two grounds: (1) It is likely to be more convincing and effective than more radical positions, and (2) even if it is not, it is good sense to determine the justification for our actual intuitions and practices before trying to change them.

As I noted in Chapter 3, the ultimate historical foundations of nature preservation are aesthetic in a broad context that encompasses the value perspectives of nineteenth-century naturalists, painters, and poets. In this context, I want to argue that existence is not simply an arbitrary ingredient in states of affairs in the world but is rather a positive value in its own right, enhancing our aesthetic/scientific appreciation of the natural world: In other words, existence is an aesthetic property of natural objects.

In taking this position, I am trying, first of all, to account for what Allen Carlson has called positive aesthetics: the view held by many environmentalists that whatever exists is in some significant way beautiful simply because it exists.[2] Second, I am relying on certain thought experiments undertaken by G. E. Moore in *Principia Ethica,* although I do not follow him in ascribing nonnatural value to the external world.[3] Finally, I am trying to develop an account that straightforwardly parallels our treatment of art objects.

AESTHETIC EXPERIENCE AND THE EXISTENCE OF ART OBJECTS

It is commonly held that our nature experiences are aesthetic and that in this context they are valuable for their own sake, without regard to their use—that is, they are intrinsically valuable experiences analogous to those we have when we view works of art in a museum. Thus a good way to begin our inquiry is to examine our intuitions about the aesthetic appreciation of art objects. It is generally held, I believe, that the value of the experience of an art object is increased if the object experienced is the original and that in cases where the original has been lost or destroyed or for some reason a reproduction has been substituted, the experience is diminished. In such cases, the existence and condition of the original art object is important to the quality of the aesthetic experience of the visitor. If the Mona Lisa were lost or stolen, the resultant uncertainty about its whereabouts and concern about the possibility that it might have been damaged would affect the quality of the experiences former visitors had when they remember their direct experience of the painting, as well as the aesthetic experiences of those who subsequently view a reproduction or look at a picture of the painting in a book. If the Mona Lisa were irreparably damaged, the quality of the aesthetic experience would likewise be diminished, and if the painting were destroyed, it would be considered a loss both to those who had previously seen the painting and to those who had not. All of these conclusions, it should be obvious, are completely inconsistent with the position of the woman who wanted Onondaga Cave destroyed in order to enhance her personal aesthetic experiences. Although the art object is in large measure valued because of the experiences it generates, when the object is threatened with damage or destruction, its protection takes precedence over the generation of aesthetic experiences in visitors.

In general, museum curators display art objects in such a way that they will not be damaged. It turns out, however, that many art objects, especially paintings, are damaged by being displayed, by being in the presence of light and air. As a result, restorers are retained by museums to monitor damage and to repair paintings and other art objects as they deteriorate. If irreparable damage should begin to occur, the object at risk is usually taken off display permanently or until such time as new techniques for display might be developed. In some cases, a reproduction is substituted for the original. Visitors generally accept these measures with regret, to be sure, but also with understanding.

This approach can and has been extended to the aesthetic appreciation of endangered natural objects as well. One interesting intermediate case is the cave paintings at Lascaux. Although we are still dealing with art objects, the problems involved are those usually encountered with the preservation of beautiful natural objects, such as delicate stalactites in caves. When caves are opened for tours, lighting of some kind, usually electric lighting, must be provided or installed. For obvious reasons, fixed lights are pointed at the features of the cave that visitors want to see. This kind of lighting leads to damage by facilitating the growth in the lighted areas of fungus that causes cracking and discoloration. Such damage also developed in Lascaux, threatening to obliterate all the paintings. The problem of visitation was solved by building a full-scale model of the cave near the original. Visitors now tour the replica rather than the original.

A similar preservation measure has been taken with regard to at least one natural object, a cave passage in Mammoth Cave National Park. In July 1954, members of the National Speleological Society exploring in Crystal Cave, at that time outside the park, discovered a passage called Turner Avenue that was extremely beautiful but so fragile that no matter how carefully the explorers moved, they still caused movement in the air in the passage that resulted in minute but visible damage to the formations nearby. Shortly thereafter, the passage was thoroughly photographed and all additional visitation was banned. After the creation of the Cave Research Foundation in 1957, a policy was developed to permit infrequent visitation if travel in the passage was necessary in connection with the CRF's master plan for scientific research in the cave system, but the ban on aesthetic viewing in the passage has continued to this day. As a result, most people's aesthetic experiences of Turner Avenue come from viewing photographs.[4]

In each case, the approach is the same. Direct aesthetic appreciation of the art object or the natural object is restricted and a representation of some kind is substituted. The representation then becomes the focus for the act of aesthetic appreciation, but not its object, which continues to be the unviewed original. To be sure, the aesthetic experience is diminished to some degree because the object viewed is a representation. However, the knowledge that the original still exists enhances the experience afforded by the representation. This is evident from the fact that the quality of the aesthetic experience is usually superior to the experience that would be generated by the contemplation of the representation alone, given that the representation is a copy and as such rarely succeeds in exactly duplicating the aesthetic qualities of the original. The deficiencies of the copy are overcome through memory (if the viewer has previously seen the original and remembers it well) or through imagination (if he or she has not, and when the memory needs supplementation). Memory and imagination are, in fact, so effective that, strictly speaking, there does not need to be a physical representation at all; the aesthetic experience can develop out of a mental representation constructed on the basis of memory and imagination (enhanced by the knowledge that the original exists safely and in good condition elsewhere).

This kind of indirect aesthetic experience is, of course, a kind of compromise. It is, to be sure, always preferable to experience the object being appreciated directly. Indirect appreciation is nevertheless adequate in most cases, and preferable to direct viewing that leads to the destruction (or consumption) of the object, which would thereby make all subsequent acts of appreciation dependent entirely upon physical representations, memories, and imaginative reconstructions. When the object is appreciated indirectly, there may be a feeling of regret that it cannot be viewed or experienced directly. However, when the object has been destroyed or so damaged that it is no longer aesthetically pleasing, the situation is far worse: The feeling of regret is replaced, or supplemented, by a feeling of loss that inhibits the emergence of aesthetic experience or prevents it altogether.

The importance of original art objects to aesthetic experience arising out of the contemplation of representations should not be surprising to anyone. The use of copies of works of art to create second-best aesthetic experience has been standard practice for centuries. In all such use, the continued existence of the original is essential to the aesthetic experience derived from the copy. It may, however, be surprising that the continued existence of natural objects may be essential to the aesthetic appreciation of the representations of those objects (for example, paintings and photographs), since here the representations themselves are frequently art objects, while the natural objects, strictly speaking, are not. It is nevertheless a well-established element of Western aesthetic appreciation.

As noted in Chapter 3, landscape painting originally developed as imaginative background decoration, secondary to the depiction of human figures. Even when landscape became the central focus, painters avoided representing places that physically existed because they believed that such paintings would lack creativity—they would be based on imitation (in a Platonic sense), not on creative imagination. Ironically, however, ideal painting, quite against the wishes of the artists themselves, fostered an aesthetic taste for natural scenery: Paintings that represented real places came to be preferred over ones that were ideal, and the places depicted came to be preferred over paintings of them. These developments were, to be sure, unexpected, but were probably, nonetheless, an inevitable consequence of the representational experimentation in painting associated with the Renaissance. Once landscape painting had established the existence of aesthetic qualities in real landscape, ideal paintings were viewed by most people as representations that lacked a physical original. Even though there was no feeling of loss, since an original, natural landscape had not been destroyed, there was a feeling that ideal paintings, because they lacked a representational relationship with the physical world, were incomplete.

MOORE'S POSITION

Although G. E. Moore, in his book *Principia Ethica,* gives no hint that he is aware of these historical developments, he engages in a series of thought experiments aimed at establishing the importance of aesthetic value in the world and its relationship to, and in many cases superiority over, aesthetic value in works of art. In all, he discusses four issues: the *existence* of aesthetic value in the world, *knowledge* of the existence of aesthetic value in the world, *belief* that such value exists in the world, and, implicitly, the *desire* for such value to exist in the world when it does not exist in external nature or when knowledge of its existence is not available.

With regard to the first two issues, the existence of aesthetic value in the world and knowledge of its existence, Moore argues that although knowing of the existence of aesthetic qualities in the world is better than not knowing of them, because such knowledge promotes aesthetic experience, aesthetic qualities in the world that are unknown still have some value and can be the basis for positive duty. In responding to a claim by Sidgwick that it is not rational to aim at the creation of beauty in external nature apart from any possible contemplation of it by humans, Moore asks his readers to imagine two worlds, neither of which can be visited by human beings: an exceedingly beautiful world and the ugliest world that can possibly be conceived. He then argues that simply on the grounds that beauty is in itself a greater good than ugliness, the beautiful world is preferable to the ugly one and that in cases where our actions can affect the unperceived and unperceivable beauty in such worlds, we have a duty to make such worlds more beautiful insofar as we can. If we admit such a duty, Moore concludes, we also admit that the existence of aesthetic value alone, independent of any knowledge of its existence, contributes to the goodness of the whole in our own world.[5]

This position, although not specifically a preservationist argument, translates into one quite easily, since the same reflections that justify a duty to make the world more beautiful can also disclose other duties, for example, the duty to protect or preserve beauty in external nature, and a family of cases in which such duties might apply. At one extreme are cases in which beauty is perceivable and known to exist and at the other extreme those in which it is unperceivable. In between are a multitude of cases in which the existence of beauty is perceivable but unperceived and there is for some reason to believe that it exists. It is to these intermediate cases that we now turn to examine the role of belief in aesthetic experience.

In moving from knowledge to belief, we also move from direct to indirect aesthetic experience. Belief comes into play only when we have some reason to doubt that the object is physically real, when we know that we are viewing a physical representation, or when we are reconstructing an object through memory and imagination. Moore cites the following cases: (1) belief in the existence of a particular group of beautiful qualities when it is true that the qualities exist, (2) an aesthetic experience without belief when it is either true or false that the qualities exist, and (3) a belief in the existence of the beautiful qualities when they do not exist. According to Moore, the first involves the appreciation of what is in nature and in the human affections, the second purely imaginative appreciation, and the third misguided affection. All three, Moore notes, represent positive goods; however, the amount of value in each varies. The value in the second category is the amount common to all three, and that value is increased when belief in the existence of the aesthetic qualities represented is true, decreased when the belief is false. This ranking, Moore believes, is readily verifiable through individual introspection, and shows (1) that the truth of belief in the existence of an art object or natural object, in lieu of knowledge of it, makes a positive difference in the value of an aesthetic experience, increasing the total value, and (2) that false belief reduces the value of the aesthetic experience significantly.[6]

Of course, some limitations to the application of Moore's thought experiment need to be addressed to ensure a positive result. First, the object being appreciated must be representational, and the aesthetic standards being applied must include a representational orientation. For example, a medieval Christian who contemplates a representation of a fish symbolically in relation to a biblical parable would be unaffected by the considerations Moore is addressing here. Similarly, the aesthetic appreciation of postrepresentational painting, for example, impressionism and abstract expressionism, which evolved out of nineteenth-century luminism, is also unaffected. Second, some representational painting, though depicting a particular place, may do so, as Berkeley points out, in such a way that the representation is taken to stand for all such places in general. For example, a photograph in a Sierra Club calendar of water running over rocks in a brook, without any additional special identifying features, may direct one's thoughts to memories of similar brooks experienced in the viewer's personal past, rather than to specific thoughts about the particular brook represented in the photograph, and as a result, belief will focus on the existence of such places in general and not on the existence of that particular place. If these special cases—symbolic, postrepresentational, and general-reference—are set aside, a person with normal aesthetic tastes and with little or no training in art appreciation who introspectively carries out the required thought experiments should agree with Moore's conclusion that knowledge and true belief about the existence of works of art and natural objects add additional value to direct and representational aesthetic experience.

The only remaining problem area is ideal painting, painting that is clearly representational but for which intentionally no original exists in nature. With regard to this difficulty, Moore asks us to compare a beautiful landscape in nature and a painting of that landscape that exactly reproduces the aesthetic qualities of the natural landscape, and he concludes that in all such cases, the natural landscape is more beautiful because the aesthetic qualities exist more fundamentally in the natural objects making up the natural landscape than in the painting depicting them. What this means is that the existence of the qualities in nature constitutes an additional element that makes the natural landscape aesthetically superior to a representation of it and in turn makes an ideal painting inferior to a representational painting of a place that actually exists in external nature. As Moore puts it: "We think that the world would be improved if we could substitute for the best works of representative art *real* objects equally beautiful."[7] In other words, the realization that an ideal painting has no natural original causes us to view the painting as incomplete and generates a *desire* that the landscape depicted actually exist in external nature.

Although Moore does not explicitly speak of this desire for things to come to be in *Principia Ethica,* it has been identified and usefully discussed in both the literary and scholarly writings of J. R. R. Tolkien. In a short story, "Leaf by Niggle," the main character works extensively on a painting of a tree; the tree and its background are subsequently actualized in heaven after the artist's death. In the first chapter of *The Silmarillion,* God creates the world first through song, then visually depicts it, and finally creates it physically in order to satisfy the desire of His angels that it should actually be. In his essay "On Fairy-Stories," Tolkien associates this kind of desire with *literary belief,* the "willing suspension of disbelief." This belief, Tolkien insists, is not simply a willingness to believe that something is true but rather a desire that it be true. For example, although he did not "wish to have them in the neighborhood," he "desired dragons with a profound desire." Longing for them to exist, he wanted to read stories about them that depict them realistically.[8]

All fiction in presenting contemporary, historical, or fantasy events strives to be convincing, to be realistic. Even when impossible events occur, the author invariably tries to ground the story in a reality with which the reader is familiar. Tolkien calls this is an attempt to express "the inner consistency of reality."[9] As Wayne Booth notes, the achievement of this effect is difficult and nearly always requires special cooperation from the reader: "He must suspend to some extent his own disbeliefs; he must be receptive, open, ready to receive the clues."[10] Usually, the reader will not be "into" a book until he has read one or more chapters, but if the author has been successful and the reader perseveres, the reader will likely develop a desire that the world depicted exist, analogous to the desire generated by landscape painting.

It is tempting to discount the significance of this drive for reality in literature and art. Booth, for example, treats it as an outgrowth of the nineteenth-century scientist's "notion of firmly constituted natural objects," which is now outdated, since "scientists have given up the claim that they are seeking one single formulation of a firmly constituted reality."[11] To Thomas Cole, who complained that nineteenth-century Americans buying landscape paintings wanted things, not ideas, it was a sign of inadequate aesthetic education and poor taste. Neither comes close to being correct. It is not simply a fad that shows preference for physical reality; it is rather a transvaluation of aesthetic value in which conformity to objective reality becomes an aesthetic standard that limits creative imagination and, especially in landscape painting, transforms physical existence into an aesthetic predicate of beautiful objects. This value change, moreover, has its roots not in science and aesthetics but in philosophy itself, as becomes clear when one carefully attends to the major themes expressed in philosophy since its beginnings in Western thought.

THE VALUE OF EXISTENCE IN THE HISTORY OF PHILOSOPHY

It has been fashionable in philosophical circles through the centuries to scorn physical existence in favor of mind. This trend is most influentially revealed in the writings of Plato, who did not attribute full existence to the external world. The questionable status of physical reality nevertheless has its roots in general Greek philosophical concerns about the problem of change and the belief that the world as experienced interfered with rational inquiry into the nature of the universe. Similarly, disinterest in the material world was also encouraged in medieval times by the belief that love of nature was in conflict with love of God as a transcendent being and by the assimilation of Greek philosophy into Christian thought. Finally, questions about the existence of the external world, arising out of Descartes' *Meditations*, likewise focused attention on the problem of mind and directed it away from external nature. All of these factors significantly shaped the aesthetic tastes of eighteenth- and nineteenth-century artists such as Thomas Cole who were repelled by the thought of accurately depicting external nature. Taken together, these factors constitute a history of ideas that supports a preference for mind over matter, thought and imagination over physical existence. They lead in the direction of the views of the woman in Onondaga Cave who valued her memories more than their physical originals. They are not, however, the whole story.

Existence has always been highly valued by Western philosophers. Our earliest records of philosophical discussion concern the existence of the world (or the universe), and this emphasis is characteristic of virtually all classical philosophical writings. The same can be said of most modern philosophy, beginning with the writings of Descartes and continuing through the early decades of this century. Even today, metaphysics, the study of existence, although it is no longer as important as it once was, continues as a specific and major subject in the curriculum of every college and university large enough to have a philosophy department. If existence had not been considered to be valuable philosophically, the field of metaphysics would never have developed, and most of what counts as the history of philosophy would never have been written.

More specifically, despite strong philosophical biases against the belief in the existence of physical objects, much of the history of philosophy is compatible with the main themes that have been discussed so far in this chapter. First, although Plato does not attribute complete reality to the physical world and does not think the natural world very beautiful, his position is completely compatible with G. E. Moore's view that the natural world exists more completely and is more beautiful than a painting of it. Second, the basic metaphysical and epistemological problems about the existence of the world originating in Descartes' *Meditations* take a form that is consistent with the representational orientation that the kinds of aesthetic experiences we have been discussing require. Descartes wanted to know if the images in his mind during sensory experience accurately represent the physical world as it really exists objectively and independently of his perception, and ever since, all philosophers dealing with the problem of the existence of the external world have followed Descartes' general approach without significant deviation. The close connection is especially clear in the writings of David Hume. The first principle of association is resemblance. As a clear example of what he means, Hume points out that "a picture naturally leads our thoughts to the original." In discussing epistemology and metaphysics, he distinguishes among impressions, memory, and imagination. He attributes independent existence to impressions; the other two he treats as derivative from impressions through operations of the mind. They are, he stresses, less forceful and vivid: "All the colors of poetry, however splendid, can never paint natural objects in such a manner as to make the description be taken for a real landscape. The most lively thought is still inferior to the dullest sensation."[12] It is a very small step from here to Moore's conclusions about real and painted landscapes, if indeed any step is required.

These philosophical connections do not readily spring to mind because of philosophical prejudices toward physical nature reflecting very questionable Greek and early modern attitudes. As Quine stresses again and again in the first few pages of *Word and Object,* our ordinary language is most fundamentally based on the belief in physical objects: "References to physical objects are largely what hold [language] together," "our ordinary language of physical objects is about as basic as language gets," and "the familiar material objects may not be all that is real, but they are admirable examples." In learning to translate from one language to another, Quine notes, physical objects are almost invariably the starting place as shown "by the almost universal belief that objective references of terms in radically different languages can be objectively compared." Philosophy has done its best to undercut physical objects and elevate abstract objects, but it has failed to alter ordinary language or the world views based on it in any significant way.[13]

Hume probably made this general point most clearly in the following passage:

> It seems evident, that men are carried, by a natural instinct or pre-possession, to repose faith in their senses; and that, without any reasoning, or even almost before the use of reason, we always suppose an external universe, which depends not on our perception, but would exist though we and every sensible creature were absent or annihilated. Even the animal creation are governed by a like opinion, and preserve this belief of external objects, in all their thoughts, designs, and actions.
>
> It seems also evident, that, when men follow this blind and powerful instinct of nature, they always suppose the very images, presented by sense, to be the external objects, and never entertain any suspicion, that the one are nothing but representations of the other. This very table, which we see white, and which we feel hard, is believed to exist, independent of our perception, and to be something external to our mind, which perceives it. Our presence bestows not being on it; our mind does not annihilate it. It preserves its existence uniform and entire, independent of situation of intelligent beings, who perceive or contemplate it.
>
> But this universal and primary opinion of all men is soon destroyed by the slightest philosophy. . . .[14]

Even though skepticism about the existence of the external world is still fashionable and sophisticated, it does not mean that such skepticism is properly philosophical and that belief in physical existence is not. Nor does it follow that valuing material objects is in any way ethically or aesthetically improper.

The aesthetic appreciation of external nature is itself fully grounded in the history of philosophy. Indeed, aesthetics as a field in philosophy got its start through extensive philosophical discussion of the aesthetic properties of natural objects, specifically, their beauty and sublimity. The fact that contemporary work in aesthetics has focused very narrowly on art appreciation and has ignored nature appreciation in no way invalidates the writings of earlier philosophers, like Burke and Kant, who took nature aesthetics very seriously.

Having established plausible grounds for accepting the view that valuing existence in general and aesthetic qualities in nature in particular are in principle activities consistent with the history of philosophy, let us now turn to the main issue in this chapter: the relationship of positive aesthetics to preservationist arguments.

POSITIVE AESTHETICS AND PRESERVATIONIST ARGUMENTS

According to positive aesthetics, nature, to the degree that it is natural (that is, unaffected by human beings), is beautiful and has no negative aesthetic qualities. The single most famous expression of the view, endlessly quoted in the nineteenth century, comes from John Constable, who claimed, "I never saw an ugly thing in my life."[15] In accordance with this view, someone who finds ugliness in nature has simply failed to perceive nature properly, has failed to find appropriate standards by which to judge and appreciate it aesthetically.

Positive aesthetics is closely associated with a specific kind of preservationist argument that asserts nature's right to exist. According to this argument, which is generally expressed very poorly, whatever exists has a right to exist simply because it exists. The argument has, I believe, been appropriately criticized by Richard Watson in the following passage:

> A very serious problem with this proposal is that it may be a claim that whatever *is* thereby has a right to exist. This is to derive value from fact, which is a procedure generally rejected by philosophers. The mere existence of "the land" is neither an explanation of nor a justification for its having rights. Consider the entirely natural possibility that these entities do not exist. If they do not exist, they do not (on this ground) have a right to exist. Furthermore, if their right to exist depends upon their existence, then if they are destroyed, their rights are destroyed. And once they no longer exist, there are no longer any rights anyone could appeal to to blame the destroyers or to deplore the destruction. The paradoxical situation would be that they have a right to existence only until they are deprived of existence.

Watson tries to improve the argument by going beyond mere existence to the function of existing things, arguing that the continued existence of "the land" is instrumentally essential to the continued existence of human beings and that "the land" ought to exist not because it has rights but because humans have rights that are protected by protecting it. In its own way, this is a good argument, but it is not the one that environmentalists are trying to articulate by asserting a right to existence for nature. To make sense out of their argument, we need to turn to matters that Watson does not consider.[16]

At the outset, let me stress that the argument is already in trouble by asserting rights for nature at all. A right is a very specific kind of concept, either moral or legal. Philosophers have generally been unable to provide any grounds that allow these concepts to be applied to nature in the way that environmentalists generally talk of the rights of nature in their arguments.[17] The most serious problem is that rights apply only to the interests of individual beings, and most environmentalists who want to assert such rights are holists who are not really concerned about protecting the interests of individual beings. Their focus is on groups of individuals and on living and nonliving elements of systems that are not individuals in any plausible sense. In this context, it is usually considered appropriate to countenance the death of particular individuals (for example, by being eaten by predators) to facilitate the harmonious good of the whole. Any conceivable rights theory, that is, one that has some relationship with what we normally mean by rights in other contexts, is incompatible with this approach. As a result, talk about environmental rights usually makes sense only in terms of emotivism, as an expression of the feelings of the speaker, not as the assertion of a justifiable moral or legal claim. Thus, to avoid confusion, it is best to rephrase the assertion so that the claim that something has a right to exist is a claim that the speaker believes for some reason that the thing in question ought to exist. An argument can then be built up by examining the reasons that might be held for making that claim. Watson has provided a traditional ethical reason, our moral duty to protect the health and welfare of human beings. What is needed to satisfy the preservationists calling for rights for nature is an aesthetic reason, one expressed in terms of intrinsic value, not instrumental value.

It could be said that mere existence is a factual ground in preservationist arguments. If something does not already exist, it is factually not possible to preserve it. Mere existence alone, however, cannot be the basis for preservationist action, for, if it were, as Watson notes, we would indiscriminately have a duty to preserve anything and everything, but only so long as it existed. Mere existence is therefore a necessary but not a sufficient reason for preserving a natural object or natural system. To provide a basis for discriminating between and ranking candidates for preservationist action, we need to go beyond mere existence to the values associated with it. In doing so, positive aesthetics begins to play its role.

Since positive aesthetics asserts that everything that exists is beautiful, a preservationist argument involving it is open to the same criticism encountered when mere existence is treated as the sole ground for preservationist action. If everything is beautiful, and all beautiful things ought to be preserved, once again there is no basis for discrimination and ranking objects when not everything can be preserved. This problem can be avoided by accepting the view that there are degrees of beauty, that some objects are more beautiful than others, and that more beautiful objects ought to be given priority for preservation over less beautiful ones.

The application of this aesthetic argument can also be broadened by including all possible aesthetic categories: for example, the traditionally beautiful, the sublime, the picturesque, and, as discussed in Chapter 3, the scientifically interesting. In accordance with Moore's argument that beauty is a greater good than ugliness, it is then possible to identify a duty to preserve appropriate objects possessing aesthetic qualities in terms of each of these categories. This duty arises, as I interpret Moore, when the object of duty, what we ought to do, is viewed as the achievement of good—by his definition, what ought to be.[18]

This outline should, I believe, serve as an adequate ground for preservationist arguments, although in fact it does not. A critic could argue that the whole position is based entirely on an analogy with the preservation of art objects and that there are basic differences between art objects and natural objects that can dilute and sometimes nullify any duty we might have to preserve natural objects. One such argument is based on the view that art objects are the products of specific acts of creation in accordance with specific standards of beauty. Although aesthetic tastes may change so that we appreciate particular kinds of art more or less at various times in human history, the standards applying to each kind provide objective grounds, independent of our current preferences, for identifying the beauty involved. Natural beauty, in contrast, is not the result of artistic creation, and no standards exist for such beauty, other than our current preferences. As a result, as Passmore puts it, the appreciation of natural beauty is simply indiscriminate delight, and there is no reason to believe that what delights us now will delight our descendants, given that what delights us now did not delight our ancestors.[19] Implicit in this argument is a fundamental criticism of positive aesthetics as a whole: If everything is beautiful, even in varying degrees, then ultimately nothing is intrinsically beautiful, and beauty depends entirely on human preference. Thus the weak spot for the preservationist argument on the basis of natural beauty is whether there really is natural beauty in the external world, rather than, in Moore's terminology, just some sort of misguided affection.

THE EXISTENCE OF BEAUTY IN THE EXTERNAL WORLD

At the turn of the century, a Harvard geology professor, Nathaniel Southgate Shaler, wrote a now little-known book called *Man and the Earth.* In a chapter titled "The Beauty of the Earth," he attempts to deal with the objective beauty of the natural world head on. Shaler concedes that most of the features of natural landscapes have developed without any design or plan and independent of any deliberate intellectual choice. He includes, for example, mountain outlines, the shapes of crystals, and celestial bodies. Nevertheless, he continues, some animals, in addition to humans, are engaged in making aesthetic choices that shape the world in ways that "embody their conceptions of beauty in the objects they shape." These choices are, to be sure, usually or mostly unconscious, but they are choices nonetheless that produce beauty in the world in accordance with identifiable standards. First among these animals are insects, who have influenced the evolution of flowers to such a degree that their efforts can in quality measure up to "our best human art." The sense of beauty of these creatures, Shaler argues, is, though unconscious, "far stronger and more dominant than in mankind." In addition, fish, reptiles, and, to a lesser degree, amphibians have also displayed "the motive of beauty" through natural selection and other influences on their environment. Birds have so transformed themselves through selection that they "are, to us, the most beautiful of all organic shapes." All of these creatures and the plants they have influenced, Shaler argues, to the degree that they exhibit discriminating choices, can be considered to be natural works of art, and human artistic beauty is itself only one more step along the evolutionary progression, after a sad relapse in natural aesthetic taste brought on by the emergence of mammals, including primates. Humans themselves were, in the beginning, as aesthetically inept as other mammals, Shaler claims, until the skill in fashioning objects reawakened the dormant motive for beauty, which then enlarged so quickly that thereafter humans could "do no manner of work that does not embody it."[20]

Shaler's position has the merit of providing a basis for some objective beauty in external nature, generated through evolutionary process in terms of the preferences or choices of animals, but it cannot, of course, provide any foundation for a belief in the existence of beauty generated by nonliving nature, since it has no preferences and makes no choices. Moreover, it can be objected that there is no real evidence of nonhuman aesthetic choice or preference, unconscious or otherwise, and that whatever counts as organic beauty has been shaped as indifferently and uncreatively as inorganic beauty. In other words, there is no creativity in nature comparable to the creativity in art.

Although there appears to be no scientific solution to this problem, it can be solved theistically by straightforwardly viewing nature as a collection of art objects planned and designed by God. If this theory is adopted, there is no significant difference between nature appreciation and art appreciation, since both nature and art are then the products of the creative activity of artists. There are, however, two significant problems. First, this theory requires the belief in a God that created the universe in a very specific way. Not all people believe in God, and not all people who believe in God believe that He created the universe in the way required by the theory. Second, the theory requires the rejection of basic elements of modern science, specifically, geological uniformitarianism and evolution, both of which present a view of natural history as neither planned nor designed, once again, in any conscious way, making it more difficult, though not completely impossible, to view nature as art. The key problem once again is creativity.

Allen Carlson has developed a scientific alternative to this theistic approach in terms of a positive aesthetics in which he takes into account the difference between art and nature on the basis of creativity but does not abandon a relationship between nature and creativity altogether. According to Carlson, "Art is created, while nature is discovered."[21] What this means is that the creation of an art object begins with a plan in the mind of an artist. This plan is, moreover, in accordance with some style, approach, or movement. After the object has been created, it is then aesthetically judged and appreciated in terms of the standards appropriate for that kind of art. Natural objects, in contrast, are not the result of any comparable plan, and since they are not in accordance with some style, approach, or movement, there are no appropriate preexisting standards by which they can be judged and appreciated. Hence they are discovered and studied scientifically, and out of this study appropriate standards gradually emerge. To Carlson, creativity still plays a role, but in the case of natural objects, the creativity is not in the creation of the objects but in the creation of the appropriate aesthetic standards.

Carlson's position has merit in that it provides what is probably a rather accurate account of how we humans go about putting ourselves in the position to judge and appreciate nature aesthetically. It is factually correct that we discover features of nature and through study of them develop aesthetic standards for assessing their beauty. It may also be true that creativity is involved in the making of these standards. Nevertheless, I believe that Carlson is in error in concluding that nature is not itself creative, for it is possible to construct a position that attributes creativity to nature, is at the same time compatible with both theistic and scientific perspectives, and is firmly grounded in traditional philosophy.

Creativity is derived from the same root as *creation. Creation* is the universe and everything in it as created by God. A *creation* is something original, for example, a work of art, the product of human imagination, invention, or design. *Creativity* is the creative ability that makes possible the creation of Creation by God or a creation by a lesser being. The latter is based on, but less than, the former. In this context, nature in its own right is said to lack creativity because it is not capable of *consciously* formulating an imaginative plan or design in advance. It is this point that I want to challenge, for I want to argue that creativity does not require conscious advance planning.

The relation of God to value was much debated by philosophers at the end of the Middle Ages. A curious paradox had to be resolved concerning the origin of good. Did God, philosophers wondered, create goodness in the world in accordance with some standard of good, or did the world become good simply because He created it? Although on the surface the first alternative seems the more reasonable, it conflicts with the Christian conception of God's omnipotence. If God created good in the world in accordance with some standard of good, this standard represents a restriction on God that limits His omnipotence. Thus to protect Himself, it was necessary for God to create the goodness in the world in a rather peculiar way, *indifferently,* without regard to any standards, so that whatever He did was by definition good. All this is summed up nicely by Descartes in the following passage:

> To one who pays attention to God's immensity, it is clear that nothing at all can exist which does not depend on him. This is true not only of everything that persists, but of all order, of every law, and of every reason of truth and goodness; for otherwise God . . . would not have been wholly indifferent to the creation of what he has created. For if any reason for what is good had preceded His preordination, it would have determined Him towards that which it was best to bring about; but on the contrary because He determined Himself towards those things which ought to be accomplished, for that reason, as it stands in Genesis, *they are very good;* that is to say, the reason for their goodness is the fact that He wished to create them so.[22]

This account of creation is important because it shows that it is impossible for God to create the world in a manner analogous to the way that a work of art is created. Although God was presumably conscious when he created the world, He was not in the position in which He could make a plan or design for what He was creating. Thus all goodness, including the beauty in nature, is an unplanned and undesigned consequence of His creative act. Goodness and beauty came first. The standards of goodness and beauty came afterward. Was the goodness and beauty of the world brought into being *creatively* as an expression of God's creativity? The answer must be yes, if creativity means creative ability—and if this is the case, creativity does not require an advance plan or design consciously conceived.

Once the importance of indifference in the creation of nature is properly recognized, it is possible to formulate theories of natural creation that reconcile the theistic and scientific accounts already discussed and provide a universally acceptable foundation for positive aesthetics. In the theistic account, uniformitarianism and evolution can be presented as the mechanisms God employed and continues to employ to maintain His creative indifference. In nontheistic scientific and even atheistic accounts, virtually nothing needs to be changed, since uniformitarianism and evolution, with or without God, sustain indifferent creativity equally well. Although belief in God is, of course, a major difference between these accounts, it makes no practical difference as far as the other elements of the account are concerned. The theistic version simply posits God as the creator of what follows.

The key issue is not whether God exists or not but whether it is appropriate on traditional grounds to attribute divine powers and abilities, in particular, indifferent creativity, to nature. Although it may appear on the surface that it is not, there are some good historical and contemporary precedents in favor of doing so. Consider the emergence of the sublime in aesthetics. The sublime did not arise out of nothing. It was actually the transfer of an aesthetic property from God to nature. The awesomeness of mountains, for example, previously treated as a symbol of God's wrath at the time of the Flood of Noah, became a direct aesthetic property of those objects. Similar, though more pleasant, associations with God attended the emergence of beauty in nature. Forests, for example, previously considered to be dark and dangerous places with little redeeming value, were flooded with light in landscape painting, suggesting the presence of God in nature or, even more radically, nature as God. Finally, the treatment of nature as God, as disclosed by the capitalizing of the word *nature,* has been widespread in literature since the end of the Middle Ages and is especially prominent in a great deal of environmental literature today (for example, in writings on deep ecology).

Perhaps the best precedent, established in this century, comes out of the writings of Jean-Paul Sartre, who attempts a transfer of God's powers and abilities to man in a parallel context. In his essay "Existentialism," Sartre argues that if God exists, man is a being whose essence precedes his existence. Like a paper cutter, man is first planned and then brought into physical existence. This situation, however, is completely changed if God is eliminated from active participation in the creative process, for man then becomes a being who creates himself. As Sartre puts it, man becomes a being whose existence precedes his essence, which means "that, first of all, man exists, turns up, appears on the scene, and, only afterwards, defines himself." In defining himself, man, like God in Descartes' account, also creates values, and these values, Sartre insists, are always good whatever they are, "because we can never choose evil." Why we can never choose evil Sartre fails to explain very fully, but it seems certain that he, following

Descartes, is invoking creative indifference: Value emerges from creative action; the action creates the standards by which it will be judged, making whatever results good by definition.[23]

There are problems with this Sartrean transfer, some of which even Sartre is willing to admit. For example, he concedes that his account of man brings with it godlike responsibilities that are too heavy for most human beings to bear, paving the way for the emergence of dark existential human emotions. There are also difficulties with man's biological nature. Although Sartre declares that our biological makeup is part of the human condition—the circumstances man faces when he is thrown into the world, and not an essence that emerges with his existence—his argument is not entirely convincing, for there is considerable evidence available that man's behavior is strongly influenced by biological factors.

Whether such problems can be overcome, or are even problems, and whether Sartre's account of man as a kind of unwilling substitute for God is entirely appropriate or "true" need not concern us here. I have introduced Sartre's account only as a precedent for taking a similar analysis of nature seriously, to show that God's difficulties with His omnipotence during creation, as described by Descartes, can have contemporary application and to introduce helpful terminology.

Consider the following argument: In Sartrean terms, nature is either an entity whose essence precedes its existence or whose existence precedes its essence. If there is a God who created and now sustains the world, and Descartes' account of creative indifference is true, nature was created without a plan in advance, and its existence precedes its essence. If there is no God, as Sartre claims, there is no one to create nature, producing the need, therefore, for nature to create itself, and since nature also does not plan its creations in advance, but instead blunders along through the mechanisms of uniformitarianism and evolution, once again its existence precedes its essence.

If this argument is accepted, we have solved two important problems, the problem of positive aesthetics—why nature is always beautiful and never ugly—and the problem of the existence of beauty in the external world. If nature's existence precedes its essence, the natural product of nature's indifferent creativity, whether through God or through itself, is and has to be good and beautiful, because whatever is so created always brings with it compatible standards of goodness and beauty. Put another way, nature is itself its own standard of goodness and beauty, making ugliness impossible as a product of nature's own creative activity. This takes care of the problem of positive aesthetics. Concerning the existence of beauty in the world, if beauty is always the result of creative activity in nature, then as long as some natural objects exist that are the unspoiled products of that creative activity, some beauty also exists in the world.

These arguments will probably not, I admit, be universally accepted. Ordinary people, who already believe in positive aesthetics and the existence of beauty in the world intuitively, will feel that no proof is necessary other than the direct evidence of our senses. Non-Westerners will probably be unwilling to accept the basic presuppositions behind Descartes' position, thereby erasing the starting point. The point of the arguments, however, is not to provide a definitive proof of positive aesthetics and the existence of natural beauty but rather to show that these positions can be defended on very traditional grounds against the claims of philosophers such as Passmore who maintain that there is no basis from the standpoint of Western traditions for asserting that nature is beautiful.

Even if it is conceded that nature is beautiful, on the grounds just given or on intuitive grounds, it still needs to be established that natural beauty is worthy of being preserved. Since it is already widely accepted that beautiful works of art ought to be preserved, an examination of the relative merit of natural and artistic beauty is a good way to continue. It is to this matter that I now turn.

THE SUPERIORITY OF NATURAL BEAUTY

G. E. Moore's thought experiment concerning the beauty of a natural landscape and a painting depicting it will invariably show that ordinary people almost universally consider natural beauty superior to most art simply on the basis of the value added by the existence, the presence, of the natural beauty in external nature. Philosophers, by contrast, have generally maintained that natural beauty is aesthetically inferior to artistic beauty. Various reasons have been given: that nature is not the product of creative imagination, that it lacks design, and that it is too alien to conform to human aesthetic standards and tastes.

It is true that beautiful natural objects are not created in the same way as works of art. We have established that nature is not the result of creative imagination. But it is not clear to me that this difference between art and nature elevates artistic beauty over natural beauty. First, beyond any doubt, nature is created and creative. It is, to be exact, self-created. Is it, however, a lesser creation, the result of a lesser creativity? Although it is conventional wisdom to claim that natural beauty is modeled on and only imperfectly analogous to artistic beauty, this position may derive its strength from the recent narrowing of focus in aesthetics on art and not be historically accurate. There is also the Western tradition that artistic creativity is modeled on the creative activity of God. In this context, creative activity of an artist would then be analogous to the creative activity of God as exemplified in nature, making natural beauty superior to and the model for its artistic counterpart.

Even if it is accepted, however, that nature as Creation is superior to the creations of art, it might be argued that imaginative creativity produces beauty that is nevertheless in some sense or at least in some cases superior to natural beauty indifferently created. Imagination is presumably capable of producing or creating aesthetically pleasing objects because it is a function of mind, which in turn is considered superior to mindless matter. There is a strong tradition in Western philosophy supporting these assumptions, but once again, they are not the whole story. Imagination is not one of the most celebrated functions of mind; usually reason and memory are considered more fundamental. Moreover, the products of imagination, for example, the imaginary and the illusory, are not generally held in high esteem on the grounds that they are not physically real. Thus the emphasis when imaginative creativity is promoted or stressed as valuable may not be on the imaginative origins of a work of art but on the fact that through the creative process an object goes from being purely imaginary in a negative sense to a state in which it exists as a physical object—for example, a piece of nonrepresentational sculpture—or at least to a state in which it seems realistic—for example, a novel or a piece of representational art.

This generally uncomplimentary view of imagination is widespread among philosophers throughout the history of philosophy, but is strongest and most appropriate for our purposes in the philosophy of Hume. As noted earlier, Hume ranks impressions, memory, and imagination in terms of their force and vivacity, putting imagination last. For him, imagination is not only twice removed from the reality found in the liveliness of impressions, but it is also the most limited. According to Hume, the human mind cannot imagine anything completely new: "The creative power of the mind amounts to no more than the faculty of compounding, transposing, augmenting, or diminishing the materials afforded us by the senses and experience."[24] I do not discount the possibility that human minds might be able to imagine something, the parts of which have no clear origin in nature; however, in art, in particular, in Humean terms, such a possibility would seem to be an exception to the rule, if it occurs at all, for close examination would, I believe, reveal empirical origins for virtually all elements of a work of art originally conjoined through imagination, whether it is overtly representational or not.

One possible exception, and an important contribution to beauty, is the creation of geometric figures. Squares, circles, cubes, straight lines, and other geometric forms do not occur in nature in any great quantity, and our use of such shapes in artistic and other craftsmanship is probably not derived straightforwardly from memory and imagination as described by Hume. More likely these figures are historically the product of abstraction based on impressions of less regular shapes in nature. Still, even here, a connection with nature remains.

Given the lowly status of imagination, it is hard to imagine why imaginative creativity has been praised so loudly in art aesthetics. One unflattering possibility might be that doing so makes the best of a bad situation by making a virtue out of a necessity. In this view, imaginative creativity is employed in the production of humanly fashioned beauty not because it makes artistic beauty superior to natural beauty but because humans are unable to create beauty indifferently and so must rely on imaginative planning in order to have any chance of achieving anything of significant aesthetic value. In other words, imagination is introduced to mask a defect in the inferior creative abilities of humans in comparison with those of God and nature.

Let us turn now to the problem of design in nature. The idea that nature lacks design will appear ludicrous to those who know nature well. The design of nature, for example, the web of ecological relationships in natural systems is, of course, so complex that rarely do we understand it fully. The amount of detail in nature is enormous. Nevertheless, arguments, or at least charges, for the claim that nature lacks design can be made: that it is chaotic, unfinished, and imperfect.

The idea that nature is chaotic seems to stem from the perception that the mind-boggling complexity of nature implies that it is somehow out of control. Although it is true that on occasion nature may really be out of control, for example, during catastrophic events, usually this perception is in error. Since *chaos* is the disorder of formless matter, to be *chaotic* is to be in disorder or confusion with regard to form. Such chaos cannot meaningfully be attributed to nature. Even the most chaotic events in nature have form, and this form can be identified in great detail when humans take the time to look.

Nature can most properly be viewed on analogy with a piece of classical music that runs the gamut from frenzied upheaval to melodious tranquility and back again. The discordant elements of the composition are not formless; moreover, they fit together with their opposites in a pattern or design that emerges as a reconciliation, a harmonious resolution. In the same way, the sublime in nature complements picturesque beauty, producing a harmonious whole. When someone cites sublimity as proof of lack of design, all that is proved is that that person lacks proper aesthetic taste and has simply failed to see the design, not that it does not exist.

The charge that nature is unfinished is, on the one hand, a factual statement and, on the other, a simple sign of aesthetic snobbery and prejudice. It is true that works of art are not truly works of art until they are finished. There are definite stages, beginning with creative imagination aimed specifically at finishing the work of art. When the object is finished, creativity ceases; it becomes a past event to be admired during future acts of appreciation. The aim of artistic creation is the production of an object that is as timeless and unchanging as physical nature permits, is complete in itself, and has fulfilled all of its potential. Granted, the results of this activity are aesthetically worthwhile to a very high degree, but does our appreciation of such objects depend on standards that, once accepted, require us to view the products of natural creativity as unfinished in the sense of being incomplete, not whole? I would be willing to consider an affirmative answer to this question if our preference for such standards were, at least in part, the result of extensive experimentation in which we had achieved mastery over unfinished creativity before rejecting it as inferior. The few experiments that have been undertaken have been of limited duration and have hardly been great successes. Put simply, the creation of something that will change continuously over indefinite spans of time, while being beautiful from moment to moment, is at least at this time beyond human artistic ability.

These considerations suggest that there is a need for a double standard, one for artistic objects and one for nature. From the standpoint of nature, to be complete need not mean to be finished, to come to an end. If the creative activity in nature were to reach an end point analogous to the completion of a work of art, the result would be failure, not triumph. The complete fulfillment of the potentiality of nature would mean the *exhaustion* of that potentiality. In this context, there is considerable traditional support for a preference for nature unfinished and continuous. As Aristotle notes in the *Nichomachean Ethics,* good can be found in both activities and the products of activities.[25] Seen in this way, the good of art is the creation of a product through artistic activity; the good of nature is the creative activity itself. While the aim of art is the production of objects that approach Platonic timelessness, the aim of nature is self-sufficient, continuous, preferably eternal activity for its own sake. As a result, although being finished in art is a virtue, being finished in nature is a defect and is irrelevant to the design that is obvious to the discriminating eye.

The charge that nature lacks design because it is imperfect derives its strength in part from the previous charges that nature is chaotic and unfinished, which we need not discuss further, but also from the belief that nature in perfect form would be in the shape of ideal geometric figures. The formal landscape garden is one triumph of this ideal. While this geometric preference can be traced back to Greek philosophy, to Plato and Pythagoras, in particular, the fixation on geometric figures as an improvement over natural forms is probably much older and not entirely a product of educated and learned Western civilization. Around 2500 B.C., when the pyramids in Egypt were built, Indo-European peoples moving across Europe began transforming agricultural lands into rectangular fields, in preference to the round or oval fields of the Neolithic peoples they were displacing, producing a checkerboard pattern across the landscape. This peculiar practice cannot be justified in terms of good farming practice alone. The best approach in terms of efficiency and productivity would have been to have planted crops in the best soil, which would rarely, if ever, exist in rectangular patches. In part, the imposition of geometric form on the landscape resulted from a primitive concept of ownership, in which the boundaries of landholdings were written on the land with the plough. Nevertheless, since landholding does not have to be geometric, it must also have been, in some sense, an aesthetic preference. At a minimum it can be viewed as an unconscious preference of the kind Shaler attributes to insects in his discussion of the evolution of beauty in flowers. Given the obvious geometric aesthetic preferences of the civilizations to the south, however, it is not unreasonable to assume that the early northern Europeans also took some aesthetic pleasure in the geometric transformation they were bringing about, just as American settlers did in the nineteenth century. Moreover, even if it was initially an unconscious aesthetic preference, it certainly became conscious long before the formal gardens of the seventeenth century.[26]

What can be said about this aesthetic preference? Does it really perfect nature? Ideal geometric forms rarely occur in nature except through the crystalization of minerals. It is remotely possible that our European ancestors may have considered this rarity a defect in nature and sought to join forces with mineral creation to bring nature into greater balance and harmony. Whatever the impact of the rarity of these forms in nature, however, it is clear that humans imposed them in the course of human conquest and domination over nature, and this is not a perfecting activity but a transformative one. Such transformations do not make nature more perfect, in the sense of better; they just make it different, in the sense of more human, more civilized, less natural. They are simply the replacement of a natural design with a less natural one. Is nature better designed when it is reshaped in terms of ideal geometric forms? It may be so from the standpoint of human aesthetic admiration for simple geometric forms, but the artificial design is nearly always less stable, less self-sustaining, less permanent than the displaced natural one, in both agricultural and landscape garden settings. To maintain these shapes for any length of time requires constant attention and continuous labor. Seen in this way, geometric design, humanly imposed, may be said to be inferior in terms of the normal standards for artistic beauty.

Regardless of these considerations, the claim that nature is imperfect because it does not imitate ideal geometric patterns has support in Western aesthetic and philosophical traditions. These traditions, however, also need to be put in their proper context and balanced against still another tradition, which we have already discussed: the common environmentalist claim that nature is perfect as it is. Although Passmore treats this claim as an aberrant primitivist view,[27] it is actually another implication of Descartes' general position on God and Creation: Nature must itself be perfect because it was created by a perfect being. Historically, this position has manifested itself as a transference of a divine characteristic, perfection, to nature in the same way that the sublimity of God became an aesthetic property of mountains, and like sublimity, it has survived translation into nontheistic contexts. From this standpoint, the perception of imperfection in nature is an aesthetic error of judgment reflecting the limitations of the finite human mind, not evidence that such imperfection actually exists in the design of nature.

Let us turn now to the final issue, the claim that natural beauty is inferior to artistic beauty because it is too alien to conform to human aesthetic standards and taste. This position has been defended in *Man's Responsibility for Nature,* where Passmore argues there that domesticated nature is preferable to wild nature, wilderness, because it is, from a human standpoint, more agreeable and intelligible. Humans understand domesticated nature because they "helped make it." In contrast, Passmore continues, "From the wilderness [man] is always in some measure alienated; it stands in a relation to him of pure externality."[28] In this context, nature appreciation is simply communion with the humanized elements in nature, and as such, at the individual level, it is communion with one's own self.

This conception of nature has common elements with, for example, Locke's theory of property, in which, as noted in Chapter 2, nature achieves value through human labor. Nature so transformed becomes property because something human, labor, has entered into raw nature and been permanently joined with it. This view of nature as something incomplete and nearly valueless waiting for a humanizing inpouring of structure, order, and value also surfaces in Hegel's philosophical writings, where he argues that because nature has no will of its own, humans have the right to use their wills to enter into any and all natural things, making them their own.[29]

Despite these good historical credentials, the claim that nature is alien is a peculiar one not only because human beings are themselves beyond any doubt part of nature but also because, as already noted with reference to Hume, human aesthetic standards are ultimately derived from nature. Given that humans are part of nature, it is impossible for nature and humanity to be completely alien to each other. Given that our aesthetic standards come from nature, it is absurd for someone to claim that nature's standards are too alien to be agreeable and intelligible from any human standpoint.

There is some historical basis for the claim that nature is alien. In early nature aesthetics, when the sublime in nature was first recognized, this sublimity was regarded as something alien to human life and values. The alienness, however, did not prevent aesthetic appreciation of nature; rather it enhanced it—it was, in fact, the alienness of the sublime that was its primary aesthetic attraction. Furthermore, this alienness did not promote alienation but rather reconciliation: Over the long term, increased familiarity and understanding of this alien nature through natural history science brought about an aesthetic revolution in which much of what was previously considered sublime was transformed and subsumed under expanded standards of beauty. Mountains came to be viewed as magnificent rather than terrifying, as being in harmony with their surroundings rather than at odds with them. The history that Passmore cites with approval ends with the informal garden.[30] At that time, it probably was true that wild nature was too alien to many people to be agreeable and intelligible. In terms of the complete history, however, it is ultimately no less agreeable and intelligible than its domesticated counterpart.

When one looks at nature from a contemporary standpoint, it is not so much alien as other, and this otherness makes a positive contribution to human aesthetic values by being a primary source for them. Given, as I have argued, that all human standards of beauty are derived from nature by direct borrowing or in reaction to nature's standards, it is probably correct to say that there would be no beauty at all if it did not exist first and foremost in nature, and in this sense, as the wellspring of beauty, natural beauty may be said to be superior to, and a necessary condition for, artistic beauty in general.

It is not true, of course, that all natural beauty is superior to all art. There are degrees of beauty both in nature and in art, and some of the best works of human art compare favorably with, and are perhaps superior to, many of nature's creations. Given, moreover, that works of art and works of nature depend on different kinds of creative activity and thus on somewhat different standards for aesthetic appreciation, it could be plausibly argued that comparing the beauty of art and nature is as inappropriate as comparing apples and oranges. This conclusion is permissible and unobjectionable as long as the interrelationships between the two are not entirely forgotten, the debt of artistic beauty to natural beauty is not overlooked, and it is acknowledged that in principle some natural beauty is as worthy of preservation as artistic beauty.

THE ONTOLOGICAL ARGUMENT FOR THE PRESERVATION OF NATURE

Traditionally, the *ontological argument* refers to various proofs of the existence of God, according to which it is asserted that the essence of God requires His existence. These proofs are metaphysical arguments without direct ethical implications. The ontological argument for the preservation of nature, in contrast, is primarily aesthetic and ethical, not metaphysical. It is not intended to prove that nature exists, which is taken as a given, but to show that humans have a duty to act so as to ensure the continuation of nature in its appropriate, natural form.

Many of the main features of an ontological argument for the preservation of nature have already been identified and discussed. In accordance with suggestive remarks and claims by Moore, the argument begins with the relationship between duty and good. In the most general terms, as I noted earlier, the object of duty, what we ought to do, is the achievement of good, what ought to be. In this context, the duty to promote and preserve beauty arises out of the recognition that beauty, whether experienced or not, is a good. In addition, the duty specifically to promote and preserve natural beauty arises out of the recognition that not only artistic beauty but also natural beauty constitutes an aesthetic good that makes up part of the general good that exists and ought to exist in the world.

The duty to promote and preserve artistic beauty is, I believe, widely accepted and completely uncontroversial. There is general consensus among nearly all humans that art objects ought to be promoted and preserved. The world is considered a better world because of the existence of works of art. The creation of additional works of art is taken as an improvement, increasing the amount of good existing in the world. The destruction of works of art is considered to be wrong because it decreases the amount of good in the world. Humans, as moral agents, are expected to take these factors into consideration whenever their actions may alter the amount of beauty existing in the world.

This duty to promote and preserve artistic beauty lends support to the duty to promote and preserve natural beauty, which also is widely accepted but is more controversial. There are two possible objections. It could be claimed first that nature is not beautiful at all or, second, that its beauty is so inferior to the beauty of art that no duty to promote and preserve it is required. Both objections have been fully refuted in my various discussions and need not concern us further here: As I already have shown, there is natural beauty in the world in a generally accepted sense, and this beauty is not in principle inferior to artistic beauty.

Our duties to promote and preserve beauty in art and nature are similar but not identical. They are similar in that existence plays the same role in the aesthetic appreciation of both natural and artistically created objects. Put simply, existence is an aesthetic property of both kinds of objects, and the quality of the aesthetic experience of a beautiful object, natural or artistic, is strongly affected by the manner in which it exists. Since the loss of both natural and artistic beauty represents a loss in the total good in the world, it is our duty to try to preserve both kinds of beauty as best we can.

It is in terms of the efforts to preserve beauty that the differences in our duties with regard to each kind of beauty begin to appear. In the case of art, a beautiful object is preserved by placing the object in surroundings where it will remain in good condition and by repairing it when necessary. In the event that the object is destroyed, much of the beauty can be retained by re-creating the object, by making copies. In the case of nature, preserving a natural object is more difficult. First, the object cannot be placed, since it already is a place, or at least part of a place. Second, repairing it can destroy its beauty. While it might be appropriate in some cases to counter unnatural influences indirectly, direct attempts to preserve a natural object usually constitute interference with natural process, reducing its beauty. Third, re-creations of natural objects, after they have been destroyed, retain little of the beauty of the original.

The reason for these differences is that existence plays a more fundamental role in natural objects than in art objects. As noted earlier, an art object is an entity whose essence precedes its existence. An art object is made in the same way that Sartre's paper cutter is made. The beauty of the art object exists in imagination before the object itself comes to be. In contrast, a natural object is an entity whose existence precedes its essence. In this case, the beauty has no prior existence in imagination and in fact no prior existence of any kind. It emerges only when the natural object takes physical form. This is a critical difference between natural and artistic beauty. It is better for artistic beauty to exist physically; nevertheless, because it has preexistence in imagination, its beauty is not directly or entirely dependent on the process of physical actualization. This point is especially clear in the case of nonpermanent, or ephemeral, earthworks, for example, Christo's *Valley Curtain.* As Peter Humphrey notes in his interesting examination of earthworks, he, like most people, became aware of this work of art by looking at plans of it in a special exhibit in a museum. In this context he goes on to ask "how important . . . our *knowledge* that there really was an enormous, orange curtain near Rifle, Colorado," is to our aesthetic appreciation of it after the fact, and concludes "that there's a possibility worth considering that such knowledge doesn't matter."[31] I am inclined to agree. If one thinks of the plans for the curtain as analogous to an ideal landscape painting, the plans themselves can be appreciated as an art object independent of whether they were or are ever carried out. Similarly, sketches for a work of art that was never finished can often serve as an adequate source for the beauty that would have been in the original. Such is not the case, however, with natural beauty. Since natural beauty does not have preexistence in the imagination or in artist sketches, it must exist physically in order to exist in any sense at all.

This is an important ontological difference. In criticizing the traditional ontological argument, Kant argues that existence is not a true predicate on the grounds that "the real contains no more than the merely possible." Since a hundred coins that physically exist do not possess any properties that are not contained in our concept of them, the physical existence of the coins is irrelevant to their properties and to predicates expressing those properties.[32] Kant's point is certainly correct with regard to objects created by humans, in which the concept precedes their creation, and would also be true of nature, for example, in a universe without evolution in which natural form was fixed and immutable, but it is not true of the objects in the natural world in the universe we actually live in. Our concepts of natural objects rarely, if ever, include all the properties those objects possess. A real, existing tree is more than a human's concept of it. For this reason, if existence is not itself a property, not a predicate of the tree, the tree's existence is nevertheless tied up with the tree's other properties in a way that the properties of the coins are not tied up with their existence.

The problem being addressed here stems directly from the limitations of the human mind, both conceptually and imaginatively. The human mind has great difficulty dealing with complexity, which is, of course, one of nature's chief characteristics. In science, humans have progressed by employing a reductionist method, by breaking nature's complexity down into its simple parts. Although this method has been very productive, it has provided a distorted and simplified picture of nature. In art, likewise, humans have progressed through simplification. The creative impulse in nature is toward the realization of beauty through the generation of complex forms and relations. The creative impulse in humans, resulting from the limitations of their minds, is, in contrast, toward the realization of simplified beauty. This trend is obvious not only in nonrepresentational art but in representational art as well. Nonrepresentational art tends to focus on simple geometric forms. While representational art tries to depict nature accurately, it must do so in a manner that presents forms that are simpler and less detailed than those of the original objects in nature. The result is art that suggests the complexity of nature but does not capture its complete reality. This is true not only of painting but also of landscape gardening, in which the elements of nature itself are used. The assemblage of the simple elements, the various plants and animals, does not produce the real thing. As landscape gardeners learned when they first began trying to imitate wild nature, they could not duplicate the inner processes, the inner reality. The methods used to produce formal gardens were also required to produce informal ones. Without careful attention, the gardens collapsed into chaos.

Recognition that complexity is a distinguishing feature of natural beauty that irredeemably sets it apart from the artistic beauty of human beings brings us back to the issue raised in Chapter 5, therapeutic nihilism. Nature knows best (or perhaps does best) in part because whatever it does through creative indifference is beautiful but also, more importantly, because the end result is a creative output that is far too complex for humans to reproduce, to go beyond, or even fully to participate in; as such, it is unique and irreplaceable. We find in the writings of philosophers such as Moore and Passmore and scientists such as Shaler, who are willing to talk about the beauty of the Earth, a willingness to accept the view that humans have a duty to improve on the beauty of nature. Such a duty makes sense insofar as artistically created human beauty is considered to be a special case within the realm of natural beauty. The generation of beauty through simplification is, of course, aesthetically valuable and something that nature can take credit for, not only because complex nature is what humans react against but also because it is the biological source of human beings and all their activity, aesthetic and otherwise. Such a duty, however, does not make sense if it calls for human involvement in the creative process of nonhuman nature, given the vast difference in the approaches of nature and humankind. Since attempts to improve natural beauty will distort, transform, and even destroy that beauty, our duty should not be to improve but rather to promote and preserve through action and inaction that does not restrict, impinge on, redirect, or bring to an end the geological and biological activity on which the indifference of natural creativity depends.

In rejecting the duty to improve nature in favor of one to promote and preserve it, we have to be careful that we do so for the right reasons. The fact that we cannot improve nature in terms of nature's own standards is, of course, an important reason, but it is not the primary one. To attempt to manipulate nature, even for aesthetic reasons, alters nature adversely from an aesthetic standpoint. Historically, manipulation of nature, even to improve it, has been considered subjugation or domination. Such manipulation limits the freedom of nature, which in turn reduces its ability to be creative. The beauty of nature arises out of self-creation, which requires freedom from nonnatural influence. Our appreciation of the beauty of nature is not focused simply on the direct sensory awareness of the moment but is also filtered through an understanding and appreciation of the creative forces that produced that moment in nature's history. Just as we want an art object to be original, the actual result of the artistic process, we want the beauty of nature to be authentic, the result of natural processes only.

The authenticity of nature arises out of the fact that its existence precedes its essence. Nature is not simply a collection of natural objects; it is a process that progressively transforms those objects, retaining some, altering and discarding others, as it selectively unfolds and actualizes its possibilities. Although many natural objects are destroyed in this way, the loss is not complete, for they remain part of the ongoing natural history that constitutes the essence of nature. Nature aesthetically is not simply what exists at this point in time; it is also the entire series of events and undertakings that have brought it to that point. When we admire nature, we also admire that history. When we interfere with nature, regardless of whether our intentions are good or not, we create a break in that natural history. We cannot help nature with its plans, for it does not have any plans. When we make plans to help or improve nature, the plans are not nature's but our own, and the result is the stifling of natural creativity and the transformation of the natural objects influenced into human artifacts. No matter how natural they may look, they are no longer original, no longer authentic: Their ontological status has been altered; they have become objects whose essence has preceded their existence.

One of the best examples of the effect of human interference on existence, or being, of wild nature is an analysis by Bruce Foltz of an exchange between Charles Park, a geologist working for a mining company, and David Brower, an environmentalist. In response to a comment by Park that he could not understand why a mining operation that was not visible in a wilderness area should ruin the quality of that area, Brower responded that "the mood would go." Foltz comments on this exchange as follows:

> What Park utterly fails to see, and what Brower merely touches upon, is that the mining operation does not let the mountain *be* a mountain. It is not just the mood of the mountain which is transformed, but its very being. Even the regions which Park would regard as completely unaffected are installed within the mining district, i.e., as the *nonproductive parts* of the installation itself. Glacier Peak would be in this instance precisely a copper mining district, deriving its being from that of the operation.
>
> Understood from this perspective, the notion of "restoration" in such a case also becomes incoherent; beyond our knowledge of the complexities of ecological succession, it must be seen that something which has been subjected to the domination of technology in this manner—which has become a resource whose yield has been challenged forth, extracted, and delivered—cannot be simply released back into its own being through technological planning. As "restored," the mountain preserves its status as a technological reserve. Ontologically, the only difference is that it is now an *exhausted* mining district.

In contrast, Foltz maintains, a firepit made by Native Americans would not have such an effect, for

> it has neither provoked the earth, nor forced anything from it. . . . It is not a question here of releasing the site of the fire from the grip of technique, since from the beginning the excavation has allowed the earth to remain earth.[33]

Numerous other examples of the effect of human activity on the reality of natural entities can easily be developed. Consider the differences between the lobo or gray wolf, the coyote, and the domestic dog. The dog is pure and simply a human artifact, bred through artificial selection over hundreds of thousands of years. It is now a part of human history, not natural history. The coyote continues to be a part of natural history, but its status, despite its popularity as an environmentalist symbol, is questionable. There is considerable evidence that extensive efforts in this century to exterminate the coyote, for example, by killing off the less intelligent members of the species, have altered the evolutionary direction of the coyote in a way that is inadvertently similar to artificial selection. Is the coyote a triumph of wild nature over humankind or a mixed creature that is partially humanized and on its way to becoming a human artifact like the dog? No unequivocal answer is possible. The lobo has retained its natural purity through extinction, but once again, by the hand of man. It remains a part of natural history, but it is a strand unnaturally severed. Its reality now is completely limited to our human concept of it, since its additional properties were lost with its extinction. Unlike species that naturally become extinct, it is not imbedded in the natural history that has followed its demise, except by omission.

What nature has lost in the extinction of the lobo can be made clearer by an examination of an animal that has survived many geological and biological epochs and remains a very visible part of our current era: the alligator. Consider the following cases: (1) an alligator in Okefenokee Swamp in Georgia, (2) an alligator on an alligator farm in Florida, and (3) a plastic alligator that is part of the safari boat ride at Walt Disney World. The alligator in the swamp has both a contemporary and historical reality. It is, first of all, a part of wild nature as it exists today; it is a representative of a species and an element in a natural ecosystem. Second, it is a direct and recognizable descendant of a creature that was both a contemporary and perhaps even a predecessor of the dinosaurs. A glimpse of that period of natural history is stored in that alligator. As a reference to that period, it and other such animals provide a depth, temporal unity, and an enlarged sense of reality to nature, aesthetically and ontologically, just as reference to past events in human history provides depth, temporal unity, and a sense of reality in a work of literature. The alligator on the alligator farm is physically identical to the wild alligator and to this extent is still a "real" alligator. It retains some of the natural history of its wild counterpart. Robbed of its natural surroundings and deprived of the opportunity to learn and carry out much of its natural behavior, however, it is a creature in transition, waiting for its transformation into a consumer product, from gatorburgers to purses and shoes, and ultimately into a biologically restructured human artifact, like the domestic cow, that can more efficiently and inexpensively yield up its instrumental value to humankind. With the plastic alligator, the connection with nature and natural history is completely severed, and no trace of the "real" alligator remains, even aesthetically. When one sees the alligator open its mouth as the safari boat turns a corner on the ride, no images of contemporary wild nature or of the dinosaurs of natural history come to mind. These have been replaced by another history, evolutionary, to be sure, but not natural, beginning with the first experimental Mickey Mouse cartoons and highlighted by such Disney animated features as *Snow White and the Seven Dwarfs, Peter Pan,* and *The Jungle Book.* Like the medieval Christian looking at a picture of a fish and thinking about the Bible, the amusement park visitor has dropped the "real" alligator out of his or her aesthetic experience.

What these examples collectively reveal is that authentic physical existence plays a more fundamental role in the creation of beauty in nature and the aesthetic appreciation of that beauty than it does in art. In terms of bare or mere existence, what exists probably does not matter. When humans look at nature, however, contrary to the teachings of early modern philosophy and physics, they do not see it as bare, valueless matter. Rather they see it as natural objects composed of large numbers of properties, historically generated in accordance with natural processes—and very strictly speaking, as Berkeley points out, they see these objects not simply in terms of those properties but also *as* those objects. In this way, existence and essence become inseparable, and concern for the continued existence of the objects is expressed in terms of those properties in the context of aesthetic, moral, and scientific valuational frameworks.

Recognition of the special significance of propertied physical existence in aesthetic experiences and in nature preservation provides the final element in the ontological argument for the preservation of nature, which can now be summarized as follows: (1) Humans have a duty to promote and preserve the existence of good in the world; (2) beauty, both artistic and natural, is part of that good; (3) natural beauty (in a broad sense that includes scientifically interesting properties of natural objects) is, in most cases, as valuable as artistic beauty and therefore as worthy of being promoted and preserved on nonexistential grounds; and (4) because the creation of natural beauty is fundamentally contingent upon physical existence, in a way that art is not—that is, because the existence of nature precedes its essence—(a) the need to preserve natural objects and systems is greater than the need to preserve works of art, and, therefore, (b) the obligation to promote and preserve natural objects, all things (including values) being equal, takes precedence over the obligation to preserve works of art on existential grounds alone.

This argument does not mean that we always have a duty to promote and preserve everything in nature or that the promotion and preservation of works of art does not come first in many cases, but it does mean that if we have a duty to promote and preserve artistic beauty, we ought to recognize a similar duty to promote and preserve natural beauty, in part for much the same reasons that we recognize a duty with regard to art and in addition for distinctive reasons concerning the ontological status of natural existence.

IN DEFENSE OF THE ONTOLOGICAL ARGUMENT

Not everyone is likely to accept the ontological argument as presented here. Among various possible objections, two of the most prominent are likely to be that it is impossible to carry out a duty to promote and preserve nature and that the argument rests on medieval assumptions that are irrelevant today. I shall conclude this chapter by dealing with each in turn.

With regard to the first objection, it could be argued that the inevitable conclusion of the emergence of human beings in nature will be the transition of all natural entities that are useful to humans into human artifacts and those that are not into paleontological concepts and cartoon caricatures: that nature as a self-sufficient other, as an independent, creative existence, is a practical impossibility. Just as humans cannot improve nature, it may be that they cannot let it be in any independent sense and that they will eventually internalize nature in such a way that nature becomes merely a part of man, rather than man a part of it. Such internalization may already be taking place. It is possible, for example, that wilderness areas, as second-growth forests clear-cut in the nineteenth century, are already human artifacts without any future as far as natural history is concerned. If so, such areas are then only re-creations, illusions of wilderness,[34] and our aesthetic appreciation of them is an example of what Moore called misguided affection. If it is factually the case that this scenario is inevitable, then for much the same reasons that I have argued that we do not have a duty to improve nature, it would also be the case that we do not have a duty to promote and preserve nature and its indifferently created beauty.

In answer, I would argue that we do not know at this time for a fact that humans are such a disruptive element that our best efforts to allow nature to continue to exist and flourish are impossible. Certainly it is possible for us to set areas aside and to avoid actively manipulating them. The key issue is whether we can control global population growth so that humans do not become so plentiful that their very presence on the planet makes natural processes impossible anywhere. Even if humans are unable to act rationally or morally in controlling population growth, it is still conceivable, and probably inevitable, that human populations around the world will crash when the total number of people on Earth finally exceeds the carrying capacity of nature.[35] Technology may put that day off, but not indefinitely, since there must be finite limits to the powers of the technological fix. Thus I reply that until we know for a fact that human population growth is completely uncontrollable and that infinite growth is feasible and technologically sustainable, people who value the existence of natural beauty, see it as a part of the total good existing in the world, and hold that they have a duty to promote and preserve such good can meaningfully continue to act in accordance with a duty to promote and preserve nature.

With regard to the second objection, it could be argued that the ontological argument depends on assumptions about the nature of natural creativity that arise only in the context of certain outdated speculations about the nature of God. In particular, someone might claim that if late medieval and early modern Christian philosophers had not been excessively disturbed about a peculiar but illusory threat to God's omnipotence, the idea of creative indifference might never have occurred to them, undercutting crucial support for both positive aesthetics and the ontological argument, which most likely, in that event, also would not have occurred to anyone.

This objection would be devastating if, in fact, the belief in positive aesthetics and the duty to promote and preserve nature depended entirely on the truth of the ontological argument. My intention in developing the ontological argument, however, is not primarily to provide such a proof but rather to show that an argument appropriately grounded in our Western traditions can be formulated. Although I do not have conclusive evidence that positive aesthetics originated in the kinds of concerns about God's omnipotence expressed by Descartes, and before him by William of Ockham and his followers, I think that it is reasonable to assume that it did, consciously or unconsciously, and that it became a part of our aesthetic attitudes in connection with the transference of various divine traits fromGod to nature beginning in the seventeenth century with the rise of the aesthetic appreciation of nature and culminating in the early decades of the nineteenth with the explicit emergence of positive aesthetics among the forerunners of the environmental movement. Moreover, whether or not the details of such a history of ideas can be delineated is probably irrelevant, for creative indifference is an essential element in any analysis of the origin of natural beauty, not because medieval precedent can be found for it but because it is a correct characterization of the process, through geological uniformitarianism and biological evolution, that does in fact generate what counts as beauty in nature. In other words, even if creative indifference had not arisen out of the concerns of philosophers like William of Ockham and his followers, and Descartes had not also accepted it and used it in his philosophy, it would still be needed by us today to account rationally for our aesthetic beliefs.

Although no explicit trail of evidence may link the ontological argument with our modern aesthetic attitudes about the beauty of nature, there is ample evidence of a growing appreciation of nature that culminates in our modern views of nature aesthetics and nature preservation. If these views are not supported historically by the ontological argument, they are nevertheless supported by a significant evolution in Western moral character associated with the rise of modern aesthetics, and these changes in moral character are themselves compatible with the ontological argument. It is thus in moral character, in the Aristotelian sense of socially approved moral traits or dispositions, that a duty to promote and preserve natural beauty can most easily and convincingly be grounded.

Passmore fails to find adequate grounding for nature preservation precisely because he overlooks the link between nature preservation and moral character. He treats the appreciation of the beauty of nature as a passing fad, a kind of entertainment of which humans may eventually tire. For him, the enjoyment of nature is simply not as universal or basic as "eating or drinking or making love," major human pleasures.[36] In taking this position, however, he inconsistently forgets a completely different analysis of the issue, used earlier as an analogous case in support of concern for future generations. In his discussion of posterity, Passmore argues that humans need some kind of fundamental moral motivation to act on behalf of future humans. Arguing that this motivation is love, in the sense that "to love is to cherish," he cites love of family and relates it to love of philosophy and love of nature:

> To love philosophy—to philosophise with joy—is to care about its future as a form of activity: to maintain that what happens to it after our death is of no consequence would be a clear indication that our "love of philosophy" is nothing more than a form of self-love. The tourist who writes his name on a tree or a rock-face in a "beloved beauty spot" makes it only too clear what *he* loves. To love a place is to wish it to survive unspoiled.[37]

By attributing to love of nature an equal status with love of family and love of philosophy in this passage, Passmore concedes everything that he later denies in his chapter on nature preservation. Humans can love nature, and this love can provide the basis for the preservation of nature. The foundation is not rational argument but moral character: People who do not simply love themselves *ought* to love nature and *wish* that *it survive unspoiled.*

Someone might want to object that Passmore is in error in giving such a high status to love of nature—claiming perhaps that such love is really metaphorical only. In response, I would argue that the history of ideas of nature aesthetics does not support such a claim. The evolution of our attitudes toward nature begins with a fear of nature transformed into a delight in the sublime, continues in enthusiasm for nature, in those days a more radical attitude than today, and concludes in love of nature. This outcome was an unlikely one, given that people in the Middle Ages avoided loving nature on the grounds that doing so offended God by diminishing their love of Him. The initial inhibition against love of nature, I submit, makes it unlikely that love of nature could have arisen in a lighthearted manner, without a strong sense of commitment on the part of those professing to have such love, making a metaphorical love of nature implausible. Rather love of nature arose, as I have indicated earlier, through two stages: love of God through nature, followed by a love of nature as such. In this way, love of nature has its origin in love of God, the strongest and highest form of love that Westerners have professed to have. This close historical association with love of God justifies the high status Passmore, perhaps inadvertently, assigns it in his chapter on conservation and concern for future generations.

Moreover, whether inadvertent or not, Passmore's comments on the love of nature provide a sound basis, completely consistent with the history of nature aesthetics as I have depicted it here, for answering the woman in Onondaga Cave who delighted in the possible destruction of the cave as a means by which her memories of her aesthetic experiences there could be increased in value. The woman's desire that the cave be destroyed in order to enhance her aesthetic experiences is, first of all, selfish. To paraphrase Passmore, she shows that she loves only herself, not others, and certainly not nature. This is a flaw in her moral character. As a moral person, she ought to want others to be able to have the same experiences that she has had, and she ought to want the cave to continue in existence as a reference for her memories of her own experiences. Although this want could be depicted as a *desire,* in accordance with my treatment of this issue in the writings of Moore and Tolkien, Passmore may be right in using the word *wish* in his own comments, if he means *wish* in an Aristotelian sense.[38] According to Aristotle, although wish determines the ends of moral choice, it is not itself a product of deliberation and choice but a manifestation of the element in moral character that unconsciously determines moral perception. When the objects of wish are not correct, it is then impossible for the moral agent to decide properly, for he or she is unable to perceive specific situations properly. This is the unfortunate situation of the woman in Onondaga Cave. Since she has no true love of nature, she cannot properly admire it, respect it, or wish that it continue to exist as part of the total good in the world. For her, nature is merely something to be used to generate pleasurable experiences, and from her perspective, the pleasure that she derives from nature is greater if others can never share it. The key flaw in the woman's perception of nature is that she sees nature as something to be used and consumed. To the degree that she loves nature, she loves it in the way that she loves ice cream.[39] It is good while it lasts, and it is better if she has some and everyone else gets left out.

Although most people do not so ardently wish the destruction of beauty in nature, the idea of nature appreciation as consumption of nature is a serious problem that often leads to confusion in the formulation of public policy with regard to natural areas. In his chapter on nature preservation, Passmore, forgetting his remarks about the relationship of love of nature and nature preservation, argues that the protection of natural areas from visitor damage is undemocratic, since it favors the aesthetic tastes of the "meditative solitary-loving few" at high cost to the majority who are indifferent about wilderness, favoring places with "picnic tables, wells, toilets, washrooms, and the like" instead:[40]

> The mere fact that, like the enjoyment of poetry, the enjoyment of solitude or private meditation is a minority enjoyment does nothing to suggest, of course, that there is no virtue in trying to ensure its continuance. Human beings differ greatly in their sources of enjoyment, minorities have their rights; the preservation of these rights is what democracy is about. But the special consideration that the enjoyment of solitary wildernesses may only be possible at the cost of greatly restricting the recreation of others raises problems not only about its political feasibility but even about its moral desirability—unless a case can be made out for its being a form of enjoyment of such value and importance that other forms of enjoyment ought to be sacrificed for it.[41]

The case that Passmore requires has, I believe, been made in this chapter. If natural beauty is as valuable as artistic beauty, as I have argued, the public policies and the moral behavior required to preserve natural beauty ought to be as stringent as those required for artistic beauty. Since the aesthetic consumption of works of art is unthinkable, the aesthetic consumption of natural objects of special beauty ought to be equally unthinkable. There are, of course, practical limits to our duty to promote and preserve natural beauty. Although Moore argues that natural beauty is a good that we ought to protect morally whether we know about it or not, most likely the cost of a public policy to protect unknown beauty would exceed the tolerance of most democratic societies. The cost involved in protecting known beauty that is being damaged by visitation, however, should be a tolerable and reasonable expense in democratic societies that recognize the value of the *existence* of natural beauty. In such societies, natural beauty, like artistic beauty, would be regarded as a good independent of its instrumental value as the trigger for aesthetic experiences, and the generation of such experiences would be restricted and even terminated, when necessary, to promote and preserve the existence of the good that beauty represents. Likewise, in such societies, the decision to preserve natural areas that were hard to reach would not be unduly influenced by projections of low visitation figures. In such societies, for example, preservationist support for places such as the Alaskan wilderness would not be dependent on the expectation that trips to such places might someday be feasible for most citizens but rather would be based on the recognition that although direct appreciation is desirable, indirect appreciation is adequate and acceptable and that the areas ought to be preserved on grounds completely independent of their instrumental aesthetic use, that is, on the grounds that their existence constitutes a significant good in the world.

NOTES

1. Ludwig Wittgenstein, *Philosophical Investigations,* trans. G. E. M. Ancscombe, 3d ed. (New York: Macmillan, 1958), par. 304.

2. Allen Carlson, "Nature and Positive Aesthetics," *Environmental Ethics* 6 (1984): 5–34.

3. G. E. Moore, *Principia Ethica* (Cambridge: Cambridge University Press, 1965), esp. ch. 6. For an alternative view of Moore on the issues discussed in this chapter, see Donald H. Regan, "Duties of Preservation," in *The Preservation of Species: The Value of Biological Diversity,* ed. Bryan G. Norton (Princeton, N.J.: Princeton University Press, 1986), pp. 195–220. I object to Regan's conclusion that natural objects, like the Grand Canyon, have no value in their own right but only as ingredients in organic wholes.

4. For a discussion of the discovery of Turner Avenue, see Roger W. Brucker and Richard A. Watson, *The Longest Cave* (Carbondale, Ill.: Southern Illinois University Press, 1987), pp. 73–75.

5. Moore, *Principia Ethica,* pp. 83–85.

6. Ibid., pp. 193–194.

7. Ibid., p. 195.

8. J. R. R. Tolkien, *The Silmarillion* (Boston: Houghton Mifflin, 1977), p. 20; "Leaf by Niggle" and "On Fairy-Stories," in J. R. R. Tolkien, *Tree and Leaf* (Boston: Hougton Mifflin, 1965), pp. 108–111, 36–41.

9. Ibid., p. 48.

10. Wayne C. Booth, *The Rhetoric of Fiction* (Chicago: University of Chicago Press, 1961), p. 112.

11. Ibid.

12. David Hume, *An Enquiry Concerning Human Understanding,* secs. 3, 2.

13. Willard Van Orman Quine, *Word and Object* (Cambridge, Mass.: M.I.T. Press, 1960), pp. 2–3, 79.

14. Hume, *Enquiry,* sec. 12, pt. 1.

15. *The Crayon* 3 (1856): 99.

16. Richard A. Watson, "Self-consciousness and the Rights of Nonhuman Animals and Nature," *Environmental Ethics* 1 (1979): 107.

17. Ibid.; Bryan G. Norton, "Environmental Ethics and Nonhuman Rights," *Environmental Ethics* 4 (1982): 17–36.

18. Moore, *Principia Ethica,* p. 115.

19. John Passmore, *Man's Responsibility for Nature: Ecological Problems and Western Traditions* (London: Duckworth, 1974), p. 110.

20. Nathaniel Southgate Shaler, *Man and the Earth* (New York: Duffield & Company, 1917), pp. 172–177.

21. Carlson, "Nature and Positive Aesthetics," p. 31.

22. *The Philosophical Works of Descartes,* trans. Elizabeth S. Haldane and G. R. T. Ross (Cambridge: Cambridge University Press, 1911), vol. 2, pp. 250–251.

23. Jean-Paul Sartre, *Existentialism and Human Emotions* (New York: Philosophical Library, 1957), pp. 14–17.

24. Hume, *Enquiry,* sec. 2.

25. Aristotle, *Nicomachean Ethics,* bk. 1, ch. 1, 1094a1–5.

26. For an interesting discussion of the transformation of the British landscape in prehistoric times, see L. Dudley Stamp, *Man and the Land: The New Naturalist* (London: Collins, 1955), pp. 8–12. For the general context in which the geometric transformation of northern Europe took place, see Geoffrey and Susan Jellicoe, *The Landscape of Man: Shaping the Environment from Prehistory to the Present*

Day (New York: Viking Press, 1975). For a discussion of the relation of field shape and ownership, see Henri Hubert, *The Greatness and Decline of the Celts* (London: Routledge & Kegan Paul, 1934), pp. 248–249.

27. Passmore, *Man's Responsibility,* pp. 38–39.

28. Ibid., p. 39.

29. Georg Wilhelm Friedrich Hegel, *Hegel's Philosophy of Right,* trans. T. M. Knox (Cambridge: Clarendon Press, 1945), p. 41.

30. Passmore, *Man's Responsibility,* pp. 36–37.

31. Peter Humphrey, "The Ethics of Earthworks," *Environmental Ethics* 7 (1985): 20.

32. Immanuel Kant, *Immanuel Kant's Critique of Pure Reason,* trans. Norman Kemp Smith (New York: St. Martin's Press, 1965), p. 505.

33. Bruce V. Foltz, "On Heidegger and the Interpretation of Environmental Crisis," *Environmental Ethics* 6 (1984): 330.

34. See Philip M. Smith and Richard A. Watson, "New Wilderness Boundaries," *Environmental Ethics* 1 (1979): 61–69.

35. Such a crash, moreover, may not be as terrible as it is often depicted. In a novelette by Philip José Farmer, for example, despite considerable initial civil disorder, both humans and nature benefit dramatically from massive population decimation in terms of quality of life and environmental quality. See Philip José Farmer, "Seventy Years of Decpop," *Galaxy Science Fiction Magazine* 33, no. 1 (1972): 96–143.

36. Passmore, *Man's Responsibility,* p. 110.

37. Ibid., p. 88.

38. Aristotle, *Nicomachean Ethics,* bk. 3, ch. 3–4.

39. Passmore himself uses this analogy in his discussion of the love of nature: "I can 'love ice-cream' without caring about what happens to it after I die." Passmore, *Man's Responsibility,* p. 88.

40. Ibid., pp. 104, 106.

41. Ibid., p. 106.

AFTERWORD
BEYOND ECONOMICS: TOWARD A BALANCED VALUE SYSTEM

Although Passmore argues throughout *Man's Responsibility for Nature* that there is no need for an environmental ethic on the grounds that any attempt to create one will be conceptually incoherent and incompatible with Western civilization, there is a third theme of nearly equal importance: that environmental problems are social problems that need to be solved through political action, in accordance with appropriate input from social and political philosophy, rather than through ethical action, in accordance with an environmental ethic. In part, Passmore, as a social and political philosopher, seems to be arguing academically about the value of social and political philosophy over ethics in solving such problems. In addition, given that he (improperly, I think) associates ethics, or environmental ethics, at least, with religious fanaticism, he is also concerned about possible abuses that (he improbably believes) might be undertaken in the name of an environmental ethic—for example, the overthrow of Western democratic institutions. His primary reason, however, seems to be that he believes that individual ethical action toward the solution of an environmental problem, such as pollution, is virtually pointless: "It may satisfy our conscience or give us a sense of moral superiority. But it will make so minimal a contribution to the problem of pollution as to be, from that point of view, meaningless."[1]

Although this last argument has some merit, since ethical action on behalf of a social problem by only a few people is indeed very ineffective, Passmore fails to note the important interconnections between ethics and politics that must exist if political action, through legislation and public policy, is to be effective and enforceable. Leopold, for example, came to the conclusion that we needed an environmental ethic only after repeatedly failing to solve environmental problems through political action. He saw that appropriate political action could not be achieved without the support of ordinary citizens and that before citizens could offer such support, they needed to develop, understand, and come to grips with their environmental values. Leopold's call for an environmental ethic, in other words, was intended not as a step toward subverting the political process but as a step toward facilitating it.

The kind of interrelationship between ethics and politics that Leopold intuitively had in mind is so well grounded in the history of ethics and social and political philosophy that it can hardly be considered controversial and certainly cannot be construed as a threat to democracy. The view comes directly from Aristotle, who saw ethics and politics as a single subject viewed from two perspectives, that of the individual and that of the group or state.[2] If we adopt this ethical/political framework, the conflict between ethics and social and political philosophy that Passmore depicts in *Man's Responsibility for Nature* dissolves. The question is no longer whether environmental problems can best be solved through ethical action or political action but rather whether these problems can be solved through complementary action at both levels.

For this dual approach to the solution of environmental problems to work, as Leopold himself clearly saw, the democratic state must educate its citizens so that they have the environmental values needed for both ethical and political action. Although the very idea of teaching values in the classroom is frequently considered dangerous, this is a misconception. People who oppose the teaching of values generally worry about two specific dangers: (1) that the wrong values will be taught, and (2) that teaching values will breed skepticism, undermining the few positive values that children and adults have somehow picked up, perhaps by osmosis. Neither concern provides adequate grounds for rejecting training in ethics and values in our society. Those who worry that the wrong values might be taught generally accept, at least by implication, that there are some right values. These values, it turns out, are traditional ones, ones that have a long history. Since, as I have argued throughout this book, environmental values are also traditional values, arising jointly out of traditional ethics and nature aesthetics, it ought to be possible to teach these values in an uncontroversial way that is acceptable to everyone. This brings us to the second concern, that efforts to teach values will breed skepticism instead. As Aristotle noted, it is difficult to teach values to humans: Usually they are either too young to understand what is being taught or too old to be willing to listen, since they have already adopted improper values and attitudes.[3] This is a problem, but not an insurmountable one. The object of value training should be not indoctrination but clarification. Although many people fear that such clarification will reveal that there is nothing to clarify, thereby generating skepticism about values, this need not be the case. As I have argued in this book, most people intuitively hold a wide range of environmental values, without being able to articulate them very well. Value training, focused on the historical origins of environmental and other social, political, aesthetic, and ethical values in Western traditions and their usefulness in making decisions in ordinary life, should strengthen these values, not erode them. Even though such training might provide some people with the opportunity to engage in skepticism about moral values, this is hardly an adequate reason to deny ethical training to those who would like to improve their understanding of their society's basic values. Surely a society of citizens who have had the chance to learn about moral matters is preferable to one in which values are only randomly and accidentally acquired and retained and examination of these values is actively discouraged as a matter of public policy.[4]

If environmental value training is to be successful, it must focus on putting in appropriate traditional perspective three approaches to value that have emerged in the past hundred years or less against the general flow of Western traditions: utilitarianism, pragmatism, and modern economics. Utilitarianism has created problems by elevating pleasure to a level that makes it synonymous with human happiness. This was not always so. Aristotle, for example, argued long ago that pleasure is an important ingredient in happiness and as such is a good but that it is not always on its own a good, since people frequently do bad things for pleasure and tire of pleasure when they have too much of it.[5] Utilitarianism may most appropriately be thought of as the democratization of ethical values. Unfortunately, in order to speak to everyone, the utilitarians converted all good into degrees of pleasure, a good that is not a higher good but has the merit of being a good that everyone can understand. Although the woman in Onondaga Cave was thinking in primarily egoistic and hedonistic terms, the pleasure that she sought in the cave and wished to have heightened through its destruction was popularized and made acceptable through the rise of utilitarianism. Pragmatism is so closely associated with utilitarianism that antienvironmental instrumental arguments are commonly regarded as utilitarian. Nevertheless, it constitutes a distinct feature of the modern anti–traditional value framework. Pragmatism, with its stress on instrumental values and its disdain for intrinsic values, is, through the conservation philosophy of Gifford Pinchot, responsible for the conversion of natural objects into instrumental triggers for the generation of aesthetic pleasures in the minds of humans. This conversion, which runs counter to the more traditional view that objects of beauty are valuable for their own sake, without regard to their use, constitutes the aesthetic relationship between the woman in Onondaga Cave and her surroundings. Finally, modern economics, a direct outgrowth of utilitarianism, has gone beyond its parent and promoted rational egoism, or selfishness, not simply as an objectively valid approach to ethical action but as the only rational approach to human action in general. In monetary terms, the woman in Onondaga Cave wished the destruction of the cave so that the purchase of her ticket for the tour would buy her pleasures that others could not subsequently have. This inordinate emphasis on money and getting good value, considered despicable in the last century, is now the standard in our own.

The tremendous influence of popularized forms of utilitarianism, pragmatism, and economics is especially clear in Passmore's chapter on nature preservation. All arguments that he presents in favor of nature preservation are instrumental arguments, although many of them could equally well be presented as intrinsic value arguments. The aesthetic arguments, in particular, in accordance with utilitarianism, are simply justifications for instrumentally drawing pleasure from nature. In the spotlight, however, Passmore places economics and economic value. Reviewing the instrumental arguments that he has mustered on behalf of nature preservation, he concludes that "they are none of them 'knock-down' arguments; they all allow that economic considerations, in a broad sense of that phrase, might under certain circumstances outweigh the case for preservation."[6] In summary, the instrumental resource value of nature, expressed in economic terms, will always, in principle, outweigh its aesthetic and intrinsic value.

This conclusion is, I submit, inconsistent with Passmore's primary claim that we ought to act in accordance with traditional values and that fundamental traditional values, the older, more established ones, ought to take precedence over less traditional values, for certainly the aesthetic and intrinsic value tradition, which has been with us since the seventeenth century, is much more traditional than the utilitarian-instrumentalist-economic tradition that has only been with us in its entirety less than a single century. Indeed, only utilitarianism can claim to be more than one hundred years old, for the other two took their contemporary form only at the beginning of this century.

It might be objected that economic value ought to have precedence over all other values by virtue of the fact that it is objectively derived from the science of economics, but this argument has little force, for economics is not a science but a renegade descendant of nineteenth-century ethical theory pretending to be a science. Modern economic theory is based directly on utilitarianism given a scientific look through the use of economic jargon in the spirit of logical positivism. Unlike real sciences, which base their theories on empirical research, economics is based on speculations about the economic behavior of the so-called economic man acting entirely in accordance with rational egoism, which is not even an especially commendable ethical theory. Economics has not shown that economic value is objectively superior to other, more traditional values; it has merely ignored those values. It has been accepted as an objective factor in public policy in part because it provides a way to quantify the value of alternatives in terms of money but also because Westerners have become increasingly confused about the objectivity of value in general as a result of the rise of emotivism out of logical positivism in the early decades of this century.[7]

To see the inadequacy of the economic approach to nature preservation, we need only apply it to our analogy, developed in Chapter 6, between artistic and natural beauty. Traditionally, the resource value of a natural object is instrumental; its aesthetic value is intrinsic. Both kinds of value can be expressed in monetary terms. In the nineteenth century, as part of the procedure for the establishment of national parks, natural history scientists were expected to assess the value of such places in terms of both kinds of value, and as noted at the beginning of Chapter 2, they tended to downplay instrumental value while extolling the intrinsic value in such a way that the first national parks were proclaimed in their reports to be instrumentally worthless and intrinsically priceless—in other words, off the monetary scale. Though these evaluations seem to support Passmore's claim that instrumental value should take precedence over intrinsic value, that was probably not the intent of the evaluators. Most likely they were simply trying to avoid political confrontation by discounting the instrumental values as the path of least resistance. The emphasis should not be placed on instrumental worthlessness as a precondition for preservationist action; rather it should be placed on the fact that everyone rated the intrinsic value of these natural areas as too high to calculate in monetary terms. This emphasis, as I shall now argue, is the one that is most consistent with our basic intuitions with regard to both artistic and natural beauty.

It is characteristic of nearly all art objects that their intrinsic value far outweighs their instrumental value. Usually, the materials out of which an art object is made are much less valuable, as scrap, than the object is as a work of art. The Mona Lisa's value as a painting, for example, cannot seriously be compared with its value as used wood and canvas. The possibility for comparison between the instrumental and intrinsic value of an art object exists only when the materials out of which the object is constructed are extremely valuable, for example, when they are made out of gold or precious gems. Because the intrumental and intrinsic values of most art objects are on quite different scales of magnitude, it would be lunacy to decide whether or not to continue preserving the Mona Lisa on the basis of a cost-benefit analysis. For such an analysis to make any sense, the intrinsic value of the painting would have to be artificially depressed so that the scrap prices for wood and canvas had some chance of winning. It is because such calculations would be absurd that they are not employed in making decisions at art museums. Unfortunately, however, this is not always the case with regard to decisions about the preservation of natural beauty.

To bolster the objectivity of cost-benefit analyses for natural areas, economists frequently circulate surveys that attempt to determine the amount of money per household in a given political jurisdiction that people are willing to pay to preserve nature. As Holmes Rolston has noted, such surveys often make little sense to the people asked to participate in them:

> The difficulty . . . is that the question is not what it appears, and even if the respondent comes to understand the pretending involved, he has no rules by which he can translate [social good] into [marketplace value], none by which he can integrate . . . value types on a scale commensurate with the market value of wildland products. The more he operates as a citizen, the more the privatized form of the questions is remote from what he is really trying to indicate, and the less his capacity to do any pricing. He may also feel that he is being forced to play this game, in the sense that no answer eliminates his opinion, and wonder whether zero bids or infinity demands (or others that the interviewer considers out of range) will be eliminated on grounds of noncooperation. If a respondent states a huge sum (a recreator who wishes to protect the rights of those who do, or an Earth citizen who holistically values ecosystems), will this make it into the cost-benefit equations, or be tossed out as a monkey-wrench answer? The citizen ought not in principle be asked to couple sufficient money with his nonmarket policy preferences; and when he is asked this, he does not in practice reliably know the answer.
>
> The respondent has no idea how to do any calculations; yet on the basis of his guesstimates, economists do metric calculations, overly refining what are really raw data. All this number crunching creates the illusion of mathematical exactitudes covering up what were, to begin with, iffy replies in a cramped hypothetical context. Nor is the user of the respondent's behavior to correct verbal misjudgments of willingness to pay reliable, because behavior is already infected with the inequities in the prevailing distribution of wealth. Meanwhile, it will take considerable intellectual subtlety for the respondent to understand the differences between willingness to pay and willingness to accept payment, between consumer and citizen dollars, between option, existence, and bequest values, between hypothetical and actual markets, to say nothing of the reliability of attaching dollar amounts to these issues.[8]

These are the same kind of doubts that would arise in the mind of someone forced to participate in a per-household survey that might decide the fate of the Mona Lisa. The participant has no more practical experience buying or selling wilderness areas or species than buying or selling major works of art and almost certainly knows no one who engages in such market activity. Furthermore, since the participant also almost certainly feels that the value of the object or objects being evaluated is priceless, that is, off the economic scale, the survey seems absurd. The situation cannot be accurately depicted as an example of willingness to pay, since the environmental value as the participant estimates it is probably beyond anyone's ability to pay; it is more like a hostage situation, in which the object of beauty is being threatened with destruction unless the participant is willing to pay as much as he or she absolutely can.

The conflict in such cost-benefit analyses arises, I believe, from the fact that the instrumental and intrinsic values being compared are incomparable on the same monetary scales. Because, like apples and oranges, they have significant qualitative differences, they cannot be easily compared quantitatively in any meaningful way. This does not mean that there may not be circumstances in which the instrumental value of a natural area might not outweigh its intrinsic value—there are large numbers of such places—but it does mean that in cases where the nature preservation question arises, the disparity between the instrumental and intrinsic values involved is likely to be so great that an analysis makes no sense, unless, as Rolston suggests, the analysts are prepared to throw out about half the surveys on the grounds that the participants, by assigning immense intrinsic value to such areas, have failed to cooperate and thus lost their opportunity to be heard.

It is important to stress that I am not claiming that economists cannot account for environmental values. It is possible for economists, through various economic contortions, to produce results that closely approximate a wide range of economic behavior. The issue here is not simply whether they can do it but whether an analysis of environmental issues through the eyes of rational economic man is appropriate. Although economists claim that they are dealing with values in a neutral manner, it is very likely that their amoral to immoral view of human motivation rather than simply factually mirroring economic behavior based on selfishness and self-interest actually encourages it. As Steven Edwards recently noted, environmental economics is complicated "by the possibility of complex preference structures such as 'preferences over preferences' whereby economic man and altruistic man might exist in the same person."[9] Although economists should certainly try to account for the behavior of these people—who by my count exist in very large numbers—it is questionable, at least to me, that altruistic economic behavior can or should be incorporated into a theory of choice that is fundamentally selfish and consumer market–oriented.

Since ordinary individual humans do not make consumer market choices about wildernesses, species, and other objects of natural and artistic beauty, it might be better to try to account for their value to us in some other way. The dollar or franc value of the Mona Lisa, however many millions it might be, is really irrelevant to any decisions about preserving it. That it is or would be worth a great deal of money should be enough. Its real value is aesthetic and historical, not monetary. The money spent protecting it, moreover, is not in any way tied directly to an estimate of its market value. Rather it is related to various factors: general overhead, security, and whatever is required to keep the painting in good condition. These are essentially social costs that are indirectly accrued and are "external" to the value of the painting itself. Similarly, the costs involved in protecting nature are most often indirect costs that also have virtually nothing to do with real market choices.

Although economists like to talk about the free market system in which all values are determined by rational economic man, this is hardly true. The production of nearly all consumer products, for example, also generate waste products that create serious environmental problems. Very little, if any, of the costs of the disposal of these wastes has traditionally been included in the price that economic man is asked to pay for the consumer product. These costs must nevertheless eventually be paid by someone, and they usually end up being social costs, paid for through the collection of taxes. These costs are called *externalities* because they are external to the market mechanisms that otherwise determine the price of consumer products. In some cases, externalities developed historically because we did not know that they were costs until, for example, the rivers began to die and it began to be difficult to breathe the air in our cities. These costs have remained externalities because incorporating them into the price of a product would make the product too expensive and thereby disrupt the system. New externalities are frequently created by local, state, and federal governments to encourage new business and industry. They remain as open-ended social costs because once in place, they are usually too difficult to remove.

Since the costs of protecting nature are really social costs independent of the market system, natural objects and natural systems, like polluted water and polluted air, are really externalities. They differ from normal externalities only in that as aesthetic entities they are positive rather than negative, good rather than bad, but as externalities, like their unpleasant counterparts, they are also, in principle, independent of what Passmore calls "economic considerations," if what he means by that phrase is free market choice.

Recognition that natural areas and species are *positive* externalities would help eliminate a lot of confused thinking about the value of nature in terms of economics and public policy. In particular, it would eliminate the need to confuse ordinary citizens further by asking them to state their preferences about hypothetical and completely impossible market choices. In this context, economic man would be still free to choose as he saw fit in the market in terms of his various selfish interests and preferences while altruistic man took care of the social costs, negative and positive, that were external to the market system.

Although it might be objected that this approach is contrary to human nature, it is only contrary to a human nature that has been culturally created in the past hundred years through the emergence of the current utilitarian, economic perspective. It is not contrary to the human nature that preceded it, when humans readily accepted a more balanced value system that included altruism in addition to self-interest and intrinsic value in addition to instrumental value and recognized goods other than the satisfaction of pleasure.

It is possible for a Western society to pass and enforce a law that protects natural beauty simply because it is good. In 1928, a law was established in Austria that required that all newly discovered caves be evaluated for possible designation as national monuments.[10] Since that time, quarry owners, for example, have been required to cease all operations until the national monument office's evaluations are complete. In cases in which it has been determined that the caves are of unusual aesthetic or scientific value, in accordance with standards that have nothing to do with economics, the caves have been declared national monuments and the quarry operations closed down. When we have a public policy toward nature in general that reflects this kind of approach, we will be a society that takes pride in the existence of nature independent of the selfish pleasures that may be drawn from it or the money that can be made by exploiting and destroying it—in short, we will be a society that lives in accordance with an environmental ethic

NOTES

1. John Passmore, *Man's Responsibility for Nature* (London: Duckworth, 1974), pp. 4–5, 57, 67.
2. Aristotle, *Nicomachean Ethics,* bk. 1, ch. 2.
3. Ibid., bk. 3, ch. 3; bk. 10, ch. 9.
4. For a more detailed discussion of these matters, see Eugene C. Hargrove, "The Role of Rules in Ethical Decision Making," *Inquiry* 28 (1985): 30–39.
5. Aristotle, *Nicomachean Ethics,* bk. 2, ch. 3; bk. 10, ch. 1–8.
6. Passmore, *Man's Responsibility,* pp. 124–125.
7. For an appraisal of economics as a science, see C. Dyke, *Philosophy of Economics* (Englewood Cliffs, N.J.: Prentice-Hall, 1981). esp. pp. 140–142. For an account of the role of positivism in economics, see Milton Friedman, "The Methodology of Positive Economics," in *Philosophy and Economic Theory,* ed. Frank Hahn and Martin Hollis (Oxford: Oxford University Press, 1979), pp. 18–35. For a good account of the emergence of economics out of philosophy in the late nineteenth century, in terms of a struggle between Henry Sidgwick and Alfred Marshall, both teachers and friends of John Maynard Keynes at Cambridge, see Robert Skidelsky, "Cambridge Civilization: Sidgwick and Marshall," in *John Maynard Keynes: Hopes Betrayed, 1883–1920,* vol. 1, pp. 26–50. Economic theory can be developed straightforwardly in altruistic terms. See, for example, David Collard, *Altruism and Economy: A Study in Nonselfish Economics* (New York: Oxford University Press, 1978). It is quite possible that the ethical stance of economics really represents the views of major economists in the recent history of economics, not the views of so-called economic

man. John Maynard Keynes, for example, summed up his ethical views with the remark, "I remain, and always will remain, an immoralist." John Maynard Keynes, "My Early Beliefs," in *Two Memoirs* (New York: Augustus M. Kelley, 1949), p. 98.

8. Holmes Rolston, III, "Valuing Wildlands," *Environmental Ethics* 7 (1985): 37.

9. Steven E. Edwards, "In Defense of Environmental Economics," *Environmental Ethics* 9 (1987): 85.

10. National law of June 26, 1928, for the protection of natural caves, *Bundesgesetzblatt* 169.

INDEX

A

B

C

K

L

M

Q

R